THE HERITAGE OF LIBRARIANSHIP SERIES,
No. 5

THE HERITAGE OF LIBRARIANSHIP SERIES
Michael H. Harris, General Editor

No. 1   *The Age of Jewett: Charles Coffin Jewett and American Librarianship, 1841-1868.* Edited by Michael H. Harris.

No. 2   *Ainsworth Rand Spofford: Bookman and Librarian.* Edited by John Y. Cole.

No. 3   *Charles Ammi Cutter: Library Systematizer.* Edited by Francis L. Miksa.

No. 4   *Melvil Dewey: His Enduring Presence in Librarianship.* Edited by Sarah K. Vann.

No. 5   *Justin Winsor: Scholar-Librarian.* Edited by Wayne Cutler and Michael H. Harris.

JUSTIN WINSOR

Scholar-Librarian

edited by
WAYNE CUTLER
and
MICHAEL H. HARRIS

1980

LIBRARIES UNLIMITED, INC.
Littleton, Colorado

LIBRARIES UNLIMITED, INC.
P.O. Box 263
Littleton, Colorado 80160

Library of Congress Cataloging in Publication Data

Winsor, Justin, 1831-1897.
    Justin Winsor, scholar-librarian.

    (The Heritage of librarianship series ; no. 5)
    Bibliography: p. 175
    Includes index.
    1. Library science--Collected works. 2. Winsor,
Justin, 1831-1897. I. Cutler, Wayne, 1938-
II. Harris, Michael H. III. Title. IV. Series:
Heritage of Librarianship series ; no. 5.
Z674.W54   020   80-19310
ISBN 0-87287-200-9

For
parents who shared their love of books

Everette and Abbie Cutler
Andrew and Frances Harris

FOREWORD

When Justin Winsor died unexpectantly in 1897, while serving his ninth term as president of the American Library Association, there was a profuse and sincere outpouring of respect and gratitude from librarians everywhere for the man who had led the fledgling profession during its most difficult years. Eulogists hailed his many contributions to the practical and philosophical aspects of librarianship, but one, Charles Ammi Cutter, pointed to Winsor's reputation as a scholar-librarian and the lustre that it shed on the status-conscious library profession, as his most significant achievement. However, Cutter was convinced that Winsor would be longer and better known as a "historian than a librarian."

Given our present perspective, Cutter would appear to have been wrong in this assessment, for Winsor's commitment to "scientific" and collaborative history is out of fashion among followers of Clio. As a result, Winsor is little known among contemporary historians. But his eclipse as a historian has been paralleled by his continued, and even heightened, relevance to modern librarianship. Winsor's missionary zeal, staunch insistance on professional autonomy, and dazzling administrative skills remain hallmarks of professional aspiration among librarians. And his example as a respected scholar-librarian retains its appeal for librarians everywhere. Last but not least, his aggressive advocacy of the library as a "mighty engine" capable of "ameliorating mankind" remains (even if less candidly stated) the credo of activist librarians in America and abroad.

Up to now, librarians have found it difficult to gain ready access to Winsor's major writings on librarianship, especially his widely read and influential annual reports. In this volume, much of that work now becomes readily available for the first time, and the careful reader will be rewarded with a better understanding of Winsor's many contributions to librarianship, and with a fuller appreciation of the relevance of his ideas for contemporary librarianship.

This volume takes its place among four earlier volumes in the Heritage of Librarianship Series. All of the Librarians considered in this series gained much of their influence because they were prolific and persuasive writers. Yet modern professionals have little conception of what concerned these pioneers, what questions they sought to answer, or how they proposed to deal with their manifold problems. By providing easy access to the writings of these influential librarians, it is hoped that the series will facilitate in some small way the modern librarian's increasingly intensive search for the purpose of the library in a post-industrial society.

Michael H. Harris
General Editor

TABLE OF CONTENTS

PART III. BIBLIOGRAPHY

PART I

JUSTIN WINSOR:
SCHOLAR-LIBRARIAN

INTRODUCTION

Justin Winsor led the American library profession into the era of national industrialization with a measure of vitality and a singleness of purpose that were worthy of even the most successful barons of mechanical productivity and financial consolidation. Always the man of energy and system, he filled his years with literary and historical pursuits in such volume that none would deny him the peerage of Boston's Brahmin elite.

Yet Winsor's mixture of intellectual abilities and personal drives were unsuited to the life of leisure, grace, and ease that characterized an earlier generation of American intellectuals. He lived in an age of industry and gave himself totally to each new endeavor, never holding back or wasting a moment. His compulsion for work and his thoroughness of organization set him apart in the unhurried currents of nineteenth-century librarianship. For Winsor, the library was not a literary retreat from reality, but a workshop for exploring, ordering, and promoting the creative forces of human progress. His library was not so much a place or an institution, but a process, a habit of producing that was ignited by an explosive passion for knowledge and sustained by a missionary zeal for self-education.

As a youth, Winsor demonstrated considerable sophistication in the study of local and family history. At age eighteen, he published *A History of the Town of Duxbury, Massachusetts, with Genealogical Registers* (1849). He would return later in life to his historical studies, but only after he had enjoyed successive careers as literary critic (1854-1867) and library leader (1868-1885).

Winsor's literary contributions brought him considerable local recognition, but his verse and prose compositions were laboriously rendered and did not survive even in the most comprehensive anthologies. He had no taste or feel for music, and his literary style suffered for the deficiency. In the field of criticism he ably recognized works of merit, but again, his remarks seldom sparkled with either charm or brilliancy. Neither as artist nor as critic could he match his appreciation for great literature.

More significant career developments came with his management of the Boston Public and Harvard University libraries. Having employed innovative statistical analysis of the library's use, he applied his findings in the promotion of his credo that libraries were more than museums of the printed word. Accordingly he devoted great attention to the compilation of bibliographies and guides to public reading. He practiced what he advocated, and his example earned him the honor of being named, in 1876, the founding president of the American Library Association. He served in that position for nine consecutive years and set the agenda for bringing librarians to a new spirit of professional cooperation and identity.

In the field of historical inquiry, Winsor distinguished himself by advancing the medium of cooperative writing. For over a decade, he won acclaim for his editing of the four-volume *Memorial History of Boston* (1880-1881) and the eight-volume *Narrative and Critical History of America* (1886-1889). In 1884, he chaired the organizational meeting of the American Historical Association, and in 1886, that organization named him its president. For twenty years, Winsor successfully combined his scholarly activities with his duties as Harvard's librarian, although from 1885 until his death in 1897, his principal interest turned upon historical research and publication projects. He was in his own person the example of what he hoped the library experience would represent for others.

As Americans of the post-Civil War era celebrated their national reunion and growing industrial strength, so social reform leaders sought to increase opportunities for individual improvement for those, and only those, most fit to apply themselves to the task of building the nation.[1] Self-improvement defined both the method and the extent of "uplift" ethics.[2]

Few Americans could fail to observe the country's tremendous growth in capital accumulation and material productivity. If the distribution of that wealth was uneven, the inequity was thought to derive either from personal inadequacy or private misfortune. Social uplift theories assumed an inevitability of human progress, not the leveling of distinctions.[3] Intellectuals often predicated their belief in education upon the same laissez-faire principles as were espoused by the giants of industrial production and financial consolidation.[4] Half a century earlier, Jacksonian democrats had enforced the laissez-faire dictum on the nation's monied interests and had applied the rule that the federal government's credit would not be used to create monopolies for private gain. Stated another way, the power of the general government would not be used to grant privileges to a few at the expense of the many. Latter-day exponents of laissez-faire employed the same "hands off" doctrine, but with a notable difference. Government would not be used to regulate the vastly increased power of corporate interests.[5] Big business intended to be free of political control as well as market competition. If unbridled competition were to be controlled, business would arrange matters itself in order to avoid its own rule.

Social uplift programs often required governmental support, and such dependence might suggest a contradiction between theory and practice. The difference was only formal, though, for reform leaders wanted no direction from or regulation by the political process. The coincidence of ideology between captains of reform and those of business combined to give cohesion and legitimacy to uplift ethics, even when exploitation of the industrial worker or family farmer was both excessive and unrestrained. Economic and political doctrines remained veiled by popular faith in the reality of national union and the promise of national progress. Americans believed in themselves even when their poverty belied their dream.

Although struggles such as those for better schools and libraries encountered considerable public inertia and demanded personal sacrifice from their advocates, such conflicts involved no radical political or economic controversies, as had the republican revolution of 1776 or the secession crisis of 1861. Reform in the industrial age touched the average citizen only to the extent that it may have activated a sense of community awareness or civic pride. Uplift action, however energetically undertaken, treated the symptoms of economic and cultural deprivation; it never challenged the established order in such terms as wealth redistribution, legalization of collective bargaining, or agricultural subsidization. For the most part, poor and rich alike accepted as "gospel" the dogmas of laissez-faire capitalism and social uplift.

Born into one of Boston's wealthy merchant families, Justin Winsor had uncommon opportunities for a successful career in business or in one of the learned professions—law, medicine, or divinity. Bored with the tedious study of classical learning so common in his day, he left Harvard College to pursue his personal tastes in scholarship. With the assistance of his family's money, he would become a "self-made" gentleman of letters; his success as librarian and historian would follow more

from the industry of his mind and pen than from his inheritance of money and property. His independent approach to education reflected the same Horatio Alger "rags-
to-riches" mentality and drive as that that glorified individual initiative and knew
"success" by no other name. By self-education, managerial skill, and incredible industry, Winsor mastered the techniques of two ancient arts and made important contributions in transforming those two crafts into respected professional disciplines.

Creation of these corporate structures, it was thought, would foster the progress
and distribution of modern learning. Membership would remain no longer the exclusive badge of wealth and gentle breeding, and objective demonstration would displace
the writing of campaign biography and polemical narratives. Professionalization
brought library economy and social science within the control of a new elite, admis-
sion to which was based on considerations other than social and political preferment.
Meritorious service and individual scholarship would govern the assortment of those
who belonged and those who did not. By letters patent, American librarians and historians proclaimed their place within the tradition of educational reform as though
professionalization itself were essential to, but detached from, the social and political
processes.

Considered apart from the ethos of the industrial age, white collar reform might
be viewed as a well-meaning, but naive and hapless confirmation of social Darwinism.
One might thus see the uplift ethic as a delusion of the masses or as an opiate administered by the wealthy to sustain their dominion over the poor. If a subsequent generation looks with scepticism at the "iron-man" ethics of the industrial age, that arrogance of modernity will not likely lead to a greater degree of understanding or historical veracity.

Americans of the late nineteenth century compared their society with that of
Europe and, on balance, found the comparison to be a favorable one. Their expanding
republic had purged itself of rebellion and slavery, had suffered greatly in that purifi-
cation process, and no longer sought governmental solutions to social problems that
might be treated by private remedies. Given the substantial advances of the nation
in its first hundred years, expectations for further progress and improvement did not
appear misplaced. Energized by an almost boundless optimism and pride, people at
all levels of society looked to the future and to themselves for self-fulfillment. That
Americans did not turn to their government revealed their basic distrust of political
paternalism. On the one hand, uplift reforms neither prevented nor cured the ills
that accompanied industrialization; on the other hand, no society has experienced
an economic revolution of such magnitude with less suffering and exploitation. The
great accomplishment may well have been that the American people preserved their
civil liberties and self-respect by setting these apart from their pocket-book concerns.
Uplift ethics reflected and supported a popular faith in values that only a self-made
generation might find both liberating and respectable.

Justin Winsor shared fully in the emerging consensus relative to the uplift ethos.
His approach to life, to scholarship, and to his labors as a librarian clearly revealed
a strong belief in the prevalent concepts of self-help, uplift, and social progress. Early
in life, he concluded that self-education constituted the most effective means of
learning, and throughout his youth, he proved a difficult pupil to his teachers. His
faith in self-education was combined with an undying belief in the ability of man to
raise himself from a lower to a higher plane of intelligence through determined and
systematic effort. Such a continued intellectual progress was demanded for two
reasons: first, because it allowed the individual to fulfill his highest potential and thus
become a happy and useful member of the larger society, and second, because the
democratic form of government assumed an educated electorate. Such an informed
electorate would insure the continued growth and stability of the republic.[6]

In the first case, Winsor reflected the apparently inescapable guilt shared by his Brahmin fellows, most of whom came in time to feel that they were in some way betraying their puritan heritage by pursuing a life of letters. Brahmin literary figures like George Ticknor agonized over their failure to do something "useful" in society, and Winsor, too, thought of his duty to serve society in a productive fashion. Opportunity to manage an institution that was committed to social reform as well as intellectual pursuits proved fulfilling beyond his greatest expectations.[7]

In the second case, Winsor's political preferences mirrored traditional Whig concerns for the future of democracy in America.[8] He shared their alarm over the rise of "rampant equalitarianism" accompanied, as it seemed, by gross violations of public morality and by widespread public disorderliness. And again, like his fellows, he subscribed to the Socratic idea that knowledge created virtue, thus, he joined them in their efforts to design and establish institutions that would educate the common people and thus maintain the traditional order in the republic.

Given these basic threads of thought, one can begin to sense the direction and intensity of Winsor's philosophy of library service. He fully subscribed to the inscription on the Boyleston Street side of Boston's Public Library: "The Commonwealth requires the education of the people as the safeguard of order and liberty." He agreed with J. P. Quincy, a fellow Bostonian, who noted that the library promised "the gradual deliverance of the people from the wiles of the rhetorician and stump orator, with their distorted fancies," and that in time, "the essential elements of every political and social question may be confidently submitted" to the newly enlightened public opinion.[9] Winsor himself, speaking to his fellow librarians in 1879, said that libraries are a "great engine in our hands," an engine that has the "power for good or evil . . . among the great masses of the people."[10]

In a similar vein, he congratulated librarians in 1881 on their growing significance in the life of the nation, and utilized yet another metaphor from industrial America to describe the library when he noted: "I think of it sometimes as a derrick, lifting the enert masses and swinging them round to the sure foundations upon which the national character shall rise."[11]

But the provision for the uplift of the "masses of readers" was only one element in Winsor's credo. For he knew from his own experience and from the frequently cited experiences of his Brahmin fellows that books and libraries were also extremely important to the aristocracy of talent that would someday guide the social, political, and literary affairs of the nation. It went without saying that libraries were essential to learning and that productive scholarship was nearly impossible without them. To him, "a great library should be a workshop as well as a repository."[12]

For Winsor, "the new significance of libraries as the necessity of the many, as well as the essential home, as it may be, of the few," could be found in their broadening of the field of observation, for the expansion of knowledge and its accessibility would make the institution "both a monument and an engine."[13] The chapters that follow explore Justin Winsor's contribution to the development of an institution that he felt combined the desirable qualities of a quiet storehouse of books, where "scholars and writers could replenish their intellectual fires," and of a "mighty engine" or an "invading army," with the power to "ameliorate mankind."

Born in Boston on 2 January 1831, Justin Winsor claimed an honorable descent and bore the conceit of his birth with modest pride throughout his life. As a child, he frequently visited his father Nathaniel's ancestral home in Duxbury, one of Massachusetts's earliest settlements. There among the reminders of his colonial heritage, he developed a taste for times past and later pursued his hobby of genealogical research. At first glance, an adolescent's preoccupation with graveyard markings might suggest an untimely seizure of morbidity. Perhaps the romance and adventure of early voyaging and settlement provided sons of New England a measure of excitement not unlike that that children now find in playing cowboys and Indians. Through his mother, Ann Thomas Howland, Winsor could trace his lineage to the Mayflower migration. In any case, Winsor found the historical company of Duxbury more interesting than the grammatical declensions of the Boston Latin School, from which he was graduated in 1849.[14]

In that same year, Winsor entered Harvard College and in his freshman term, completed a lengthy compilation of oral memories, local traditions, and public records, all of which he published under the title, *A History of Duxbury, Massachusetts, with Genealogical Registers* (1849). At eighteen, the young author's book exhibited his taste for historical adventure and his great capacity for meticulous detail. Unfortunately for his academic career, he took little interest in classical instruction and instead devoted considerable energy to collecting and reading modern literature and biography.

Always possessed of a free spirit, the recalcitrant scholar probably read as much and worked as hard as any of his classmates. Yet his mind resisted preparation for class recitations, and apart from the lure of local dramatic productions, nothing distracted his near total immersion in belles lettres. Winsor prepared notes on much of what he read and occasionally tried his hand at artistic composition. His parents wanted him to complete his schooling, and to honor their wishes, he submitted to the regimen as best he could. At the end of his sophomore year, he stood next to last in his class; in the middle of the following year, the faculty suspended Winsor for one semester. This disciplinary action failed in its intended effect, and Winsor began preparations for leaving Harvard in favor of the less rigid instruction in European universities. In his eyes, a classical education smothered the creative spark of the literary novitiate. It would require fifteen years of failure to convince this headstrong youth that his talents lay elsewhere.[15]

Apart from the urgency of his need to chart an independent course of study, Winsor took to Europe a diverse trunk of unfulfilled intellectual curiosities, particularly those related to Shakespearian textual criticism and to the famous drama circle led by David Garrick. Even as a student at Harvard, young Winsor had begun compiling notes on his favorite playwrights and thespians. Inspired by productions of Richard Sheridan's comedies, Winsor had composed theatrical farces with irreverent haste and had offered them to a Boston drama company. Once he devoted an entire day to the writing of a comedy, which bore the unheeded injunction, "Don't Get into a Passion." His second effort in three days took the more prosaic, though autobiographical title, "The Sophomore." Winsor confided to his diary that he had written W. H. Smith, manager of the Museum Theater, a cover letter urging attention to the enclosed manuscript:

> Dear Sir, you have before you the production of a novice—a student
> who has stolen a few hours from his work, and one who can as well
> rest with respect as attention. Read it, and if you find it unworthy of
> attention, burn it; if a better fate be decreed, perhaps you would
> like to confer with the author . . . . [16]

Failure to play in Boston did not freeze Winsor's pen, and the outpourings of an immature artist later would find a more receptive response in the mediums of poetry and literary criticism.

Winsor's two years in Paris and Heidelberg (1852-1854) allowed him a degree of leisure not experienced in his school years. Now he could taste and savor library treasures previously unavailable even in the literary capital of America. He studied French and German with eagerness, and tested his new skills by translating enough poetry to compile a volume of such labors. Yet he was not overly optimistic about its immediate publication. On returning home, the young poet would get it into shape and put it to the test. Selections from the manuscript did find their way into print, but not collectively.

Some of Winsor's letters to his parents, written during his travels through France and Germany, demonstrated a strong determination to earn his living by writing. He wrote his father from Germany in early 1854 that he wanted to publish a collection of original and translated poetry, but that such an effort would not "see the light at any risk" to his father's purse. Speaking of future career plans, Winsor added that if he were "to succeed in any line," it would be "in that of literature." He did not expect wealth from his vocation, "for that may not come with fame, if fame itself come . . . ." Cryptically, he concluded that "many things may happen to open something . . . here or there."[17] Many years of desultory writing would pass before Winsor found the coincidence of his native ability and vocational opportunity.

Arriving home in September 1854, Winsor assisted his family in moving to a spacious new dwelling on Boston's fashionable Blackstone Square. From Europe, he had sent instructions on the design and decor of the library, the extravagance of which was not unlike that of Winsor's literary ambitions. By correspondence he had arranged the setting for his life work; also by letter he had proposed marriage to Caroline Tufts Barker, a young lady whom he had courted while he was at Harvard. About a year after his return from Europe, Justin and Caroline were married and given quarters in "Winsor Castle," as the residence had come to be known locally. The would-be Brahmin of letters surrounded himself with beauty and order; he took up his vocational labors with all of the benefits that physical and emotional security might afford. Now Winsor could work at being Winsor.[18]

New York City's new *Crayon* magazine provided an outlet for much of Winsor's unsold collection of verse. From its beginning in 1855 to 1858, that journal alone published 26 of his essays and 36 poems, many of which were English translations of works by German romanticists. Winsor served as literary editor of the *Crayon* for two years, during which tenure he frequently selected poems and essays that painted word pictures of nature and stressed its ordered perfection. In Winsor's "Country Correspondence," the quaintness of rustic life charms the urbane visitor-author, and for nine additional installments, this quaint charm renders great splashes of verbal landscapes that are uniformly ponderous and exceedingly contrived.[19]

In 1860, Winsor became Boston's literary correspondent for Richard Grant White's new daily, the *New York World*. Although he supplied regular reports of publishing news, he offered almost nothing of his own. Unable to serve in the Massachusetts militia because of poor eyesight, Winsor remained at his desk during the great rebellion. During this period, he published occasional verse and book reviews for

Henry and Charles Humphreys Swietser's *Round Table*, a journal of opinion published in New York. From 1863 to 1868, Winsor's letters and literary notes appeared in the *Round Table* and treated a wide variety of topics, although the definition of art and Shakespearian criticism attracted more of his attention than other subjects. In reviewing books, he almost never gave false praise for the sake of local or national pride; perhaps his iconoclastic reviews were more popular in New York than in Boston.[20]

During the war years, Winsor drafted a lengthy manuscript on the life of David Garrick, whose theatrical career had attracted Winsor's attention as early as 1850. On returning from his intellectual pilgrimage to Europe, he had begun intensive research on Garrick in the Boston Athenaeum. By 1860, he had begun the near-impossible task of pulling together his countless number of notes. After four years of writing, he had completed ten folio volumes, which were replete with front matter, references, maps, appendices, and index. Yet "Garrick and his Contemporaries" was not complete, for its author continued to collect data and revise the initial manuscript. He enlarged the scope of his work, and the final manuscript came to be entitled, "The Life and Times of David Garrick: A View of the Eighteenth Century in England, in its Social, Literary, and Dramatic Relations, and Their Influence upon Continental Life and Letters."[21] Perhaps the length and scholarly character of Winsor's work on Garrick discouraged publication, for neither the original nor the revised draft ever went to the printers.

In the winter of 1866, Winsor developed a close, though decidedly platonic relationship with Lillian Woodman Aldrich, who had married Thomas Bailey Aldrich the previous year. Every afternoon at four o'clock, Winsor called upon his lady friend and shared an hour before her fire taking tea and enjoying conversation about his favorite subject, David Garrick. The limitedness of Winsor's range of interests was memorable, for his companion recalled the visits with great detail many years later:

> The program of the hour was ever the same. The largest and easiest chair drawn to the fire, and while the tea was brewing the long fork held and toasted the bread. Sometimes there was pleasant talk, and sometimes long silence, but always the two were the most companionable of comrades. Although Mr. Winsor could in truth be named a veritable bookworm—versed in all literature, a man of letters in the fullest sense of the word—in this hour books were rarely talked of. Mr. David Garrick was often present, real and tangible as Hamlet's ghost, he appeared and disappeared, and came again, often making a third in many a cheerful duet.[22]

Mrs. Aldrich remembered that as the months passed "the intimate bonds of his friendship seemed loosened."[23] At the end of the year, Thomas Aldrich took his bride to a new residence in another part of Boston, and the affair ended with but two or three subsequent visits. Fortunately for Winsor, Mrs. Aldrich had spoken of him to another friend "high up in the city's affairs." Winsor accepted an offer, channeled through Mrs. Aldrich, to serve on the Board of Trustees of the Boston Public Library.[24]

Upon his initial appointment to the Board of Trustees, Winsor was selected to head the Finance Committee, but the Trustees were so impressed with his prodigious efforts to learn every detail of the library's operations that they unanimously decided to name him chairman of the Examining Committee for 1867. The latter committee was charged by the governing regulations of the library to assess critically the operations of the library and to make such suggestions as they deemed appropriate for its future management. That Winsor should be selected for the chairmanship of such an important committee so soon after his appointment to the Board was evidence of the vigor with which he undertook his responsibilities as a new Trustee.[25]

The five-member Examining Committee completed its review in the fall of 1867, and the other members were so impressed by Winsor's knowledge of the library's affairs that they asked him to write their report. This document, the 1867 Report of the Examining Committee, was to prove the most thorough and constructive ever prepared by the Trustees, and more importantly, it was to demonstrate Winsor's remarkable mastery of the whole range of activities undertaken by Boston's public library. So impressive was his report that librarians and friends of libraries across the country took notice of it, and Winsor was quickly recognized as an authority on public library management. This unexpected development positioned Winsor perfectly for his sudden and meteoric entrance into the library field.

On the afternoon of 8 January 1868, Charles Coffin Jewett, Superintendent of the Boston Public Library, suffered a severe attack of apoplexy while working at his desk in the Library's new building on Boyleston Street. Realizing that he was near death, the 52-year-old librarian pleaded to be carried to his and family in nearby Braintree. There, attended by his wife and several friends, he passed away early the next morning.[26]

Jewett had come to Boston in 1855, after experiencing the indignity of being removed from his position as librarian at the Smithsonian Institution in Washington. However, despite this embarrassment, he was still considered the nation's leading professional librarian. Joining the staff of the Boston Public Library, he served first as cataloger, then as advisor in matters related to building the book collection. Within three years, he was appointed Superintendent of the Library.

In seeking their first superintendent, the Trustees of the Boston Public Library had stressed the fact that they were searching for a man "of extensive knowledge of books, ancient and foreign languages, and of science and literature generally." Furthermore, they admitted that such individuals were not easily found, for "the general management and administration of a first class library requires an efficient and responsible head, possessing a degree of ability and qualifications, intellectual and literary, of a higher order than can be expected" from most members of the profession.[27]

A decade later, the Trustees retained their emphasis on experience and professional stature when they eulogized that "in the death of Charles Coffin Jewett this Library is deprived of a steadfast friend, and an officer of such ingenious mind and such rare knowledge apposite to his duty, that we hardly know where to find his equal . . . ."[28] Ironically, the man who was to replace Jewett, and who in time was to eclipse completely his achievements as a librarian, was totally inexperienced in the library profession.

Indeed, Winsor himself acknowledged this fact when he described his appointment in the following fashion:

> It was much the same process as in the New England Seaboard towns, in old times, a young man sometimes attained command of a ship without apprenticeship before the mast, by "crawling in through the cabin windows," that I got so conspicuous a place in the librarian's calling.[29]

But, while he lacked experience in library affairs, he was remarkably well suited for the position in other ways. First, he was quite the proper Bostonian. His local reputation as a "literary man," his family's financial connections, and his identification with the best of genteel Boston made him a very desirable candidate for the job.[30] As William E. Foster was to recall, "if . . . you should have in your mind a mental picture of a representative Bostonian of that period, here is a man who is a typical embodiment of that ideal."[31]

A second important qualification was his deeply felt need to prove "useful." After experimenting with various literary pursuits, the "independent man of letters" was growing dissatisfied with his desultory life.[32] The Boston Public Library post offered him a concrete and definable focus for his missionary zeal to be of service, and he brought enormous stores of energy and determination to his work.

Third, he was a man of great self assurance. He once noted that he could get more done in an hour than most men could in two.[33] His confidence in his own abilities and his reputation for hard work impressed the Trustees.

Finally, Winsor had demonstrated by means of his work on the 1867 Examining Committee a facility for administration, especially the statistically based management practices then gaining wide acceptance in America. Indeed, Judge Mellen Chamberlain later remarked that Superintendent Winsor might well have succeeded as a captain of industry, for his administrative talents would have amply suited him for competition in the business arena of the Gilded Age.[34]

And so, family tradition and social connections, literary inclinations and a commitment to serve his fellow men, boundless energy and a latent genius for management, all combined to make Justin Winsor ideally suited for the job, so much so that "even latter-day Bostonians would agree that his appointment was in the nature of a remarkable providence."[35]

Given these qualities, one would justifiably expect Winsor to serve with distinction as superintendent of the Boston Public Library, but no one foresaw the awe-inspiring nature of his achievements during his tenure at the helm of the nation's premier public library.

Upon assuming the leadership of the Boston Public Library, Winsor was faced with a rather confused operation. For one thing, Jewett had not been an able administrator. He had failed to give balanced attention to the whole operation and had focused on questions relating to the acquisition and cataloging of books. Consequently, as Charles Ammi Cutter has noted, Winsor inherited an "organization which, to say the least, creaked a little."[36]

Jewett's limited administrative ability only partially explains the problem. Although he had been on the very cutting edge of library development at mid-century, by the time he assumed the leadership of the Boston Public Library, he had become increasingly conservative and had resisted reforms in library management.[37]

Librarian Jewett had not implemented all of the Trustees' objectives for the Boston Public Library, as outlined in the famous 1852 Report of that body and in other subsequent documents.[38] The Library had been established by Boston's "Best Men" in response to a number of disturbing trends in their community. Especially disconcerting was the flood of immigrants coming to the city. More than 230,000 entered between 1845 and 1855, and an overwhelming number of them, mostly Irish, remained in Boston.[39] Members of the Standing Committee of the Boston Public Library were convinced that these new residents thought "little of moral and intellectual culture." The Committee raised a lament then being voiced by many concerned Bostonians: "where is the remedy for this influx of ignorance?"[40]

The city's "Best Men" came to feel the need for institutions that would contribute to the process of assimilating into society these new and potentially dangerous classes. This strongly felt need, coupled with their faith in the efficacy of the printed word as a means of influencing human behavior, led to the establishment of an integrated system of common schools, libraries, and other "public" institutions.[41]

The founding of the Boston Public Library was dominated by George Ticknor, the city's leading literary and social figure. He insisted that the new institution be made as accessible as possible, for he believed that an open library might be used as a proper means of educating the immigrants, thus guarding the established order against demagoguery.[42] Ticknor predicated this belief upon the assumption that the library would be regularly and profitably frequented by the common man.[43] He vigorously noted that "it is of paramount importance that the means of general information shall be so diffused that the largest possible number of persons should be induced to read and understand questions of social order."[44] As far as Ticknor was concerned, "if people will not come to your library you may as well establish none."[45] Accordingly, he held that the Boston Public Library should cater to public taste for "healthy general reading," that is, material that would contribute to "moral and intellectual improvement" among "the middling-classes."[46] The objective was to contribute to the uplift of Boston's new residents, and the library was to serve as a "conservator of order." That the library should also provide access to the world's most worthwhile knowledge for the "natural aristocracy" that would one day lead in the social, political, and intellectual affairs of the nation was self-evident.[47]

While Jewett seemed quite willing to provide for the needs of Boston's intellectual leadership, he appeared unwilling, or unable, to design programs necessary to make the library a "popular institution." Thus he failed to achieve both parts of Ticknor's objective. Justin Winsor would bring order to the management of the Boston Public Library, and he then would move to extend and popularize services. In so doing, he would test the efficacy of Ticknor's scheme to civilize Boston's turbulent element.

When Jewett died, leaving the library in need of immediate attention, William Jillson, the assistant librarian, could not be elevated to the head post, for he was dying of consumption. Responding to this distressing situation and "having in view the large work already in preparation for the year, and the necessity of familiarity with all parts of our system of labor, the Trustees selected for the position, Mr. Justin Winsor, at that time a Trustee of the Institution, who at once entered upon the service."[48] The Trustees then issued a judgment that was to be echoed by dozens of Winsor's most perceptive contemporaries:

> His energetic administration of affairs, the order, promptness and accuracy with which the various work has been arranged and carried forward, and his earnest efforts to make the Library fulfill public expectation, have, each and all, fully justified the choice.[49]

Justin Winsor possessed a hidden brilliance for management, and the Trustees has stumbled upon the man who, due mainly to his "great executive ability," was to become, in Charles Ammi Cutter's opinion, "the best known librarian in the country."[50] Writing after Winsor's death, Cutter concisely summarized Winsor's assets in this way: "forceful personality . . . great executive ability . . . the born organizer's eye for the choice of subordinates . . . the power of impressing himself on them . . . an inexhaustible supply of energy."[51]

Cutter also noted that Winsor was not well known for any "special originality in library economy" but instead, was simply a superb, if somewhat conservative, administrator. Upon assuming the position of Superintendent, Winsor set out to become "thoroughly acquainted with the minutest details of every subordinate position," and in time, "reduced the whole management of the library to a regular system which worked like a charm."[52] He worked, worked, worked: "days between breakfast and dark were devoted to library work," and as he said himself, when making improvements in the administration of the library, he had never acted without "due deliberation."[53]

Indeed, his careful, thoughtful, and "scientific" approach to management was to become his hallmark. One of the first tasks he undertook was to request information on the management of libraries from other librarians across the land. He carefully studied this information and became, in a short time, fully conversant with every aspect of library affairs in this country and abroad. Further, he pioneered in the systematic and extensive use of statistics as an administrative tool. As he wrote in 1876:

> There is no branch of library economy more important, or so little understood by a librarian as helps to himself, as the daily statistics which he can preserve of the growth, loss, and use (both in extent and character) of the collection under his care. The librarian who watches these things closely, and records them, always understands what he is about, and what he accomplishes or fails to accomplish.[54]

Winsor invariably justified his administrative decisions with an awesome presentation of statistical data; he believed that such presentations helped "patrons . . . comprehend better the machinery of the library." His annual reports were considered masterpieces of statistical data collection, analysis, and presentation, and they were widely read and cited by librarians both in this country and in Europe. The attitude of library interests was reflected in this comment found in the *Fifth Annual Report of the Trustees of the Holton Library of Brighton, Massachusetts [1869]*:

> By the aid of statistical tables of comparison with other libraries, large and small, in this country and abroad, and with most loving zeal and care, he has performed his work to the utter discomfiture of all superficialists in similar departments of service.

As an administrator he was firm, disciplined, and fair-minded, and by the end of the first year of his superintendency, the several departments operated with military precision.[55] Winsor had resolved a whole series of administrative difficulties, most of which involved personnel policies. The Superintendent's staff received explicit instructions on even the most elementary questions, such as the length of rest periods, use of the telephone, and avoidance of unnecessary conversation. One Examining Committee applauded the results of Winsor's regimentation, observing that the administration of the Library was "its most credible feature. It is believed that, in this respect, it stands in the front rank of similar institutions."[56]

Perhaps Cutter paid him the ultimate compliment by noting that when Winsor left the Boston Public Library, it was "running so smoothly that for a long time after he resigned the charge, it was not perceived that there was no librarian. . . ."[57]

In their 1852 *Report*, the Trustees specifically stated that they expected the library to be popular in nature. George Ticknor, the author of the *Report*, was instrumental in formulating this basic philosophy. In 1860, he gave his private collection to the Library and had occasion to recall that from the beginning, it had been his desire that this institution "should be made useful to the greatest possible number . . . , especially to such of them as may be less able than they would gladly be to procure pleasant and profitable reading. . . ."[58]

Not only did Ticknor and his fellow Trustees require that library membership be open to all classes of society, they insisted as well that the collection itself be inclusive of all classes of books:

III. *Books that will be often asked for*, (we mean, the more respectable of the popular books of the time,) of which copies should be provided in such numbers, that *many* persons, if they desire it, can be reading the same work at the same moment, and so render the pleasant and healthy literature of the day accessible to the whole people at the only time they care for it,—that is, when it is living, fresh and new . . . . We may hope to create a real desire for general reading. . . . An appetite like this, when formed, will, we fully believe, provide wisely and well for its own wants . . . and when such a taste for books has been formed by these lighter publications, then the older and more settled works in Biography, in History, and in the graver departments of knowledge will be demanded.[59]

And so, articulately and forcefully, we find the most influential statement of the "uplift" theory to appear in early library literature, one that was to become the very credo for most of the country's public librarians. Light reading, even fiction—lest it be "unprofitable" or "pernicious trash"—was to become the "carrot" used to entice the populace.[60]

Trustees frequently reminded their librarians not to forget the higher purpose of the library, for work, not recreation, was the central theme of uplift ethics. As the Boston Public Library Trustees wrote in their 1875 Report:

Notwithstanding any popular notions to the contrary, it is no part of the duty of the municipality to raise taxes for the amusement of the people, unless the amusement is clearly seen to be conducive to higher ends of good citizenship, like the encouragement of patriotism, the promotion of public health, or the undermining of immorality.[61]

Unlike Jewett, who seemed reluctant to invest in the "carrot," Winsor set out with vigor to implement the "uplift" theory in Boston. To do so, he had to take a forthright stand on the question of light fiction in libraries, for he knew that without the lure of light reading, few of the "sinewy-minded" people of Boston would frequent his library. He was convinced that if he could only induce them to use the library, they could be molded into the "earnest and thoughtful readers" so desired.

In two widely-read papers published in 1876, Winsor clearly articulated the position that he had been advocating since 1867. In one of these papers, "Reading in Popular Libraries," Winsor maintains that reading tastes are both relative and changeable:

Thus it is: A spurns as trash what elevates B, who looks down on the highest reading C is capable of, and so on till you get down to the mere jingle that amuses a half idiot . . . . If this principle is understood, the whole question lightens up. It is by no means to be inferred that, however we take things, we must leave them as we find them. Librarians do not do their duty unless they strive to elevate the taste of their readers, and this they can do, not by refusing to put within their reach the books which the masses of readers want, but by inducing a habit of frequenting the library, by giving readers such books as they ask for and then helping them in the choice of books, conducting them, say from the ordinary society novel, and then to the proofs and illustrations of the events or periods commemorated in the more readable of the historians. Multitudes of readers need only to be put in this path to follow it.[62]

In the second paper, entitled "Free Libraries and Readers," he emphasized that books are "the librarian's tools to accomplish his work, and as the work of moulding readers is multiform, his tools must be as various—some course, some fine." And he offered explicit directions on how this "moulding" was to be accomplished. He reminded librarians that Americans are not easily "driven either in their reading or in their politics":

> The fact is, a library must reach the summit of its usefulness naturally, as most agencies do. It fails as a hot-bed. . . . you must foster the instinct for reading, and then apply the agencies for directing it. You can allure, you can imperceptibly guide, but you make poor headway if you try to compel. . . . Let the attention be guided, as unwittingly as possible, from the poor to the indifferent, from this to the good, and so on to the best. . . . [63]

But how was such imperceptible guidance to be exerted? Again, Winsor supplied a careful and articulate answer. It came in the form of two publications: *The Chronological Index to Historical Fiction* (1871) and *A Catalogue of Books Belonging to the Lower Hall of the Central Department of the Classes of History, Biography and Travel . . . With Notes for Readers under Subject References . . .* (1873). Winsor explained his scheme for his fellow professionals in his 1877 *Annual Report*:

> In 1873 the Library made an innovation in the bibliographical matter which was made an adjunct of its popular Catalogues. The new departure was a natural one, and followed as a matter of course in the development of the influence which it was the aim of the fathers of the Library to bestow upon the public. . . . With the growth of any collection the ease of consultation naturally gives way to an indecision in the face of accumulated titles on every subject. . . . A consideration of these difficulties ripened the plan. As [a] preliminary the thought occurred of alluring the pastime reader, of whom all Libraries, in any degree popular, have a large following, by easy steps, to become a reader of better purpose. I am too much a believer in the general straightforwardness of ingrafted impulses ever violently to counteract them. I believe men must be led rather than pushed. . . . This assistance was accordingly invoked in a list of historical fiction, which was prepared in chronological groupings under countries, as calculated to instigate a study by comparison, and lead the mind to history and biography by the citing of the critical faculties. . . . This was but a trial. The next step was the most serious one of endeavoring to direct the ductile perceptions of the less learned among readers. The effort was not to propound positively any course of reading, for there is danger always in dogmatism, however right its foundation may be. The notes which were appended to the subject-references in the History, Biography, and Travel Catalogue of the Lower Hall, in 1873, served to render the ordinary reader more able to choose to his liking when an undistinguishable mass of equivalent titles perplexed him.[64]

In short, the catalog was annotated in order to give it an "educational character," and the innovation, referred to by Charles Francis Adams, Jr., as "a new and creditable Boston idea," was to be widely imitated by librarians throughout the land.[65] As Winsor himself remembered in 1877, "I have reason to believe the idea was not a futile one," and he frequently noted with pride the nature and extent of the increased circulation attributable, at least in part, to his "educational catalogue."[66]

Unquestionably, library use was increasing.[67] Winsor's careful reports clearly demonstrate this fact, but most observers were so convinced of the malleability of the human intelligence that they assumed an improvement in the quality of reading as well as the quantity of material read. For instance, the president of the Board of Trustees, William W. Greenough, told the crowd gathered for the dedication of the South Boston Branch of the Boston Public Library that the opening of the library clearly evidenced the "intellectual and moral cravings" of the city's citizens. He continued:

> that those desires were not, on the average, of a more elevated character, at first produced some disappointment in the friends of education, but when it was remembered that people would only read the books which they wished to read, and not those expressly provided, as it were, without their consent, for their intellectual advancement, the disappointment gave way to the reasonable expectation that, in forming a taste for books, the average understanding would raise itself, step by step, from the perusal of innocuous works of fiction, or from inconsequential and sporadic reading, to a better and higher and more useful class of literary productions. Experience has shown that this expectation has proved measurably correct.[68]

And then Trustee Greenough offered a generally unsubstantiated disclaimer: "though, throughout this country and in England, three-fourths of the whole amount of average circulation is made up of fiction and juveniles, it is yet found that the demand for better books is steadily and regularly making progress."[69] Evidence of such an increase in the quality of reading generally rested on personal observation. For example, Winsor claimed that "it has been noticed that . . . the less prepossessing and poorly clad neighbor showed an appreciation of a volume of science, art or history."[70] Mathew Arnold reported in the *Library Journal* that he was more impressed by the sight of a shoeless newsboy seated in one of the plush chairs of Bates Hall reading the *Life of Washington*, than anything else he had seen in America.[71]

Winsor sought to get books used in many other ways as well: he worked for the establishment of branch libraries; he extended the hours of opening for the library; and he relaxed use restrictions.[72] But in every case, the purpose was to bring men and books together so that the printed work might "ameliorate mankind."

Winsor promoted the public library movement with the same intensity of commitment that led men and women of his day to the missionary field in China.[73] For nearly three decades, he poured much of his time and energy into the organization of that cause. Yet building the institutional structures of the library profession would prove more successful than maintaining the vital piety of the new dogma.[74]

Winsor served the Boston Public Library precisely at that time when librarians appeared most committed to the uplift ethos, and he never lost his faith in the efficacy of the printed word in the struggle to lift the "inert masses" to the "sure foundations upon which the national character shall rise."[75] During his last year at the Boston Public Library, he addressed his colleagues, urging them not to forget their social creed: "Your life as a guardian of a library is one of constant wariness and struggle. In fashion, in low tastes, in unformed minds, you have an enemy who must be made to surrender."[76]

In his "President's Address" for 1877, Winsor displayed a rare bit of anger over a situation that had become a *cause célèbre* among librarians. He observed that, despite advances since the 1876 meeting:

> there are still corporators and civic councillors who conceive that the extent of a librarian's duties is to pass books over a counter, and who fancy there is no special training necessary to administer a library. They say to us, we have nothing to do and are fully equal to it. We must expect to find such people using authority vested in them on general principles to control purposes of which they have no conception; upon whom popular suffrage has bestowed the right to an opinion, but upon which nature has put a veto.[77]

Those reading Winsor's speech in the *Library Journal* knew well that he referred to Boston Alderman Hugh O'Brien and several other members of the City Council. They also knew, or felt they knew, the story of O'Brien's disgraceful treatment of Winsor, and their sympathy for the librarian whom many viewed as the most accomplished in the country surged through the library profession with such force that Winsor was pushed to the stature of a folk-hero almost overnight.

Justin Winsor, the nation's premier public librarian, suddenly had resigned his post at the Boston Public Library, and it appeared that the "ignorant masses" had finally had their say about the Public Library's management. The problem arose over a question of salaries, but from the beginning, Winsor, president of the newly formed American Library Association, interpreted the dispute as an attack on his professional integrity. Pursuing a policy of fiscal retrenchment, the Committee of Aldermen arbitrarily recommended the reduction of Winsor's salary from 3,600 to 3,300 dollars. The cut, and the manner in which it was administered, struck Winsor as totally unwarranted, and he threatened to resign. While he vacillated some in fulfilling that threat, his high regard for the principle of library autonomy and his general distaste for the partisan nature of Boston city government required that he resign from the institution that he had served so devotedly for ten years.[78]

Winsor's friend, Horace Scudder, understood the decision and later wrote the following explanation:

> With his generous nature he was keenly sensitive to any act of meanness; he had come once or twice into collision with members of the city government when he was administering the library, and he had a profound distrust of municipal politics as he saw it in operation.[79]

The "act of meanness" that prompted Winsor's resignation surfaced at the City Council's meeting of July 2, 1877. Choate Burnham, speaking on behalf of the Library Board, had presented a laudatory plea for an increase in Winsor's salary and had emphasized Winsor's invaluable contributions to the Library's administration.[80] Unimpressed with Burnham's argument, Alderman Hugh O'Brien boldly challenged the professionalism of library management:

That Mr. Winsor is a very valuable man and very efficient in the performance of his duties, I have no doubt of it. But, Mr. Mayor, I doubt
the expediency of bringing in an order of that kind, and saying to the
City Council and to the 350,000 inhabitants of Boston that Mr. Winsor is the only man who can fill that position. We have educated Mr.
Winsor in that position, and I propose to give some other man a chance.
. . . I propose that we shall become public benefactors in the administration of public business. Having educated him, I say we ought to
educate more. I believe there are hundreds of citizens who could fill
that place after a few weeks' experience with just as much ability as
Mr. Winsor; and if Mr. Winsor has an offer of a position in Harvard
College I should advise him to take it. . . . It appears to me there is
a little too much red tape about this Public Library. The men who
instituted that library never dreamed that it was going to be such an
expense as it is . . . .[81]

The City Council voted to increase the superintendent's salary. But when
Winsor learned that the new rate would be allowed for only the remainder of the
fiscal year, he decided to accept the directorship at Harvard, a position that would
place him beyond the reach of "city demagogism" and in a setting more conducive
to the pursuit of his scholarly interests.

The public prints filled their columns with both recrimination and applause
over the news of Winsor's resignation. The debate reached the point that one paper
remarked that the whole thing appeared "a little overdone." But while it may have
seemed that way to many Bostonians, it was quite another matter to the members
of the emerging library profession.[82]

As far as Winsor's colleagues were concerned, his leavetaking under pressure
represented the forces of evil at work in American life. They blamed ignorance and
demagoguery for this slap in the profession's face. An editorial writer in the *Library
Journal* vividly presented the profession's views:

The Public Library, we had said to ourselves, was the one thing in Boston which Boston would not permit to be touched, and Boston was
the one city in which institutions were intrenched behind intelligence.
Yet in the City Council of Boston itself we hear the very same voice
which is making itself heard in other parts of the country though the
rapine and bloodshed of the railroad strikes—the voice which insists
that intelligence is worth no more than ignorance, and that every man
must be ranked on an equality with the lowest—and this voice is attacking that best gift of the people itself, the public library. This is of
dreadful significance, but it presents a fresh motive to the friends of
public libraries, in the fact that they furnish the most effective weapons
against the demagogic ignorance that glorifies ignorance and challenges
civilization. Light is the one cure for darkness, and every book that the
public library circulates helps to make Alderman O'Brien and the railroad rioters impossible.[83]

Writing in 1877, Winsor confirmed their faith in the power of libraries, noting:

It is well that we encounter foes as well as friends: the conflict will
sharpen our wits; and I know of no profession whose followers have
greater need to know men as they are, since a mission that is to

ameliorate mankind must have its base of operations in a thorough knowledge of it.[84]

Of course, by this time he had accepted a new position at Harvard, and the future looked bright and peaceful.[85] But Winsor never lessened his commitment to public libraries and their important mission in society. As a result, he played a consistently central role in the affairs of the American Library Association, a subject that we will consider prior to examining his years of distinguished service at Harvard.

In a way, Winsor's embarassing and disquieting encounter with Alderman O'Brien provided a rallying ground for those who felt that the librarian's calling deserved respect and autonomous status. Further, this incident led Winsor to a much more active interest in professional organization. It is no coincidence that the American Library Association was founded at this time, or that the pages of its official proceedings and the early issues of its official journal, *The Library Journal*, were filled with reports and editorials on the "disgraceful situation" in Boston.[86]

Winsor's important role in the American Library Association has been celebrated on many occasions and in many publications.[87] That he served as president of the ALA for the first ten years of its existence was ample evidence of his continuing commitment and significance to ALA. Historians who have examined those early years generally conclude that the record shows little Association activity outside of the sporadic conferences, and that little else was accomplished.[88] Such a narrow interpretation, however, discounts several significant contributions made by Winsor and his colleagues to the consolidation of professional librarianship. Perhaps a consideration of Winsor's three roles—as symbolic leader, professional prophet, and conference manager—will more fully illuminate the early years of professional librarianship in America.

As early as 1869, Winsor had clearly articulated the need for increased communication and solidarity among the nation's librarians. In the 17th *Annual Report of the Boston Public Library*, he asserted that there was not "a library in the country of a public nature but we are glad to be in correspondence with it." He noted further that "the interchange of bibliothecal experience is almost alone wanting to carry the knowledge of library science to the limit of proficiency." What was most needed, he argued in the same report, was an "organized medium for such inter-communication." Such a medium would have to await the establishment of the *Library Journal*, but until that time, Winsor's annual reports at the Boston Public Library constituted at once a widely-read compendium of "bibliothecal experience" and an influential call for the significant role played by the library in American society.[89]

His desire to cultivate a sense of professionalism was readily apparent during the years immediately preceding the founding of the Association. Many library trustees and would-be librarians turned to him for information and advice. This assistance Winsor readily provided, although he acknowledged on several occasions the inconvenience it caused him. In addition to providing novice librarians with a thorough knowledge of the practice of librarianship through apprentice-like service in the Boston Public Library, he instilled in his charges a sense of the professional nature of the field.

Given this long-standing concern for professionalism, it is little wonder that he reacted so obstinately to the reduction of his pay in Boston in 1876. And it is for reasons of like concern that he and his colleagues vehemently denounced Alderman O'Brien, the man who had audaciously suggested that "there are hundreds of citizens who could fill that place [Superintendent of the BPL] after a few weeks' experience with just as much ability as Mr. Winsor."[90]

In addition to supporting the librarians' claim to professionalism, Winsor urged librarians to assume responsibility as well as the perquisites. In 1876, he insisted that the profession had too long been characterized by individuals who had failed in the schoolroom or in the pulpit. What was required, he repeatedly said, were individuals committed to librarianship; he looked for men and women of "pluck" and "energy" who could earn for the profession the general public's respect.[91] Thus, by 1876, Winsor had become the very symbol of the librarians' drive for recognition.

Yet Winsor became more than just an important symbolic figure for the emerging profession. Realizing that librarians required a significant social mission to couple with their increasing technical expertise, Winsor proclaimed a new role for the library in American society. The library should commit itself to a crusade for combating the dangerous assaults on American moral and social standards by the "salacious" and "injurious" literature being consumed in ever greater amounts by the American public. Librarians had come to share the anxieties of the nation's intellectual elite about the future stability of the republic. These conservatives were greatly alarmed at the rise of "rampant egalitarianism," accompanied as it seemed, by gross violations of public morality and widespread public disorderliness. Furthermore, they fully subscribed to the Socratic idea that knowledge, albeit "true knowledge," created virtue. Influenced by these concerns, Winsor forcefully identified with a movement that might project librarians onto center stage and afford them the opportunity of rescuing mankind from the corrupting influence of low culture. Thus, he provided an insecure profession with a higher rationale for its existence.[92]

Winsor repeatedly admonished his colleagues that their great mission was nothing short of the amelioration of mankind. "Your life as guardian of a library is one of constant wariness and struggle," he told his fellows in 1876, for, "in fashion, in low tastes, in uniformed minds, you have an enemy that must be made to surrender."[93] In a ringing metaphor, Winsor articulated the profession's commitment to social and cultural uplift; he saw the library as a great "derrick, lifting the inert masses and swinging them round to the sure foundation upon which the national character shall rise."[94] Winsor's was not the only "voice in the wilderness," but among the high priests of the new community of librarians, none had suffered martyrdom for his conviction save the innocent victim of Alderman O'Brien. Winsor's sacrifice bespoke the meaning of his message.

A third aspect of Winsor's contribution to the struggling young profession came in the form of his wise, and unchallenged, management of the American Library Association's conferences from 1876 to 1885. Winsor was selected by the 103 delegates at the first meeting in Philadelphia to serve as the meeting's president, and he was continued in that post for the first ten years of the Association's history. Much of the profession's overwhelming confidence in Winsor must be attributed to his symbolic significance to the field and to his role as spokesman for the emerging profession, matters already discussed.

However, Winsor also possessed a manner and confidence that made him an ideal president of the Association. The literature of librarianship is replete with recollections by his contemporaries of his masterful handling of ALA meetings. Mellen Chamberlain, Winsor's successor at the Boston Public Library, noted that "I never saw Clay, Blaine, or Reed in the Speaker's Chair; but I have served in both houses of the General Court [of Massachusetts] when they were presided over by men of distinction, and I think I may say without exaggeration that I have never known any presiding officer who sooner got control of his assembly or handled it more efficiently or judiciously for the progress at hand."[95]

Josephine Rathbone, herself to be a president of the American Library Association, left a vivid portrait of a tall, portly, dignified Winsor who was somewhat haughty in bearing. She remembered "the graying brown hair parted in the center, the quiet and self-assured voice, and the heavy eyeglasses with stout guard chain that every little while would amusingly fall from his fleshy nose with such a clatter into his lap, and whose appearance in no way denoted or encouraged approach-ability or familiarity." His way was firm, and there was clearly no mistaking who was in charge of the meeting when Winsor was present. Rathbone, acknowledging his gentle way with most people, nevertheless recorded the fact that "one would *address* rather than *talk with* him."[96]

In those first years of the history of the ALA, the strong and respected presence of Winsor was reassuring to the self-conscious librarians. William Foster remembered that Winsor's "predominating quality was sanity of judgment" and that he left on all of the Association's proceedings "the impress of his strong per-sonality and his organizing mind."[97]

Winsor's enduring presence was not without disadvantage, as his strong hand and formidable demeanor often weighed heavily on the proceedings of the various conferences. As one reporter noted of the 1881 Conference, "there was from the beginning an overpowering sense of Cambridge, Harvard and Boston—a feeling among the inferior planets that they were revolving around the Hub." It was clear to that reporter, at least, that those attending the meeting were clearly in awe of Winsor, and that his presence stifled discussion and debate.[98]

Despite his tendency to overpower his colleagues, Winsor's important contri-bution to the American Library Association cannot be overestimated. That its members chose to honor him with the presidency once again near the end of his life (in 1897) is evidence of their enormous esteem for "Mr. Winsor." Perhaps Charles Ammi Cutter made the point best when he casually noted that Winsor was simply "the best known librarian in the country."[99]

That his position in the field was unrivaled was attested to by all, but most librarians chose to emphasize the great significance that his presence in librarian-ship had had for the recognition of the librarian's worth. Lamenting his death, his staff states that debt clearly when they noted that every librarian would find his "work dignified, his place in the community elevated, because of the life work of Justin Winsor."[100] In this sense, there is credence in Francis Peabody's eulogistic remark that "as librarian it is not enough to say that he was at the head of his profession; he may almost be said, so far as this country is concerned, to have created his profession."[101]

A number of students of Winsor's work at the Boston Public Library have concluded that he left the post with considerable regret, and only after the most severe provocation. While it is true that he was clearly upset by the "uncivilized" behavior of Alderman O'Brien, it must be remembered that Winsor had placed his very considerable scholarly interests in abeyance during the hectic and challenging years at the BPL, and he increasingly yearned for an environment more congenial to both his administrative and scholarly inclinations.

Scholars writing of his work as librarian at Harvard tend to devote the majority of their attention to his administrative activities, with only passing attention to his awesome scholarly productivity during the same period. They do so despite the ample evidence that his scholarly research, especially his mammoth cooperative histories, increasingly overshadowed his library interests.

That Winsor was determined to secure a position that would allow him ample time for his scholarly researches is explicitly stated by Harvard's President Eliot himself, who at Winsor's death, recalled his initial appointment in the following way:

> Although Mr. Winsor's administration was absolutely diligent and thorough, his knowledge of the whole subject was so comprehensive, and his quickness in executive work was so great, that from his first coming to the Library in 1877 he had much leisure. . . . This leisure he used with extraordinary diligence for twenty years in historical research, editorship, and authorship. The precious fruit of these congenial labors are well known to this society. It was understood in 1877, between the New Librarian and the President of the University, that such leisure as he might get would be used in this scholarly and serviceable way.[102]

Eliot hit upon a paradox that would trouble library historians for years: "The Harvard chronicler of this period will probably remain in doubt whether the University then enjoyed the services of a librarian who was an historical scholar, or of an historical scholar who was a librarian." The best evidence available suggests that the scales, especially during the last decade of his tenure at Harvard, may well have tipped toward the latter of Eliot's labels. Winsor tacitly acknowledged this fact when he dedicated his most significant scholarly work, *The Narrative and Critical History*, to Eliot with these words: "you took me away from many cares and transferred me to the more congenial service of the University."

This point does not diminish Winsor's very real contributions to academic librarianship during his twenty year tenure as Harvard's Librarian, but rather, it confirms his unrivaled significance to the nascent library profession. It is our contention that Winsor's elevated status among librarians was based upon three factors: 1) his impressive achievements as an innovative library administrator; 2) his martyrdom at the Boston Public Library; and 3) his recognition as historical scholar. Many of his colleagues viewed his historical contributions as being a very positive and significant part of his work.[103] Because of his dual career, Winsor emerged as the prototype of the ideal academic librarian, and the scholar-librarian has become among the most cherished of the profession's darlings.

Librarian Winsor assumed his new position at Harvard at a propitious time, a fact that surely did not surprise a man who always viewed his life as blessed with signal good fortune. In 1877, American higher education was entering a period of rapid growth and change. Indeed, it was a period characterized as revolutionary by some historians—and the way was cleared for those educators who had visions of significant alterations in the pattern of American higher education.

One of those men was Charles Eliot, President of Harvard. Eliot sought the expansion of Harvard, both in size and mission, and quickly set about this task. Possessed of increased funding for the nation's premier institution of higher education, Eliot agressively enlarged the faculty, revised the curriculum, introduced an elective system of course offerings, and struggled to redefine the University's role so that it might include research and publication along with teaching. In the latter emphasis, Eliot, like so many other of his contemporaries, was heavily influenced by the emerging model of German higher education. Of particular significance was the German insistence that education should be conducted on a seminar basis, as opposed to the more traditional lecture-recitation model, and that the university's principle role should be the pursuit of knowledge through research and publication conducted by faculty and students.

The nature and extent of that revolution in American higher education has been the subject of much, and of late varied, interpretation, and space limitations preclude any lengthy analysis of the matter here.[104] However, one fact appears clear: the changed emphasis and the rapid growth of American higher education posed some obvious opportunities (or problems, depending on one's viewpoint) for the libraries serving those institutions. First and foremost, the new emphasis on research (and ultimately specialization) among faculty and students assumed ready access to large collections of printed materials. Second, the transition from lectures to more informal and materials-oriented pedogogical methods increasingly required the assembly of substantial libraries designed to support the course work of students.[105]

That both of those needs were obvious to members of the faculty at Harvard prior to Winsor's assumption of the post of librarian is apparent from the records of the University. For instance, in 1875, Henry Adams addressed a petition to the Harvard Corporation, noting in part that "the Undersigned, Assistant Professor of History, . . . has the duty of instructing a number of students in the department of History. He requires of them that each one shall use to the utmost possible extent the resources of the College Library. Without doing so, they cannot acquire the training which it is his principal object to give them. As the Library is at present arranged it is impossible for them to use it to proper advantage." Noting that "this inconvenience is wholly unnecessary," Adams went on to suggest a simple method of improving student access to the Library's collections, and his suggestion was promptly acted on.[106]

Similarly, Eliot frequently reiterated his support for the development of a large and well staffed library, even if that meant the inclusion of "masses of dead books." Perhaps he said it best when he argued that "the justification of the enormous expense which is involved in the accumulation and maintenance of a great university library is not to be found in the daily use which the mass of the students will make of it." Instead he said, reflecting the intensifying interest in research, "the justification must be found in its indispensableness to teachers, authors, and other thorough scholars, and to students having exceptional work in hand."[107]

Into this heady atmosphere of reform entered Justin Winsor, a man totally committed to the idea of in-depth scholarly research, free and ready access to books, and efficient administration.[108] Winsor's vision for the radical reorientation of the University Library's role within the changing institution is clearly and forcefully stated in his *First Report (1878)* to the Corporation. In this *Report*, Winsor not only outlined his plans for the Library, but more significantly, provided the justification that was to be so widely copied from his day to the present by academic librarians attempting to justify the enlarged scope and essential role of the library in the college or university setting. Given its importance, the *Report* will be carefully analyzed here, as well as reprinted in full in part II of this work.[109]

Winsor began noting that his *Report* was based on a thorough survey of the "Library and its sphere of usefulness." He noted that his overriding concern was to make the library the "centre of the University system," "indispensable and attractive to all." And then he launched into a series of ringing calls for changes designed to insure such a role for the library. First, there must be more books; but these books must be readily accessible, for "a great library should be a workshop as well as a repository." Second, the catalog must be improved for the "usefulness of any library depends largely on the character of its catalogue;" the new librarian expounded at length on this, one of his favorite topics. Third, the faculty must be better informed of new acquisitions through the improvement of the Library's *Bulletin*, or quarterly list of accessions; here his plan was not only to inform the faculty of new books but also to attempt a more "prudent" expenditure of the system's book monies. Winsor viewed departmental expenditures as frequently duplicative, and he clearly hoped to encourage the "beginnings of a perfected system of partially unified administration" of the resources of both the main Library and the independent departmental libraries. Fourth, he would liberalize the Library's use policy. As he noted in his *Report*, "I consider nothing of more importance than the provision of large classes of books to which unrestricted access can be had." Numerous changes would be required to implement this objective: students would be given freer access to the shelves; hours would be extended through the installation of electric lights; more efficient use would be made of the available space, thus allowing more students to study in the library; and a "Notes and Queries" system would be established in a prominent place in the Library to help the perplexed user with unanswered questions. Regarding his recommendation of electric lights, which the Corporation viewed as a fire hazard, Winsor noted that the evening hours made possible by such lights would contribute a "moral as well as an intellectual good" by encouraging students to spend their evening hours productively in the Library rather than in a less suitable and unnamed haunt. Winsor concluded the *Report* with his usual impressive array of statistics detailing progress already made in cataloging, circulation, and book purchases.

Even before the publication of his famous first *Report* as Harvard Librarian, Winsor had made impressive gains in his plans to make the Library the "centre of the University." Prior to his appointment, he had been instrumental in convincing Eliot, over Sibley's objections, that a new and much more efficient book stack system should be constructed at Harvard. This new six-story bookstack, so widely copied, greatly improved the efficiency of the book storage operation.[110]

Further, at the time of the publication of his *Report*, Winsor had already done a number of things to improve student access to materials in the library. In the first year, he implemented a model "reserve system" and adopted a policy of free access to the alcoves, for as he noted, "absolute contact with books is . . . humanizing."[111] The demand was clearly there, as indicated in Adams's letter quoted above, and Winsor's innovations met with quick success—so much so that Henry Ware noted in 1880 that "a new life and spirit seem to pervade the place; and it is safe to say that a public library does not exist to which readers are more cordially welcomed, or more intelligently and courteously aided in their researches, than the library of Harvard College under its present enlightened and modern management."[112] Indeed, the program had become so successful that Winsor complained to Eliot that his reserve system was proving a trial as well as a triumph, for "the pressure is constant to buy duplicates," something Winsor insisted be done sparingly. He lamented the fact that students had become so dependent on the Library for their course reading, and concluded that "I deem it one of the most unsatisfactory phases of our student life that there is a disinclination to count the ownership of books among the necessities of a college course."[113]

Winsor's successful implementation of his plans to "get books used" led to some of his more vexing, and in one case insurmountable, problems. From his appointment in 1877, Winsor struggled mightily to convince the Overseers to install electric lights in the Library. The need was obvious. Winsor noted frequently that the insistence on the use of natural light demanded that the Library's closing hour be determined "according to the state of the sky." Winsor tried to overcome the Overseers' insistence that electric lights constituted a fire hazard by noting the lack of such modern conveniences led "thoughtless persons" to light "matches in their search for books," a practice considered far more dangerous than the installation of lights, at least so far as Winsor was concerned.[114] Despite his early arguments in favor of the lights, they were not allowed until 1895.

Even more troublesome was the always frustrating problem of finding space to house a burgeoning collection and the increased services mandated by Winsor's desire to encourage library use. A typical lament was voiced by Winsor in 1892, when he wrote to President Eliot, "I wish to notify you that of this day, at the beginning of cold weather, we are all blocked in our Reading Room, and every chair, we can find space for on the floor and in the gallery is filled, and many of the sitters are without table facilities." With obvious consternation, he literally cried out for help:

> Our Cloak room is packed, and we have been obliged to let students carry their overcoats into the reading room. Our delivery room is crowded to the detriment of its administration. Our stack is gorged, and confusion is increasing.[115]

Given Winsor's constant complaints about the lack of space, and his well known reputation for making do, it is probable that his appeals fell on deaf ears.[116] One of his more novel justifications came to hand during the Thanksgiving Day recess of 1889; Winsor advised President Eliot that a fifty-pound ornament gracing the wall of the reading room had fallen onto one of the tables "where on ordinary days a student might be sitting."[117] Despite his constant pressure, and weighty arguments of the need for a new library building, Winsor was generally unsuccessful in increasing the amount and quality of space available to the Harvard Library.[118]

Nevertheless, Winsor did not lose sight of the new and significant role that the Library should play in academic life. Repeatedly—in his reports, published writings, speeches, and private correspondence—he advocated the role of the library as the "heart of the university." For Winsor, the fact that library use would increase was preordained given the new emphasis in the university. As he noted in 1879,

> The Library will become the important factor in our higher education that it should be. Laboratory work will not be confined to the natural

sciences; workshops will not belong solely to technological schools. The library will become, not only the store-house of the humanities, but the arena of all intellectual exercise.[119]

He always retained his faith in the increased usefulness of libraries. All that was necessary to insure this enhanced role for the Library was diligent and enlightened administration. He stated this view matter-of-factly in 1879:

> The use of books goes on increasing naturally if the conditions are favorable. It is a librarian's province to watch those conditions and to prevent relapse. Diligent administration, considerate forbearance, care that no rule is enforced for the sake of mere outward uniformity, and the establishment of reciprocal confidence between the govern- ment and the users of the library, open the way to many relaxations of old-established prohibitions, which could not be safely allowed if a less conciliatory spirit prevailed. There should be no bar to the use of books but the rights of others. . . .[120]

While Winsor's example at Harvard was surely influential in demonstrating the potential effectiveness of the "new" library, it was probably in his role as spiritual leader, as forceful and respected library advocate, that he proved most effective and influential. Winsor constantly pursued this theme in his written work, numer- ous speeches, and highly significant consulting activities. Indeed, it might be safely said that it was in those ways that Justin Winsor made his most significant contri- bution to the rise of the modern academic library.

The influence of Winsor's reports, in a day when library literature was scarce and people relied heavily on them for guidance in library matters, has already been discussed. It remains only to survey briefly his other writings and consulting activities before turning to a consideration of his historical research.

Winsor's catholic interests are readily discernible in his published writings of the period 1877-1896.[121] He wrote general expositions on the academic library in such papers as "College and Other Higher Libraries" and "The College Library and the Classes."[122] In the former paper, one finds ample illustrations of the inspirational quality of Winsor's work, and his colleagues were moved and stimu- lated by remarks such as those on the role of the librarian: "the librarian lives in an atmosphere of possibilities; but there is also about him an ether, charged with his own electricity that makes in every alcove, the dead alive!"[123] Winsor also found cause to address himself to more specific aspects of academic librarianship and wrote papers dealing with nearly every aspect (i.e., circulation, cataloging, selection, and reference) of the librarian's work.

His published writing and his well-known achievements at Harvard placed Winsor in great demand as a consultant to librarians and library interests through- out the country and abroad. In an unusually mirthful letter to his close friend, Charles Soule, Winsor revealed the extent of those activities. He noted that over the years he had given freely of his time and wisdom "to every grade of applicant, from the United States to the humble village" and that if he "could have charged fees as lawyers and doctors do," he would now be able "to found the Winsorian College for Librarians and Bibliographers." He then listed the following soliciters of his counsel: the United States Government, the Tilden Trust of New York, the City of Chicago, the Imperial government of "Tokio," the state officials of Mas- sachusetts (who were "getting notions on a state library board"), and the President of the Pacific Railroad ("who wanted to give a library to some town on the line of his road"). Winsor concluded by admonishing Soule not to "give this note to any one who is getting up a Biographic Bibliothecaria," for he already held a reputation as being "a man who gives services for nothing."[124]

In a more serious vein, he illustrated the range of his influence in his *Report* for 1889:

> Early in the year Mr. Tanaka, an assistant librarian of the Imperial
> Library of Tokio, came with credentials from the Japanese government,
> in accordance with a request which had been made earlier, that a mem-
> ber of the staff of that library should be allowed the opportunity of
> acquiring experience in library work according to American methods.
> Under my direction, Mr. Tanaka not only became familiar with every
> department of our own library work, but I introduced him to other
> libraries. . . .

Winsor concluded by noting that Mr. Tanaka, "has now gone to Europe, with intro-ductions which I gave him to the principal European libraries."[125]

Winsor was particularly esteemed as a building consultant. His article, on "Library Buildings," was viewed as gospel by most librarians, and his experience at the Boston Public and Harvard enhanced his early reputation in this area.[126] As a result, he was frequently consulted regarding new library buildings. In January 1881, for instance, he described to William Frederick Poole the following consulta-tion: "architect of the new national Library in Washington, has been here to see me, and I have spent several hours with him going over the plans, and he returns to Washington tomorrow. . . . He has not embodied my ideas of such a thing exactly; but has been indoctrinated enough to take some of their essential features . . . the building . . . is capable of being a fair one."[127]

Also highly sought after as a speaker, Winsor frequently addressed the Amer-ican Library Association meetings. In addition, he gave numerous addresses at vari-ous public exercises such as the opening of a new library building. In 1883, for instance, he delivered a long address at the dedication of the new library building at the University of Michigan. His speech, which consumed over a dozen closely printed pages in the proceedings of the day's events, emphasized the increasing importance of libraries in the university setting and played recurrently his convic-tion that librarianship constituted a noble calling. "The work of the librarian," he noted at one point, "is only now sharing the perplexities, which all sciences exper-ience in that transition stage when they are passing the purlieus of pretense to the recognized status of a department of knowledge."[128] Little of Winsor's speak-ing style is known, but William Warner Bishop, who later made his own mark in librarianship, recalled Winsor's commencement address at the University of Michi-gan in 1892 with the following observation: "I cannot claim that I profited greatly by the address, for I heard but one phrase of it, 'in the year 1668.'" Bishop quickly noted that the problem was not a lack of attentiveness, but rather that "Justin Winsor had a bushy beard, and he talked into it."[129]

While Winsor may not have impressed Bishop overly much, it is clear that Harvard's librarian was one of the most effective recruiters that the profession could boast. His prominence as a library administrator, his influential connections with potential employers, and his inspirational insistence that librarianship constituted a noble and professional calling all contributed to his popularity in this regard. He was frequently consulted about the qualifications of novice librarians, and he re-ceived countless requests from would-be librarians seeking advice on the best way to enter the field. Many of the latter were encouraged to join him at Harvard, where, upon completion of a thorough indoctrination in the operation of a library, they were recommended to that institution as qualified employees.

In the course of his twenty years as Harvard's librarian, Winsor devoted an increasingly large part of his time and energies to historical studies and publications. As with his advent into the library world, so it was with his emersion into the third and final phase of his career: opportunity presented itself, and new directions were taken up with both quickness and enthusiasm.

His most sustained and arduous historical efforts were devoted to three major projects: a four-volume *Memorial History of Boston* (1880-81), an eight-volume *Narrative and Critical History of America* (1886-89), and four works on America's early exploration and development.[130] Even the most detailed assessment of these works would not in itself identify Winsor's place in the historical fraternity.[131] For purposes of the present volume, no attempt need be made to describe or assess Winsor's works themselves. However, the relationships between Winsor the historian and Winsor the librarian are important and require explanation. The young scholar who compiled the early documentary history of Duxbury is the same man of letters who wrote word pictures of New England farm life; the innovative superintendent who produced statistical profiles of the Boston Public Library is also the historical editor who prepared exhaustive and critical surveys of historical erudition on early Americana. Although Winsor gave short shrift to theoretical history, he did allow for the possibility that in biography one might find "permeating the record a reasonable constancy of purpose."[132] Winsor's thread of constancy can best be found in his approach to historical investigation.

At the close of his exhaustive editorial labors on the cooperative histories of Boston and of the Americas, Winsor reflected upon "The Perils of Historical Narrative." He did not offer in that essay a systematic theory of historical investigation and reporting, for such he decidedly eschewed; but he did catalogue some of the more common fallacies. For example, historians of his day laid great stress upon factual accuracy; yet neither they nor the layman understood that historical accuracy was "the most fleeting of vanities." The annalist (not *analyst*) seldom erred in compiling facts, yet the historian must go further:

> But the difference between an annalist and a historian is, that the mere facts of the first as used by the latter become correlated events, which illumine each other, and get their angles of reflection from many causes external to the naked facts. These causes are the conditions of the time, which gave rise to the facts; the views of the period in which they are studied; and the idiosyncrasies of the person studying them. Hence no historical statement can be final.[133]

Thus one might question the accuracy of the historian, but his answer could never be absolute or fully satisfying. For Winsor, the search for unquestioned historical accuracy was "like the vital principle of life." One might seek it, but never find it.[134] Correlated historical interpretations were frequently "nothing more than probability" as it lay "in one mind."[135]

Winsor's first peril might well have been intended as a rejection of exaggerated claims made by both romantic and scientific historians. Although both schools of writing observed high standards of source criticism, each subscribed to the notion that historical truths were knowable. Romantics discovered in history the fateful hand of cosmic design forming patterns of progress toward the idealization of man and society. History was value-laden, personal, and at times, mysterious. On the other side, scientific historians found in history the natural evolution of man and society. History was value-free, collective, and demonstrable. The struggle between romanticism and science was also a contest between age and youth, amateurism and professionalism, spiritualism and materialism, and in a very broad sense, individualism and collectivism. By the end of the nineteenth century, young professorial historians would effect their independence from art, literature, philosophy, and other humanistic studies searching for relationships between reality and ultimate meaning. History would imitate natural science and look only for the precise relatedness of measureable things, one to another. Claims on both sides were exaggerated. Romantic historians were more critical than their opponents allowed, and scientific scholars were not the pedants whom their seniors decried. Both groups shared the same social values and agreed to work together for the preservation of historical records.[136] Yet Winsor was in one essential regard unlike either romantic or scientific historians—neither theories of world spirit or of evolutionary development would bring him to accept historical interpretations as final truths.

Perhaps Winsor knew too many books, manuscripts, and authors to be exclusively romantic or scientific. His personality and erudition were such that he was accepted and respected by both schools; his perspective on history was at once transitional and distinctive. No scholar had a greater love of fact or detail. One has but to peruse Winsor's critical notes following each chapter of the *History of America* to appreciate his passion for knowing his craft. In several instances, he knew the sources and facts better than the specialist assigned to write the narrative section. It had been Winsor's original intention to edit only a critical history, but for fear that such would lose the popular audience, the work's plan was modified to include a narrative as well as critical chapter on each topic. Literary accounts would make the book readable and marketable; Winsor's critical commentary would render the work useful to subsequent scholarship. In this, his most famous cooperative venture, Winsor bridged the conversion of history from literature to science.

Willingness to accommodate both sides of the methodological debate did not require Winsor's loss of identity. He loved erudition, but he understood and appropriated the techniques of Boston's business community. In discussing the "perils" of history, he wrote that the successful historian "employs the same faculties which make for the merchant his fortune. It is penetration of evidence, judgment of probabilities, that enable the historian to give the seeming of fact; and, after all, it is but a seeming."[137] In another place in the same essay, Winsor likened the perfect historian to Thomas Macaulay's definition of the perfect law-giver, one who exercises "a just temper between the mere man of business, who can see nothing but particular circumstances."[138] Winsor rejected philosophical history, not because "causes and effects do not exist; but because the elements of the problem do not remain constant. The times are different, the conditions of life are altered, the peoples are not the same."[139] Environmental influences were often of such force that human nature was not a constant factor.

Winsor likewise rejected historical forecasting, for there was "a flexibility in the relations of cause and effect that is quite beyond gauging."[140] So too, he argued, "God in history . . . appears to be a noble phrase, but the ways of Providence are no less inscrutable to the historian than laws of the natural world that are not understood."[141] As for the school of historical positivists, Winsor judged that the "theories of Comte, Buckle, and Spencer are interesting; but the life of the world goes on willfully, nevertheless."[142] Commenting on their methods, he observed that one "may strike an average from the wildest helter-skelterism, and this average may be reasonably steady if long enough followed; but an average is not a law,—it is the proof of the absence of law."[143]

Aware that young students of history were asking whether or not their discipline was a science, Winsor admitted that he knew of no question that he would not rather "shuffle out of sight." He answered his rhetorical question first by dismissing the idea that natural laws governed the affairs of mankind—the power of human will should not be discounted so greatly. Then Winsor reflected on the fact that scientific research was producing a considerable "body of correlated material in which the historical student finds much to study."[114] He applauded the scientific historian's emphasis on detail, for like a camera, historical research ought to photograph the past and develop it into a picture in which all objects, trivial and otherwise, might be seen in their true relationship. Winsor closed his discussion of narrative history with the following observation:

> In conclusion, I may confess that I have made of history a thing of shreds and patches. I have only to say that the life of the world is a thing of shreds and patches, and it is only when we consider the well-rounded life of an individual that we find permeating the record a reasonable constance of purpose. This is the province of biography, and we must not confound biography with history.[145]

Winsor's perception of history followed his observation of reality. His realism anticipated the relativism of a later generation of historians, many of whom would discard the absolutism of their scientific predecessors.

Winsor's pragmatic realism manifested itself in almost all aspects of his library career. Like the great captains of the industrial age, he was a man of action and management. He did not study librarianship as an abstract or theoretical discipline. Rather, he examined every function of his library and converted his study into action. In his view, each of his fellow librarians must look to his or her own institution and determine what ideas were workable or impractical, as the case might be. Sharing experience often proved useful; on the other hand, codification of management principles should not become an end in itself. Demands for professionalization arose, not from any desire to enforce uniform standards of practice, but from fear that public libraries might become pawns of political demagoguery. Library autonomy was a necessary prerequisite for experimentation and fulfillment of the institution's goals. Winsor's librarianship was that of the "rugged individualist" who would not be regulated by ward politicians. He insisted that the results of his stewardship warranted his being given a free hand. Always pragmatic, Winsor measured his library's value in terms of its use. Thus, job security was a factor of the librarian's utility, not his partisan politics.

In Winsor's view, municipal politics did not touch the question of basic societal values. He worked, experimented, managed, saved, and achieved. His was a life of stern self-discipline, yet he was not without compassion for weaker individuals. Because the life of mankind was willful and not subject to natural laws, society might progress only by the efforts of individual action. Each man must will his own improvement; his success or failure must be his own. Capitalist ethics apportioned rewards to each according to ability, not need. That there was at times a great distance between theory and practice did not dissuade the true believer.

Winsor recognized that large numbers of Boston's immigrant population lacked adequate opportunity for testing native abilities. Branch libraries must be opened to afford everyone the opportunity of self-education and thus, self-advancement. Reading guides would assist patrons to appreciate and adopt the moral values of those in an advantaged situation. If political demagoguery threatened to thwart the public library's educational mission, the public's control over that institution must be retrenched. Professionalization of librarians would insure sufficient autonomy to protect programs against capricious political influence. Those who sought to uplift the masses never intended to foster that degree of intellectual independence that might lead to preferences for a non-capitalist social order. For the most part, public schools and public libraries provided didactic instruction, the vocational utility of which was the measure of its worth. After all, it was the individual who must be reformed, not society. In pursuit of such "democratic" goals, Winsor proved to be both reformer and authoritarian. In the idiom of the industrial age, he interpreted *democracy* to mean *free enterprise*.

While Winsor's increasing interest in historical research "withdrew him to a considerable extent from active participation in library progress," he nevertheless retained interest in the library profession's activities. As a result, despite a busy schedule, he consented "to the unanimous desire of the leaders in the association" and assumed the ALA presidency again in 1897.[146] His selection was deliberately timed to place the profession's most prominent scholar-librarian at the head of the American delegation to the Second International Conference of Librarians in London that same year.[147]

Ever a vigorous advocate of library interests, Winsor assumed this role with his usual zeal and represented the Americans with dignity and strength.[148] However, his travels proved wearing, and his system could not counteract a cold, which he nursed throughout his homeward voyage. His malady grew more severe and reached a critical stage on 21 October 1897. Struggling through the night, he finally breathed his last on the morning of 22 October. His funeral, attended by many scholars, librarians, and distinguished citizens, was held on 26 October, and his body was buried on a hill in Boston's famed Mount Auburn Cemetery.[149]

The final judgment must be that Winsor, the scholar-librarian, was more a "doer" than a thinker. The library was not a museum of printed books containing fixed truths; it was an active process of gathering and sorting books and ideas. Similarly, history was neither a theory nor a demonstration of the meaning of past realities; it was rather a process of inquiring into "the bits and pieces" of the past and giving such stories "the seeming of fact." Above all other considerations, Winsor the librarian wanted his books to circulate, for as he put it, "absolute contact with books is . . . humanizing." So it was for Winsor the scholar—his "seeming" brush with past realities proved equally humanizing. In his writings the perils of interpretive history seldom arose, for as one of his generation's leading authorities on historical fact, he never forgot that "after all, it was but a seeming." For Winsor it was not "the truth" that was humanizing, but the search for it.

1. Several works summarize the nature of American society during the years covered here. Those that we found particularly helpful were Samuel P. Hayes, *The Response to Industrialism, 1885-1914* (Chicago: University of Chicago Press, 1957); Howard Munford Jones, *The Age of Energy; Varieties of American Experience, 1865-1915* (New York: Viking Press, 1971); Bernard A. Weisberger, *The New Industrial Society* (New York: Wiley, 1969), esp. his chapter on "Critics and Uplifters"; and Robert Wiebe, *The Search for Order: 1877-1920* (New York: Hill and Wang, 1967). Daniel Boorstin's *The Americans: The Democratic Experience* (New York: Random House, 1973) treats this period in a provocative fashion and provides bibliographic essays for each aspect treated.

2. A number of recent monographs treat the "self-help" or "self-made" idea in American history. For example, see John G. Cawelti, *Apostles of the Self-Made Man: Changing Concepts of Success in America* (Chicago: University of Chicago Press, 1965); Richard Weiss, *The American Myth of Success* (New York: Basic Books, 1969); and Irvin G. Wyllie, *The Self-Made Man in America: The Myth of Rags to Riches* (New Brunswick, NJ: Rutgers University Press, 1954).

3. The impact of Darwinian thought on America is brilliantly treated in Richard Hofstadter, *Social Darwinism in American Thought*, revised edition (New York: George Braziller, 1959); but Paul F. Boller, *American Thought in Transition: The Impact of Evolutionary Naturalism, 1865-1900* (Chicago: Rand McNally, 1969) is a more recent assessment and is accompanied by an extensive bibliographic essay.

4. The standard treatment of the subject is Sidney Fine, *Laissez Faire and the General Welfare State: A Study of Conflict in American Thought, 1865-1901* (Ann Arbor: University of Michigan Press, 1969). It appears clear that the majority of Americans accepted the government's obligation to secure individual and corporate property against theft or destruction. The establishment of schools and libraries designed to "stabilize society" certainly qualified under the definition of the "negative"state powers of government.

5. This is the ideological switch that Clinton Rossiter has unforgettably labeled the "great train robbery of American intellectual history." Clinton Rossiter, *Conservatism in America: The Thankless Persuasion*, 2nd ed. (New York: Vintage Books, 1962), p. 128.

6. David Tyack, *Turning Points in American Educational History* (Waltham, MA: Tyndale Publishing Co., 1967), p. 122, noted that "when every man might be his own politician, the patrician decided that every man must be educated." In 1862, the Rev. George Thayer, addressing an audience at the dedication of the South Boston Branch of the Boston Public Library, noted that "this is a democracy,—everyone a sovereign, and it is of the highest importance that all should be intelligent sovereigns" (*Dedication of the South Boston Branch of the Boston Public Library, 16 May 1862*, p. 18).

7. The nagging desire to do something "useful" was felt by many of New England's "literary men." For a discussion, see David B. Tyack, *George Tickor and the Boston Brahmins* (Cambridge, MA: Harvard University Press, 1967), pp. 187-192.

8. On the front of Winsor's desk was a half-life-size bust of Daniel Webster, thus designating the famous Whig Senator as his preference among America's statesmen. For treatment of Whig contributions to American political thought and

action, see Richard Buel, Jr., *Securing the Revolution: Ideology in American Politics, 1789-1815* (Ithaca, NY: Cornell University Press, 1972); David Hackett Fischer, *The Revolution in American Conservatism: The Federalists in the Era of Jeffersonian Democracy* (New York: Harper, 1965); and Kinley J. Brauer, *Cotton versus Conscience; Massachusetts Whig Politics and Southwestern Expansion, 1843-1848* (Lexington: University of Kentucky Press, 1967).

9. Quoted in J. P. Quincy, "Free Libraries," in *Public Libraries in the United States of America: Their History, Condition and Management* (Washington: Gov. Print. Off., 1876), p. 402.

10. Justin Winsor, "President's Address," *Library Journal* 4 (1879): 223-25.

11. Justin Winsor, "President's Address," *Library Journal* 6 (1881): 63-64. Winsor's use of industrial metaphors suggests his affinity with the new industrial age. Many of his contemporaries were more inclined to draw analogies between themselves and the more traditional professions, like medicine or law. For instance, Cutter likened the librarians' customers to "patients," and the librarian was like a "city physician" administering aid from a "bibliothecal dispensary" (Charles Ammi Cutter, "The Public Library and its Choice of Books," *Library Journal* 3 [1878]: 73). Another writer varied the allusion somewhat by referring to the librarian as "a mental doctor for his town" (*Library Journal* 6 [1881]: 39).

12. Justin Winsor, *First Report (1878) of Justin Winsor, Librarian of Harvard University*, p. 11.

13. Justin Winsor, "President's Address," *Library Journal* 6 (1881): 63.

14. Perhaps the most intimate and sensitive treatment of Winsor's early years is that by Horace E. Scudder, "Memoir of Justin Winsor, LL.D.," *Massachusetts Historical Society Proceedings*, 2nd series, 12 (1889): 457-82. For a more detailed account see Joseph A. Boromé, "The Life and Letters of Justin Winsor," Ph.D. diss., Columbia University, 1950, pp. 1-64.

15. Boromé, "Justin Winsor," pp. 35-40.

16. Scudder, "Memoir of Justin Winsor," pp. 462-65; quotation, Ibid., p. 463.

17. Justin Winsor to Nathaniel Winsor, January 28, 1854; quoted in Scudder, "Memoir of Justin Winsor," p. 469.

18. Boromé, "The Life and Letters of Justin Winsor," pp. 46-52.

19. *Crayon*, Vol. III, pp. 220-21, 251-53, 281-82, 314-16, 346-47, 378-79; Vol. IV, pp. 57-58, 125-26, 284-85, 317-18.

20. That Winsor published most of his poems, essays, and reviews outside Boston (the "Athens of America") lends credence to this interpretation.

21. The ten-volume draft and six volumes of alterations thereof are in the Theatre Collection, Harvard University Library.

22. Lillian Woodman Aldrich, *Crowding Memories* (Boston: Houghton Mifflin Company, 1920), p. 94.

23. Ibid., p. 95.

24. Ibid., pp. 94-95.

25. Boromé, *Life and Letters of Justin Winsor*, pp. 80-82, discusses his effort in detail.

26. Jewett's life and career are covered in Joseph Boromé, *Charles Coffin Jewett* (Chicago: American Library Association, 1951); his years at the Boston Public are treated in Walter Muir Whitehill, *The Boston Public Library: A Centennial History* (Cambridge, MA: Harvard University Press, 1956); and finally, for a more up-to-date assessment of Jewett accompanied by a selection of his writings, see Michael H. Harris, ed., *The Age of Jewett: Charles Coffin Jewett and American Librarianship, 1841-1868* (Littleton, CO: Libraries Unlimited, 1975).

27. This report, and many other documents of relevance to the history of the Boston Public Library, will be found in Horace G. Wadlin, *The Public Library of the City of Boston: A History* (Boston: The Library, 1911), p. 63+.

28. Quoted in Whitehill, *Boston Public Library*, p. 75.

29. Quoted in Whitehill, *Boston Public Library*, p. v. When Winsor resigned his post as superintendent of the Boston Public Library, the library profession curiously complained that his successor, Judge Mellen Chamberlain, was an inexperienced man. Even stranger was Winsor's own solecistic lament, in 1879, that too many people came to librarianship only after they had "failed in the shop, in the schoolroom, and in the pulpit." Justin Winsor, "Presidential Address," *Library Journal* 5 (1879): 5.

30. Oliver Wendell Holmes caught the essence of "Proper Boston" when he noted that, all things being equal, he preferred a "man of family." Librarians of Winsor's period were quite candid in pointing out the importance of good breeding in the making of a good librarian. See for instance, James L. Whitney, "Selecting and Training Library Assistants," *Library Journal* 7 (1882): 137-38. And the noted director of the Library Company of Philadelphia, Lloyd Pearsall Smith, stated flatly that a good librarian "must belong to the Brahmin Caste." See his "The Qualifications of a Librarian," *Library Journal* 1 (1876): 73. It should be noted that Winsor displayed less of this class consciousness than some of his colleagues. Dee Garrison, in a study of library leadership in the country from 1876-1910, concludes that "the most prominent library leaders were preeminently aware of their special standing as the 'best men' in American society—the men of breeding, education and taste." See her "Cultural Missionaries: A Study of American Public Library Leaders, 1876-1910," Ph.D. diss., University of California at Irvine, 1973, p. 8.

31. William E. Foster, "Five Men of 76," *ALA Bulletin* 29 (1926): 313.

32. Joseph Boromé, "Justin Winsor," p. 59.

33. Ibid., p. 125.

34. Mellen Chamberlain, "Tribute to Justin Winsor," *Massachusetts Historical Society Proceedings*, 2nd series, 12 (1899): 37-38.

35. Whitehill, *Boston Public Library*, p. 77.

36. Charles Ammi Cutter, "Justin Winsor," *Nation*: 65 (1897): 335.

37. Michael H. Harris, ed., *The Age of Jewett*, p. 41.

38. For a full discussion of the motives of the founders, and for extensive notes relating to research on the subject, see Michael H. Harris and Gerard Spiegler, "Everett, Ticknor and the Common Man; The Fear of Societal Instability as the Motivation for the Founding of the Boston Public Library," *Libri* 24 (1974): 249-76. *Report of the Public Library in the City of Boston, July, 1852.* City Document No. 37 (Boston, 1852) is frequently cited as among the most articulate and influential documents ever promulgated relative to the management of public libraries. It is reprinted in full as an appendix to Jesse Shera, *Foundations of the Public Library; The Origins of the Public Library Movement in New England, 1629-1855* (Chicago: University of Chicago Press, 1949).

39. For details on Boston's population growth during the period covered here, see Oscar Handlin, *Boston's Immigrants; A Study in Acculturation*, revised and enlarged ed., (Cambridge, MA: Harvard University Press, 1969); Peter Knights, *The Plain People of Boston, 1830-1860; A Study in City Growth* (New York: Oxford University Press, 1971); and Stephen Thernstrom, *The Other Bostonians* (Cambridge, MA: Harvard University Press, 1973). Knights noted that by 1855, the population of Boston was slightly over 161,000 and that 53 percent were foreign

born. Theodore Parker observed that Boston, once fondly likened to an American "Athens," was quickly becoming an American "Dublin."

40. This report is fully quoted in Horace G. Wadlin, *The Public Library of the City of Boston: A History*, pp. 27-28. See also Harris and Spiegler, "Everett, Ticknor and the Common Man . . . ," pp. 263-64.

41. Massachusetts, and more specifically Boston, has been the subject of a considerable body of research demonstrating the process and motivation for the founding of schools and other "reformative" agencies in nineteenth-century America. See especially, Michael Katz, *The Irony of Early School Reform: Educational Innovation in Mid-Nineteenth Century Massachusetts* (Cambridge, MA: Harvard University Press, 1968); Marvin Lazerson, *Origins of the Urban School: Public Education in Massachusetts, 1870-1915* (Cambridge, MA: Harvard University Press, 1971); and Stanley K. Schultz, *The Culture Factory: Boston Public Schools, 1789-1860* (New York: Oxford University Press, 1973). As Nathan I. Huggins notes, the poor were "a problem to be acted on, dealt with, reformed, and uplifted." (*Protestants against Poverty: Boston Charities, 1870-1900* [Westport, CT: Greenwood Press, 1971], p. 201). For an extensive list of works on Boston, see Michael H. Harris, *The Role of Public Library in American Life: A Speculative Essay* (Urbana: University of Illinois, Graduate School of Library Science, Occasional Paper No. 117, 1975), ftnt. 13. Contemporary examples of "uplift" thinking are plentiful. For example, the Trustees of the Stoneham, Massachusetts, Public Library noted in their Report for 1868: "The public library has come to be one of the institutions of New England, ranking with the church and the school house. . . . A good library which is generally used tends not only to create an intellectual, but also a moral elevation of character. . . . As a rule the more intelligent men become, the better they will be. . . . " (quoted in Francis G. Collier, "A History of the American Public Library," Ph.D. diss., Harvard University, 1953). Or, as the Rev. George Thayer said in Boston in 1872, "this is a democracy,—everyone is a sovereign, and it is of the highest importance that all should be intelligent sovereigns. . . . The great problems of civil and religious liberty, which we are endeavoring to solve in this country, are becoming more complex as we receive large immigrations. . . . If there hangs over any city or state of America an ominous cloud foreboding mischief to our institutions, its source and nourishment are among the ignorant classes." He then proposed the public library as one cure for the problem (*Proceedings at the Dedication of the South Boston Branch of the Public Library of the City of Boston, May 16, 1872* [Boston: Rockwell and Churchill, 1872], p. 18).

42. Ticknor is the subject of a thorough biography that touches his efforts on behalf of the Boston Public Library: David Tyack, *George Ticknor and the Boston Brahmins* (Cambridge, MA: Harvard University Press, 1967). For a detailed treatment of Ticknor and the Boston Public Library, see Harris and Spiegler, "Everett, Ticknor and the Common Man. . . ."

43. Ticknor authored the most important parts of the 1852 *Report of the Boston Public Library*, and they clearly articulate his insistence on this point.

44. Ibid., p. 15.

45. Ticknor made this remark in 1827, in response to a request from the Rev. D. Nichols relative to selecting books for a social library in Portland, Maine. Quoted in Tyack, *George Ticknor*, pp. 208-209.

46. All phrases are from a letter, Ticknor to Everett, 14 July 1851, published in *Life, Letters, and Journals of George Ticknor*, edited by George S. Hillard, Mrs. Anna Elliot Ticknor, and Miss Anna Elliot Ticknor (Boston: James R. Osgood and Co., 1876), II: 301-302.

47. For the development of this two-edged conception of the library's role in society, see Michael H. Harris, *The Role of the Public Library in American Life*, pp. 4-9.

48. *Sixteenth Annual Report of the Trustees of the Public Library, 1868* (Boston, 1868), p. 8. For a detailed description of Winsor's first year's work at the Boston Public Library, see Boromé, "Justin Winsor," pp. 90+, and Whitehill, *Boston Public Library*, pp. 75-82.

49. *Sixteenth Annual Report of the Trustees . . .* , p. 8.

50. Cutter, "Justin Winsor," p. 335.

51. Ibid. Winsor's contemporaries, within and outside the library profession, all writing in different places at his death, described Winsor the administrator in remarkably similar terms. Francis Peabody, speaking at a memorial ceremony in the Appleton Chapel in Cambridge noted that "he directed our library as a great executive officer should control a department of state; with scrupulous discipline, with large confidence in subordinates. . ." (*Justin Winsor: Memorial Address in Appleton Chapel*, 26 October 1897, p [2]). Edward Channing noted that Winsor was a great administrator in all of his many activities and that "he chose his assistants with care" ("Justin Winsor," *American Historical Review* 3 [1898]: 200). James L. Whitney recalled his "great executive force and tenacity of purpose" ("Justin Winsor," *American Antiquarian Society Proceedings*, new series, 12 [1898]: 234). Samuel A. Green observed that "Mr. Winsor was a great organizer, and he had the happy faculty of selecting the right persons for subordinate places . . ." ("Tributes to Justin Winsor," *Massachusetts Historical Society Proceedings*, 2nd series, 12 [1899]: 31).

52. Channing, "Justin Winsor," p. 201. Channing further wrote that while Winsor was at the Boston Public Library, "he trained himself to interruption, stopping his pen in the middle of a sentence instead of at the end. In this way he was able to take up the unfinished thought at once upon the departure of his visitor."

53. Judge Mellen Chamberlain emphasized that his predecessor at the Boston Public Library was not an "idealist, still less a mere theorizer. He was the most practical man I ever knew in bringing things to pass" (Mellen Chamberlain, "Tribute to Justin Winsor," p. 201). Of course, the Board of Trustees of the Boston Public Library had little interest in radical and irresponsible change. As they noted in 1876, the library's general success might well be due to the fact that they had avoided "rash innovations and bold experiment by ill-advised and inexperienced though doubtless well-intentioned men." And while in this instance they were talking about the Board of Trustees itself, the message was certainly not lost on the library administration (*Twenty-fourth Annual Report of the Trustees of the Public Library, 1876* [Boston, 1876], p. 13).

54. Justin Winsor, "Library Memoranda," in *Public Libraries in the United States of America: Their History, Condition, and Management* (Washington: U. S. Bureau of Education, 1876), p. 714.

55. Winsor carefully selected members of his staff and groomed them for responsible posts in the library field. Thus, positions in the Boston Public Library during his tenure were eagerly sought, even though the superintendent was a hard taskmaster and not infrequently treated his employees much like factory laborers. Josephine Rathbone provided a rare insight when she wrote that "Mr. Winsor was a large, fine-looking, dignified man—today he might be called pompous—with whom no one (not even, I am sure, his wife and daughter) ever took liberties. . . . I never . . . ventured to address him (and one would *address* rather than *talk with*

him) . . ." (Josephine A. Rathbone, "Pioneers of the Library Profession," *Wilson Library Bulletin* 23 [1949]: 778).

56. *Twenty-fourth Annual Report of the Trustees of the Public Library, 1876* (Boston, 1877), p. 12.

57. Cutter, "Justin Winsor," p. 335.

58. Quoted from a letter from Ticknor relating to the donation of his library to the Boston Public Library, 16 April 1860, in Whitehill, *Boston Public Library*, p. 62.

59. *Report of the Trustees of the Public Library in the City of Boston, July, 1852*, p. 15. Wilhelm Munthe, a prominent European librarian, visited this country in 1936 and still marveled at the American librarians' commitment to this ideal, for as he noted, "in the minds of Europeans, the American library movement stands out primarily as that gigantic endeavor to persuade a large, heterogeneous, pioneer population to turn to the book as the great fountainhead of culture" (*American Librarianship from a European Angle* [Chicago: American Library Association, 1939], p. 16).

60. It was William I. Fletcher who suggested that the librarian was in a position similar to that of the cook who followed an old recipe for preparing rabbit. The initial step was rather elemental: "first catch your hare." For a study of Fletcher and his application of "uplift theory," see George S. Bobinski, "William Isaac Fletcher, an Early American Library Leader," *Journal of Library History* 5 (1970): 101-18. For a comprehensive study of the use of fiction in nineteenth-century American libraries, see Esther J. Carrier, *Fiction in Public Libraries, 1876-1900* (New York: Scarecrow Press, 1965). A more interpretive treatment of the uplift ethos has been supplied recently by Dee Garrison in her incisive and provocative studies, "Cultural Custodians of the Gilded Age," *Journal of Library History* 6 (1971): 327-36; and "Cultural Missionaries: A Study of American Public Library Leaders, 1876-1910," Ph.D. diss., University of California at Irvine, 1973.

61. *Twenty-third Annual Report of the Trustees of the Public Library, 1875* (Boston, 1875), p. 17. This theme runs through all of the public library reports of Boston and every other community in New England. In 1879, the Rev. J. F. Clarke, a member of the Boston Public Library's Board of Trustees, noted that libraries are provided for the "same purpose as the Public Garden, Public Baths, music on the Common provided by the city, or fireworks on the Fourth of July. Why do we provide these things at public expense? Because they tend to refine and elevate the people . . . to make them more contented, cheerful and happy . . ." (*Library Journal* 4 [1879]: 356). Such thinking was current on the eastern seaboard prior to 1900; see Sidney Ditzion, "Social Reform, Education, and the Library, 1850-1900," *Library Quarterly* 9 (1939): 156-84. Richard Hofstadter shrewdly observed that Americans generally feel that a book "merely read for enjoyment is misused" (Richard Hofstadter, *Anti-Intellectualism in American Life* [New York: Alfred Knopf, 1969], pp. 307-308).

62. Justin Winsor, "Reading in Popular Libraries," in *Public Libraries in the United States of America: Their History, Condition and Management*, p. 432.

63. Justin Winsor, "Free Libraries and Readers," *Library Journal* 1 (1876): 64.

64. *Twenty-fifth Annual Report of the Trustees of the Public Library, 1877* (Boston, 1877), pp. 40-41. This report, which surveys Winsor's ten-year tenure at the Boston Public Library, is reprinted in part II of this volume. In "The Boston Fiction Lists," *Library Journal* 1 (1876): 257-58, Winsor had described more briefly the purposes of his reading guides.

65. Winsor took considerable pride in the fact that the idea was being widely copied. Thus, he was rather disturbed to read Charles Francis Adams's criticisms of the scheme in his book, *The Public Library and the Common Schools* (Boston: Estes and Lauriat, 1879). Adams reported that he had originally encouraged the institution of an "educational catalogue" in the Quincy Public Library, "freely imitating" the Boston model. However, he concluded after some experimentation that it was "labor well-nigh lost." Winsor reviewed Adams's book for the *Boston Daily Advertiser* of 24 September 1879, and while he applauded Adams as a "vigorous and unimitative" friend to schools and libraries, he differed at some length with him over the relative value of the "educational catalogue," noting that its "great effect was as well proved as such things can be." On the morning of 24 September 1879, Adams sent Winsor a letter which began, "I recognized your hand in this morning's Advertiser" and good-naturedly differed with Winsor where the "educational catalogue" was concerned, noting only that he thought it less useful than did Winsor. "Anyhow," he said, "one thing is indisputable. You are the originator of the educational catalogue . . . it is a great conception . . . it is a new and creditable Boston idea" (Charles Francis Adams, Jr., to Justin Winsor, 24 September 1879, ALS, Adams Family Papers, Massachusetts Historical Society).

66. In a letter to Miss N. E. Browne, 17 September 1895, Charles Ammi Cutter, who was in Boston during the years of Winsor's experimentation with the "educational catalogue," wrote, "I remember when the Bost. Pub. first touched 1000 in one day, which no library had ever reached before. How proud Mr. Winsor was!" (ALS in the James I. Wyer Collection, American Library Association Archives).

67. Any superficial examination of Winsor's detailed reports will clearly show this fact. In his 1877 *Report*, Winsor noted that circulation in the Boston Public Library had risen from 200,000 a year to 1,200,000 volumes a year during his tenure. Part of this increase was attributed to his "educational catalogue."

68. William W. Greenough, "Remarks" at *The Dedication of the South Boston Branch of the Boston Public Library, 16 May 1872* (Boston, 1872), p. 7.

69. Ibid.

70. *Twenty-third Annual Report of the Trustees of the Public Library, 1875* (Boston, 1875), p. 18.

71. *Library Journal* 12 (1887): 228.

72. For details on these innovations and the day-to-day operations of the library during this period, see Boromé, "Justin Winsor," pp. 96-125, 130-73; and Whitehill, *Boston Public Library*, pp. 75-102.

73. In her study of public librarianship in America, 1876-1910, Dee Garrison argues persuasively that "because it was necessary eventually to please the masses, upon whom their living depended, public librarians were forced to modify their reformist attitudes and ultimately to tolerate public 'vulgarity'" (Dee Garrison, "Cultural Missionaries . . . ," p. 47).

74. Garrison insists that the turn of the century heralded the "decline of the missionary-librarian" and the rise of a pragmatic group of professionals determined to get out of the "miracle business" (Ibid., p. 290). For a similar assessment, see Harris, *The Role of the Public Library in American Life: A Speculative Essay*, pp. 9-17. Faith in uplift came to be viewed as overly optimistic by even the most generous of critics. Samuel Swett Green wrote, "Perhaps Mr. Poole and Mr. Winsor had too high hopes of raising the character of the reading of users of libraries who remain comparatively stationary in respect to education and, in the absence of the thinking power, fail to improve." (Samuel S. Green, *The Public Library Movement*

in the United States, 1853-1893 [Boston: The Boston Book Company, 1913], p. 21).

75. Justin Winsor, "President's Address," *Library Journal* 6 (1881): 63.

76. Justin Winsor, "Free Libraries and Readers," p. 65.

77. Justin Winsor, "President's Address," *Library Journal* 2 (1877): 5.

78. See Boromé, "Justin Winsor," pp. 243-59; and Whitehill, *Boston Public Library,* pp. 103-15.

79. Horace E. Scudder, "Memoir of Justin Winsor," *Massachusetts Historical Society Proceedings*, 2nd series, 12 (1899), 475.

80. *Proceedings of the Board of Aldermen, City of Boston, July 2, 1877.* pp. 468-71.

81. Ibid., p. 469. Modern librarians, generally free of the authoritarian and elitist leanings of their nineteenth-century predecessors, will perhaps be inclined to sympathize somewhat with Alderman O'Brien. After all, the annual reports of the Boston Public Library frequently made reference to the "ignorant," the "less intelligent," and the "masses," all of whom needed to be "ameliorated." Perhaps part of O'Brien's opposition was in response to the smug insistence that Winsor, the Trustees, and the staff of the Boston Public Library, knew what was best for the "middling-sorts," most of whom were Irish. However well meant, paternalism did not always inspire respect and gratitude.

82. The *Library Journal* 1 (1877): 401-402, printed a full description of the events leading to Winsor's resignation, concluding that "Boston has suffered the fate of cities less renowned for intelligence and culture, and the lower classes of politicians seem to have obtained the upper hand in the legislative branch of the city administration."

83. *Library Journal* 1 (1877): 395.

84. Justin Winsor, "President's Address," *Library Journal* 1 (1877): 5.

85. In a letter addressed to Charles C. Soule, Winsor revealed that the break with the Boston Public Library was final in 1877: "I have studiously avoided expressing any opinion, in any way to the public, about the affairs of that library, ever since I left it" (ALS Justin Winsor to Charles C. Soule, 17 October 1890, James I. Wyer Collection, American Library Association Archives).

86. See especially the *Library Journal* 1 (1877): 401-402.

87. This literature is particularly voluminous, especially with the recent celebration of the ALA centennial in 1976. The items cited below were particularly useful in preparing our account, but for a much fuller list, see Michael H. Harris and Donald G. Davis, Jr. *American Library History: A Bibliography* (Austin: University of Texas Press, 1978), pp. 164-73. Far and away the best introduction to the origins of the American Library Association in 1876 is Edward Holley's *Raking the Historic Coals: The ALA Scrapbook of 1876*, Beta Phi Mu Chapbook No. 8 [Chicago: Lakeside Press], 1967. In addition to providing an insightful analysis of the first meeting, Holley's work contains the very enlightening correspondence between the principal organizers of the ALA. For a recent, and concise, study of the organization of the ALA, see Michael H. Harris, 'An Idea in the Air'–*Library Association Review* 78 (1976): 302-304. A detailed but generally descriptive treatment of the organizational meeting will be found in Sister M.A. J. O'Loughlin, "Emergence of American Librarianship: A Study of Influence Evident in 1876," Ph.D. dissertation, Columbia University, 1971. Lucy Maddox, "Trends and Issues in American Librarianship as Reflected in the Papers and Proceedings of the American Library Association, 1876-1885," Ph.D. dissertation, University of Michigan, 1958, carries the story through Winsor's tenure as president. Three histories of the evolution of the ALA, and by implication, of the American library profession, are

also of real value. The most detailed is Dennis Thomison, *The History of the American Library Association, 1876-1972* (Chicago: American Library Association, 1978); while two shorter, and more interpretative, accounts are Michael H. Harris, "Portrait in Paradox: Commitment and Ambivalence in American Librarianship, 1876-1976," *Libri* 26 (1976): 311-31; and Edward Holley, "ALA at 100," in the *ALA Yearbook* (Chicago: American Library Association), 1976, pp. 1-32. Finally, Boromé's "Justin Winsor" treats ALA activities in some detail.

88. See Thomison, *History of the American Library Association*, p. xi.

89. O'Loughlin, "Emergence of American Librarianship," pp. 94-104, illustrates the great significance of Winsor's reports and catalogs by quoting extensively from correspondence with librarians both here and abroad. In his *Report* for 1869 (the *Seventeenth Annual Report* of the Library), Winsor commented at length on his efforts in this regard:

> There is not a library in the country of a public nature but we are glad to be in correspondence with it, and to exchange the data of our experience and practice. The measure of our gift in this way, may be, in the nature of the case, in many instances greater than the return; but we have not failed to profit by what has been given to us. . . . During the past year, I have done much to establish relations of good fellowship with the libraries of this continent; and our exchange list now numbers over four hundred different libraries, over one-quarter of which are foreign.

90. See note 80 above.

91. Justin Winsor, "Free Libraries and Readers," *Library Journal* 1 (1876); 67.

92. For a detailed explication of this theme see Michael H. Harris, "Portrait in Paradox," pp. 285-86.

93. Winsor, "Free Libraries and Readers," p. 65.

94. Winsor, "President's Address," *Library Journal* 6 (1881): 63.

95. Chamberlain, "Tribute to Justin Winsor," p. 40.

96. Rathbone, "Pioneers of the Library Profession," p. 778.

97. Foster, "Five Men of '76," p. 3.

98. J. K. H. Hoyt, *Newark Daily Advertiser*, 12 February 1881, p. 15.

99. Cutter, "Justin Winsor," p. 335. There is considerable evidence that America's librarians called Winsor to the ALA presidency again in 1897 so that he could head their delegation to the Second International Library Conference in London in 1897. In doing so, they acknowledged once again his preeminence in their eyes. See Budd L. Gambee, "The Role of American Librarians at the Second International Library Conference, London, 1897," in *Library History Seminar 4*, ed. by H. Goldstein and J. Goudeau (Tallahassee; Florida State University School of Library Science, 1972), pp. 52-85. Winsor also lead the delegation to the First Conference held in London in 1877. For his important role in that meeting, see Budd L. Gambee, "The Great Junket: American Participation in the Conference of Librarians, London, 1877," *Journal of Library History* 22 (1967): 9-44.

100. Remarks reported in William C. Lane and William H. Tillinghast, "Justin Winsor, Librarian and Historian—1831-1897," *Library Journal* 23 (1898): 13.

101. Francis Peabody, *Justin Winsor*, p. 1.

102. Charles W. Eliot, "Tribute to Justin Winsor," *Massachusetts Historical Society Proceedings*, 2nd ser. 12 (1889): 34.

103. While most recent students of Winsor's library career overlook this important point, the significance of his scholarly reputation was clearly important to his contemporaries. All seemed to view him as the most important scholar to grace the profession, but a few examples must suffice. William E. Foster noted, "there are few men of his time who have united in their own persons so exceptional an equipment of scholarly tastes and accomplishments with so exceptional a capacity for administration" (Foster, "Five Men of '76," p. 2). His colleagues at Harvard noted:

> He believed that the position of librarian, placed in control of a large accumulation of books to be arranged for the best interests of a community of scholars, was an honorable position of grave responsibility, and should rank in the academic scale with the professor's chair. Administrative ability was an essential qualification, but not, if the contradiction be allowed, the most important; a capacity for sympathizing with the scholarly life, a self devotion to intellectual pursuits were no less essential. Thus he raised the work of the librarian everywhere in dignity . . . (Lane and Tillinghast, "Justin Winsor," p. 11).

At the 1898 meeting of the ALA, Herbert Putnam labeled Winsor "the foremost *librarian* of his time," due to his rare combination of scholarship and administrative abilities. "In the aggregate," Putnam concluded, "therefore, his career offers the best we have offered or are likely to be able to offer in one man of those administrative capacities in which, as a group, we may perhaps excel the members of our profession abroad, and those scholarly attainments in which as individuals we are fairly their inferiors." Putnam's remarks are in his presidential address to the American Library Association, (*Library Journal* 23 [1898]: 1, 2). Finally, to cite just one more of many witnesses, Charles Ammi Cutter remarked that Winsor's fame would probably rest on his scholarly abilities. "No doubt," he said, "he will be longer and better known as a bibliographer and historian than as a librarian . . ." (Cutter, "Justin Winsor," p. 335).

104. The literature relating to the rise of the American university during the last quarter of the nineteenth century is voluminous, to say the least. However, a number of seminal works need to be cited here. Of special significance is Laurence R. Veysey, *The Emergence of the American University* (Chicago: University of Chicago Press, 1965). Recent scholarship on the period in question has tended to emphasize the emergence of professionalization among scholars in the nation's universities. Three of the most provocative of these new studies, all of which throw considerable light on the drive to create a value-free social science equal in rigor to the natural sciences—a theme central to Winsor's thinking—are Burton J. Bledstein, *The Culture of Professionalism: The Middle Class and the Development of Higher Education in America* (New York: W. W. Norton Co., 1976); Mary O. Furner, *Advocacy & Objectivity: A Crisis in the Professionalism of American Social Science, 1865-1905* (Lexington: University of Kentucky Press, 1975); and Thomas L. Haskell, *The Emergence of Professional Social Science: The American Social Science Association and the Nineteenth-Century Crisis of Authority* (Urbana: University of Illinois Press, 1977). More specifically related to the rise of Harvard is the standard treatment by Samuel E. Morison, ed., *The Development of Harvard University since the Inauguration of President Eliot, 1869-1929* (Cambridge, MA: Harvard University Press, 1930). More recent, quite revisionist, and accompanied by excellent bibliographic notes is Robert A. McCaughey, "The Transformation of

American Academic Life: Harvard University, 1821-1892," *Perspectives in American History* 8 (1974): 239-332.

105. The literature related to the rise of the academic library during Winsor's tenure at Harvard is extensive. The classic treatment is Kenneth J. Brough, *Scholar's Workshop: Evolving Conceptions of Library Service* (Urbana: University of Illinois, 1953), which considers Winsor's contribution at length. Also of real use is Samuel Rothstein's *The Development of Reference Services through Academic Traditions, Public Library Practice and Special Librarianship* (Chicago: Association of College and Reference Libraries, 1955). A recent collection of essays—Richard D. Johnson, ed., *Libraries for Teaching, Libraries for Research; Essays for a Century* (Chicago: American Library Association, 1977)—throws considerable, if diffuse, light on the period covered here. One essay in that collection, Edward G. Holley's "Academic Libraries in 1876," is a painstakingly detailed, very insightful treatment of the academic library scene upon Winsor's ascendency at Harvard.

106. Adams's petition is quoted in full in Robert W. Lovett, "The Undergraduate and the Harvard Library, 1877-1937," *Harvard Library Bulletin* 1 (1947): 223.

107. Quoted in ibid., p. 228.

108. A great deal has been written about the Harvard University Library, and much of that treats, in more or less detail, Winsor's work there. For a complete list of this material, see Harris and Davis, *American Library History: A Bibliography*, pp. 111-14. For a complete list of materials on Winsor's tenure, see the bibliography in part III of the present work. It remains to note the most important of these studies. By far the most detailed is Boromé, "Justin Winsor," which covers his day-to-day activities in depth. Other works utilized here were W. C. Lane, "The Harvard College Library, 1877-1928," in S. E. Morison, *The Development of Harvard University*, pp. 608-31; W. C. Lane and William H. Tillinghast, "Justin Winsor's Administration of the Harvard Library, 1877-1897," *Harvard Graduates Magazine* 6 (1897): 182-88; and a more recent, but rather traditional work, Robert E. Brundin, "Justin Winsor of Harvard and the Liberalizing of the College Library," *Journal of Library History* 10 (1975): 57-70. Also note the works cited above in references 105-106.

109. *First Report (1878) of Justin Winsor, Librarian of Harvard University.* Each Winsor *Report* was issued separately and also published as part of the annual president's *Report.*

110. Lane, "The Harvard College Library, 1877-1928," p. 610.

111. *First Report (1878) of Justin Winsor . . .* , p. 8.

112. Quoted in Lovett, "The Undergraduate and the Harvard Library, 1877-1937," p. 224.

113. Justin Winsor to Charles W. Eliot, 17 October 1887; quoted in Lovett, "The Undergraduate and the Harvard Library," p. 227.

114. *Fifteenth Report (1892) of Justin Winsor, Librarian of Harvard University*, pp. 14-15. Winsor further noted that "the old part of the building is highly inflammable, and a lighted match carelessly dropped in a dark corner might lead to a serious disaster." He concluded most of his reports prior to 1895 with a plea for lights.

115. Justin Winsor to Charles W. Eliot, 2 December 1889, quoted in Lovett, "The Undergraduate and the Harvard Library," pp. 224-25.

116. Winsor generally reserved the last paragraphs of his annual reports for a strident appeal for more space (and electric lights, too, of course). In his *Fourteenth Annual Report* (1891), for instance, he warned of the "absolute repletion" of the library's stack space and insisted that the only way to avoid "the calamity"

was to enlarge Gore Hall. The next year, he wrote, "I have in earlier reports exhausted the language of warning and anxiety, in representing the totally inadequate accommodations . . . which Gore Hall affords. Each twelve months brings us nearer to a chaotic condition" (*Fifteenth Annual Report* [1892], p. 15).

117. Justin Winsor to Charles W. Eliot, 2 December 1889; quoted in Lovett, "The Undergraduate and the Harvard Library," p. 225.

118. Gore Hall was remodeled and expanded in 1895. For a history of the Harvard Library buildings during the late nineteenth and early twentieth centuries, see Lane, "The Harvard College Library," pp. 623-28.

119. Justin Winsor, "The College and Other Higher Libraries," *Library Journal* 4 (1879): 402.

120. *Second Report (1879) of Justin Winsor, Librarian of Harvard University*, pp. 10-11.

121. These works are listed in part III.

122. "College and Other Higher Libraries," *Library Journal* (1879): 399-402; and "The College Library and the Classes," *Library Journal* (1878): 5-6. Another influential paper in this category was an essay that Winsor wrote, "College Library," which was part of a pamphlet entitled *College Libraries as Aids to Instruction*, published by the Bureau of Education in Washington in 1880. In the latter work, which is reprinted in part II, Winsor emphasized the librarian's bibliographical skills as being the very foundation of professionalism.

123. "College and Other Higher Libraries," p. 400.

124. Justin Winsor to Charles C. Soule, 20 March 1880; in J. I. Wyer Autograph Collection, American Library Association Archives, University of Illinois Library, Urbana.

125. *Twelfth Report (1889) of Justin Winsor, Librarian of Harvard University*, p. 7.

126. "Library Buildings," in U. S. Bureau of Education, *Public Libraries in the United States of America: Their History, Condition and Management* (Washington: Gov. Print. Off., 1876), pp. 465-75.

127. Justin Winsor to William Frederick Poole, 21 January 1881; ALS in the Manuscript Division of the Boston Public Library.

128. "Address by Justin Winsor," printed in the *Public Exercises on the Completion of the Library Building of the University of Michigan, December 12, 1883* (Ann Arbor: Published by the University, 1884), p. 38.

129. William Warner Bishop, "The American Library Association: Fragments of Autobiography," *Library Quarterly* 19 (1949): 38.

130. Winsor's four major works on exploration, all published by Houghton, Mifflin and Co. of Boston and New York, were: *Christopher Columbus and How He Received and Imparted the Spirit of Discovery* (1891); *Cartier to Frontenac: Geographical Discovery in the Interior of North America in Its Historical Relations, 1534-1700* (1894); *The Mississippi Basin: The Struggle in America between England and France, 1697-1763* (1895); and *The Colonies and the Republic West of the Alleghanies [sic], 1763-1798* (1897).

131. For a thorough description of Winsor's editorial labors and method, see Joseph A. Boromé, "Winsor's History of America," *The Boston Public Library Quarterly* (1953): 119-39. Winsor's historical scholarship earned him a leadership role in organizing the American Historical Association in 1884. Named one of the Association's founding vice-presidents, he was elected president at the Annual Meeting of 1886.

132. Justin Winsor, "The Perils of Historical Narrative," *Atlantic Monthly* 66 (1890): 297.

133. Ibid., p. 289.
134. Ibid., p. 290.
135. Ibid.
136. For details on the transition between the romantic and scientific schools of historical writing in the United States, see John Higham, *History: Professional Scholarship in America* (New York: Harper Torchbooks, 1965), pp. 89-103.
137. Winsor, "Perils of History," p. 290.
138. As quoted in Ibid., p. 293.
139. Ibid., p. 294.
140. Ibid.
141. Ibid.
142. Ibid., p. 295. References are to Auguste Comte, Henry T. Buckle, and Herbert Spencer.
143. Ibid., p. 295.
144. Ibid., p. 296.
145. Ibid., p. 297.
146. Cutter, "Justin Winsor," p. 335.
147. Ibid., p. 335.
148. Budd L. Gambee, "The Role of American Librarians at the Second International Library Conference, London, 1897."
149. Boromé, "Justin Winsor," p. 584-85.

PART II

SELECTED WRITINGS OF JUSTIN WINSOR

PUBLIC LIBRARIES

1. REPORT OF THE EXAMINING COMMITTEE [1867]

The Examining Committee appointed by the Trustees of the Public Library for the year 1867, ask leave to

REPORT.

They directed their attention to the

I. BUILDING,

and learned that its history shows the usual experience with public edifices, of inconveniences discovered in use that had not been anticipated in the accepted plans. It was a condition of Mr. Bates's original gift that the building should be an architectural ornament to the city—a provision which Mr. Everett, two years before in a letter to the Mayor, had feared might yet be interposed, while in his opinion the attempt at architectural display would end in failure. Mr. Bates's condition—whatever we may think of the way in which it was met—did not of course forbid any of the requirements of fitness, and Mr. Winthrop, who made the address at the laying of the cornerstone, believed that the building, when completed, would be found to have few edifices of a like character, to equal it in practical appropriateness and convenience; and the Trustees at that time reported that it would compare favorably with any public building in the world for position, convenience and adaptation. When the Library was dedicated, it was suggested that no disappointment should be felt, if the building should be found deficient in some details, and that it would not be surprising if alterations might finally become necessary. It is not strange, perhaps, that the Commissioners, in their joint capacity, did not successfully guard against any such future development, since libraries are various in character, and have produced diverse experiences, while those who have made their construction a study are not at all agreed upon the prime necessities of their plan. Besides, a free circulating library like this, and of its destined magnitude, did not exist, whence the tests of actual trial could be drawn. After the building had been occupied three or four years, we began to hear complaints of its construction from the Examining Committees, supported by those, who were deriving from the management of the institution, a practical insight into its defects.

WHAT ARE ITS MAIN DEFECTS? A want of light in some of the alcoves of the Bates Hall, of ventilation in the lower story, and the absence of working-rooms. Moreover, a mistake had been made in the height of the alcoves, since movable steps are required to reach the higher shelves,—a fault too late, probably, now to remedy.

In the matter of *light*, the defect is often very inconvenient. The needless fluting of the exterior walls, devised to afford light to the Lower Hall, and which has not proved of use, both enhanced the cost of the edifice, and deprived the Bates Hall of valuable room. To reconstruct the walls not so as to make a straight line, would, we are informed, cost an amount that it is hardly desirable to expend in view of the future, if not immediate necessity, of an additional building in the rear. It is practicable, perhaps, to cut through long, narrow loopholes in the outermost parts of the wall, in the two lower ranges of alcoves (the upper range being light enough) and the expense might not be disproportioned to the benefit.

In regard to *ventilation*, your Committee found the atmosphere of the lower Delivery Room invariably very bad, and that of the Reading Room not so good as it should be, when

Source: Fifteenth Annual Report of the Trustees of the Public Library, 1867. Boston: Alfred Mudge & Son, 1867. pp. 11-64.

many are occupying it, particularly in the evening, when the gas is burning. The matter, we learned, had often been investigated without any satisfactory result. The only effectual remedy in the Delivery Room would seem to be the removal of its present false-ceiling, and even this might not be sufficient without some contrivance for facilitating the draught in the flues. It is possible some artificial appliance for this end may work relief in the Reading Room.

The need of *working accommodations* seems to your Committee to be seriously felt, and the arguments for special rooms, in our opinion, outweigh those in favor of using the galleries and alcoves, as is now the case, for work which, it seems to us, requires greater room and more fitting conveniences, to insure facility and accuracy. All the labor upon the newly-received books—the collating, the varied cataloguing, and other work of preparing them for the shelves—is at present done in so narrow a space that two persons can barely pass beside the tables; and the room is very insufficient for assorting the books, as may be necessary, in making proper classifications. The crowded condition of this part of the gallery causes more or less confusion, and the neighboring shelves of books are exposed to an increase of dust. In the alcoves where binding and repairing to bindings have been done since 1863, these last considerations seem more valid, while the workmen are necessarily put to some inconvenience in timing the noisy parts of their trade to intervals when the hall is free from readers.

The large collection of *pamphlets* is kept in a low and dark apartment over the Delivery Room, and their assortment and examination requires light as well as space. If the ceiling of the Delivery Room, which makes the floor of this apartment, is removed, accommodations will have to be provided for this collection elsewhere.

A small room in one of the rear towers is now devoted to the *British Patent Specifications and Reports*, and its shelves can receive but a few volumes more of a collection, which, through the liberality of the British Government, is constantly growing. It is probable that space must be gained by some temporary expedient, before another room could be furnished, even if an enlargement of the present building be deemed desirable.

The *records* of the institution in volumes and slips have now reached an inconvenient bulk, if no regular place of deposit is provided for them. At present they are necessarily disposed in various corners and spaces, and a suitable room for their regular arrangement is to be desired.

The collection of the *Fine Arts* now small, is well begun, and the time cannot be far distant, when the hall at present devoted to their reception will be wholly inadequate.

The *Reading Room* at times is filled in every part, and might well, even now, be enlarged.

The assistant, who has charge of the *monetary accounts*, is at present only provided for in a much frequented passage-way, with extemporized conveniences for the work.

There is no apartment at present furnished for the keeping and showing of *maps* and large sheets of *plans or engravings*.

Some of the higher range of alcoves in the Bates Hall are now used for storing *sale-duplicates* of books and pamphlets; but the increase of the Library is gaining upon those alcoves, and some place of deposit, not now in view, should be made ready for them, since a large library, receiving donations, must always be burdened with such duplicates.

In the matter of *shelving*, a cursory examination of the Library might seem to show that sufficient room existed for the accumulations of several years to come. The building was calculated to hold about 200,000 volumes in the Bates and 40,000 in the Lower Hall, and it now contains about 136,000 volumes in both, exclusive of some 35,000 pamphlets. But the measure of further accommodation in the Bates Hall is not wholly determined by a difference of some 80,000 or 90,000 volumes. Every large library, to be useful, must be classified, and the classifications must be preserved locally with some degree of distinctness. Hence it is very undesirable to allow the overflowings of one department to encroach on the neighboring one, which is sure in time to eject the intruders, and cause much confusion in the catalogues. Accordingly, though the shelves of the Bates Hall will still accommodate a large accession of volumes, not many thousands more can be received without departing locally from the classifications so needful to make a library useful. Already some inroads have necessarily been made on a strict system. The Parker collection had, by a condition of the gift, to be kept together, and the most eligible position for it compelled the division of the Fine Arts collection, which is thus inconveniently halved and put in separate corners of the building, and similar disturbances have been made in the departments of bibliography and literary history. Of course, the Library, in accepting other equally extensive collections, may be obliged to take them on similar conditions. Such could not, on the present shelves, be accommodated without the greatest disturbance to the library's classifications. It seems very desirable that a series of independent rooms should be provided, of various sizes and suitable arrangements, to relieve the present hall of these minor consolidated collections, and not only to lodge, but to invite further accessions of a like character.

It has been held from the beginning that the *ordinary* annual increase of the Library would be about 6,000 volumes; and in 1854 it was reckoned, on this basis, that it would contain in fourteen years a hundred thousand volumes. Experience has shown that, for the ordinary increase, the calculation was nearly correct; but since, before reaching the end of fourteen years, we have fully 136,000 volumes, the difference shows that there are *extraordinary* accessions, like the Parker library and the gift in books of Mr. Bates, which are not calculable. Two more such windfalls now would find the present shelving insufficient to receive them. Your Committee then feel, that though there may not be pressing need of shelf-room, but a few years can elapse before such will be the case; and it possibly may be, at any day.

WHAT IS THE REMEDY? This state of affairs induces your Committee to suggest the occupation at some early day of the ground in the rear, provided for such an emergency. They will not devise a plan, but leave that to be determined by the necessities of the case, as understood by the Trustees; but, in general, it seems to be desirable that the ceiling of the Delivery Room be raised to the height of the adjacent apartments, and the lower library be moved back into the proposed new structure, which should contain also the grand staircase (removing the existing one); and by this means to secure ampler space in the lower story of the present building for a Delivery Room, a Reading Room, and a Fine Arts Room. The new structure need not be costly from ornamentation within, or from exterior finish, as it is chiefly needed for working-rooms, and for supplementary collections. The present Bates Hall would still be kept as the chief architectural attraction of the library.

In case of such enlargement, it may be deemed best to exchange the present defective mode of warming the building for the apparatus of steam or hot-water heating. Your Committee understand, that the furnaces now in use are only kept in order by constant repairs, and something before long will have to be done with them, if no change in the manner of heating is made.

Your Committee would suggest that any radical change in the Lower Hall, by which the shelf-numbers of the books would be altered, ought, if possible, to be made before the consolidating of the Finding Lists now in progress is effected in a new printed Catalogue of that Hall. The same consideration will apply, though not so urgently, to the Bates Hall.

II. BOOKS.

HAS THE INCREASE BEEN SATISFACTORY? The number of volumes in the *Bates Hall* as reported, Aug. 1, 1866, was of

Located books		96,819
Prince Library, not then located		1,952
Sale duplicates		4,955
Making a total then of		103,726
Located 1866-67	5,100 vols.	
Not yet located	1,678	
Parker duplicates	186	
Excess of duplicates received over exchanges	191	
		7,155

The present number in the Bates Hall, 110,881

An actual count might fall a trifle short of this; first, because about one hundred volumes are missing from the shelves, either lost, or charged to borrowers and not yet returned; and second, because, in re-binding, two volumes have been in some cases put together and now stand on the shelves as one.

In the *Lower Hall* the shelf-lists show that, including 3,002 volumes added during the past year, there have been placed in this collection from the beginning $\qquad$ 31,802 vols.

An actual count the present year gives $\qquad$ 25,199 "

$\qquad$ 6,603 "

Deduct transfers to Bates Hall $\qquad$ 360 "

And we have $\qquad$ 6,243 "

which must be understood to cover all missing and worn-out books since 1858 to the end of the last library year.

Your Committee reckon, then, for a total enumeration, not far from 136,000 volumes. There is reason to believe that the Boston Public Library is destined to become the largest on this continent, while it is unequalled for its accessibility among the great public collections of the world. It is now, we believe, only surpassed, as to size, in this country by the Library of Congress, now that the Library of the Smithsonian Institution, and that of Hon. Peter Force, have been joined to the national collection. They calculate, at the British Museum, that 40,000 volumes will take a mile of shelf-room, which proportion would give this Library over three miles of occupied shelves.

To this collection of books, we must add an increase for the year, of 7,877 *pamphlets*, making a total of 44,443, united to the collection from the beginning. It must be borne in mind, however, that, say from four to five thousand of these, have been culled from the mass as of sufficient importance to bind separately, and are now enumerated as books. Moreover, perhaps a thousand have been bound in groups, and an equal number exchanged, for which there has not been received an equivalent *numerical* return. Roughly, then, from this computation, the Library may be said to contain about 35,000 pamphlets; and the accessions of this sort the past year have been largely in excess of any previous year, owing to the several thousand liberally turned over to the Library by Mr. William Everett, from the collection of his lamented father.

Your Committee consider this record of increase very satisfactory.

DOES THE RECORD OF DONATIONS SHOW ON THE PART OF THE PUBLIC A SUSTAINED INTEREST IN THE LIBRARY? Nearly one-half of the collection of books, and a vast preponderance—say all but about 2,000—of its pamphlets, have been the gift of 3,279 persons and institutions, not enumerating anonymous donors, and counting the same source each time that it appears on the *annual* return of donors. This one-half is independent of the purchases with the interest of the trust-funds, which are, in fact, likewise the fruit of private munificence. If we add these to the casual presentations, it would show that the vast majority of our books is the result of other causes than the City appropriations. The average yearly number of casual donors has been about two hundred and nineteen, and the past year there were three hundred.

Mr. Edwards, in his "Memoirs of Libraries," affirms that "casual donation is a totally untrustworthy source for the formation of public libraries under any circumstances," but we are glad to say the experience here is quite the reverse. Half, indeed, of our total donations of books have come in large bulk, but an accumulation of between 30,000 and 40,000 volumes in lesser gifts, varying from a single volume to two thousand, is no small benefit from casual responses to our needs. Indeed, Mr. Edwards, who at the time was librarian of the Manchester Free Library, so far qualifies his statement as to say, "In Boston there has been precisely that co-operation between corporate functionaries on the one hand, and independent citizens on the other, which is, I think, to be desiderated here." Your Committee think no other large free library in the world will show so large accessions from casual donors. We have seen no recent enumeration of the British Museum, but of its 540,000 volumes in 1857, only 218,000 had been given. In four of the chief free libraries of England established under the Public Library Acts, almost coincidently with this institution, their aggregate volumes in five years amounted to 140,000, and of these only 30,000 were gifts. In the libraries of this country, that of Harvard College is made up to a considerable extent of donations; but as a collection for general use it is greatly inferior in the quality of its books to ours, very deficient in recent and current literature, and its garnering from private sources shows a much greater proportion of mere literary lumber. Private munificence has rarely bestowed a more solid value in books upon any institution, than came from the second gift of Mr. Bates. The Astor Library is so emphatically the creation of a single family that it is hardly to be reckoned either as a public endowment or as the outgrowth of an ordinary private benefaction. In the choice of its books, it is to be doubted if its foundation was laid in any better manner than, or even as well, as ours. The library of the Boston Athenaeum is in effect a subscription one, and has grown from private aid to be a valuable collection, but, in the nature of the case, it does not make the same appeals to the public interest. Subscription libraries cannot ordinarily depend upon further private assistance than comes from the payments naturally accruing to their treasury. The most flourishing, perhaps, in the country, that of the New York Mercantile Library, while it increased its collection by some 9,000 volumes in 1865-66, found that only one hundred and seventy were given. The records of the Boston Public Library then show, eminently, we think, that it has invited the contributions of the public with a success not elsewhere equalled in libraries of its character.

DO THE BATES AND LOWER HALLS MAINTAIN RELATIVELY A PROPER SIZE TO THEIR COLLECTIONS? The Bates Hall was designed to contain about five times the volumes of the Lower Hall; and this, with slight fluctuations, has been the proportion kept up. It is about the ratio preserved at Manchester, between their central library and the *average* of their five branch or lending libraries. Your Committee see no reason to object to this proportion at present, but they question if it be desirable to increase the bulk of the Lower Hall much over its present numbers, for two reasons. First, because, in a collection circulating so extensively, it is not desirable to use galleries, if as many volumes as will maintain a lively circulation can be shelved on a single floor; and, secondly, because the system of recording loans, now in operation, will show year by year the books that are least called for, thus pointing out at the season of each new consolidating of the catalogue, what books can be transferred to the Bates Hall, to make room in the Lower for the fresher publications, and those in more active demand.

The growth of these two halls is, in the nature of the case, somewhat determined by the relative amounts of the Trust Funds' interest and the City appropriation; the former, being out of regard to the expressed or implied wishes of the donors, spent for works of solid and permanent value, which find their place commonly, though not always, in the Bates Hall, while the money allowed by the City Council is entirely devoted to the demands of the Lower Hall and the Periodical Room.

DO THE VARIOUS DEPARTMENTS OF LEARNING IN EITHER HALL SHOW RELATIVELY PROPER PROPORTIONS? In the *Bates Hall*, if we exclude the Parker, Bowditch and Prince collections (which may be put apart as characteristic in themselves, making together over 16,000 volumes), and throw out something over 5,000 sale duplicates, we shall have an aggregate of about 90,000 volumes, thus far located, and they are divided in classes thus:

Periodicals and Transactions	12	per cent.
English History and Literature	12	"
American History and Literature	11	"
Theology and Ecclesiastical History	10	"
French History and Literature	7	"
Italian History and Literature	5	"
Medicine	5	"
Mathematics and Physical Sciences	5	"
General History and Geography	4	"
German History and Literature	4	"
Greek, Latin and Philology	4	"
Bibliography and Literary History	3	"
Other History and Literature	3	"

Metaphysics	3 per cent.
Fine Arts	3 "
Jurisprudence	2 "
General Cyclopaedias	1 "
Political Economy	1 "
Useful Arts	1 "
Miscellaneous	1 "

The accessions of the last year show, relatively, a large increase in Theology and Ecclesiastical History; an increase in American history and literature, and a decrease in English and French history and literature. The department of American history and literature stands to English history and literature about as ten to eleven, which, considering the extent of the two in printed books, shows that our collection affords a more complete examination into our national life and letters than it does into any other, and your Committee think this extensive garnering of our own literature and history most commendable. If the average call for books in the two departments might be taken as a criterion, our national history and literature might be thought to be unduly cherished, for, of readers in the Bates Hall, those calling for English history and literature to those asking for American, has been for five years an average of seventeen to nine. The proportions of demand and classifications in other departments have run comparatively even, except that the demand for works in the useful and fine arts is probably somewhat in excess of the relative supply in that department.

Your Committe learn, that, from the first gathering of the Bates Hall collection, the aim has been to make each department of relative importance to the needs of this community, and they cannot see that the Library is other than a success in this respect. They are told, that, through the instrumentality of Mr. Ticknor, men distinguished for proficiency in special fields of investigation were invited, early in the history of the collection, to furnish lists of the most desirable works, and that from the thoroughness of these returns the Library has gained much. A special effort was made in 1857 to secure all that was rare and valuable in books on America, and a list prepared by Mr. Greenough was printed and distributed among dealers with orders to buy, and about one-third of that list has not yet been acquired.

Your Committee learned that the system of the Trustees is to establish regular agents of the Library in the chief European book-marts, and in this capacity Mr. Henry T. Parker is employed at London; Doctor Flügel at Leipzig; Monsieur C. Porquet at Paris; and Chevalier Albèri at Florence. Sums of money are periodically placed to their credit in the hands of Messrs. Baring, Brothers & Co., and these agents, who are statedly furnished with lists of books to be purchased, are instructed to draw upon those bankers to a specified extent. The London agent has a considerable margin allowed him to purchase current books, not ordered; and a lesser margin is sometimes allowed the continental agents for important books, though not ordered. Invoices from the London agency are constantly arriving, and those from the continent come seldom oftener than once a year. For current literature in foreign tongues dependence is placed upon an importer in New York, as the most expeditious way of procuring them. Of the current American publications *all* are sent for examination to the Library by an agent, Mr. Burnham, and none are rejected but the positively frivolous, immoral or needless. Your Committee deem this system well devised to keep the Library supplied with a due variety of books in all the classifications.

The *Lower Hall* shows naturally a very large proportion of fiction, say 7,000 to 8,000, or about one-third of its entire number of volumes,—a proportion not relative to the demand, but in your Committee's opinion quite large enough, as we shall later show. There has been no strict account published of the classifications in this hall since 1860, but the proportion is not perhaps much changed since. It is not always easy to compare the classifications of two libraries, they are so generally kept on different bases in some particulars; but we should say that while in the circulating department of the Manchester Free Library, history and biography have a larger share of books than with us, in the sciences and the arts the preponderance is on our side. The percentage arrived at in 1860, regarding the classifications of this hall were as follows:

Novels and Amusing Miscellanies	37.4 per cent.
Science and Arts	12.3 "

Biography	10.3 per cent.
Travels	9. "
Foreign Books	8.8 "
Poetry and Drama	6.7 "
Miscellaneous History	6.5 "
Religion	4.7 "
American History	4.3 "

Since 1860 the department of Foreign books has been advanced nearly one per cent of the whole, and at present it contains of

German books	1,036
French books	1,042
Italian books	221
Total	2,299

The selection seems to your Committee to be well made.

There has been no enumeration of the *entire* library by *languages* since 1863, and then there were of

English books	59 per cent.
French books	18 "
German books	9 "
Italian books	8 "
Latin books	4 "
Others	2 "

It is to be expected, as the Library grows, that more and more attention will be bestowed upon the foreign literatures, since recourse can be prudently had to further explorations among them, as the most desirable parts of English literature become more and more gathered in.

IS A DUE AMOUNT OF CURRENT LITERATURE PURCHASED? It has been the aim, as your Committee understand, to keep the collection promptly up to the times, purchasing, as a general thing, books of long standing with what moneys are left after supplying the current publications. This plan is subject, however, to some conditions. The Library has, at present, in interest from the Trust Funds, in currency about $7000, chiefly to be spent for books of permanent value (the conditions of one of the funds require the books to be of five years' standing), and unfortunately there is but a small portion of current publications, which a catholic judgment can pronounce in that category. The great dependence for this end is, then, the City appropriation. For the three years previous to the past there has been an average yearly accession of this current description, of 1,570 volumes. During the past year there has been received the following:

English books	635	
American books	1,154	
Continental books printed in English	104	
Foreign books	539	2,432
Duplicates		97
Total		2,529

This is much in excess of the recent average, and of this number a larger proportion are foreign, than last year.

Your Committee learn, with satisfaction, that measures have been taken to make known these fresh accessions, as soon as they are prepared for circulation. Something further was clearly needed than the entries in the interleaved catalogues. A book of accessions of current publications, posted week by week, fully meets the requirement. Besides this, periodically, perhaps monthly, a printed list of all accessions is to be distributed.

ARE THE PAMPHLETS INCREASING BEYOND THE PRESENT MEANS OF MANAGING THEM? The collection, as before stated, numbers about 35,000, and such as have been assorted, are arranged within presses, in pamphlet cases, in an alphabetical order of their case-title, so that any pamphlet on a particular subject is easily found. The system of assortment pursued is to place them one by one in these cases, as the subject requires; and by a periodical examination of the cases, it is ascertained when a sufficient number on one subject, or of the proper sequence are obtained, to make a volume for binding to put upon the shelves. In this way, some valuable accessions are made yearly to our catalogue of books. Other pamphlets are judged of sufficient value to bind separately, and however thin they may be, a device in the hands of Mr. Goldsmith, the library-binder, makes the back of sufficient breadth to receive the title and shelf-number, without necessitating the accumulation of blank paper within the covers.

Your Committee ascertained that this assortment is now in such arrears that six months' labor of the usual assistant in this department, would not more than suffice to bring them up; meanwhile the collection is growing daily. Your Committee also learned, that it is impossible, with the various other duties requiring service in the Library, to allow this assistant more than a fraction of his time for this labor; and they cannot but see, that with the present force in the Library, these arrears are becoming more and more unmanageable, and must inevitably get into such bulk and confusion, as to be discreditable to the institution. Your Committee then most earnestly recommend that in the appropriations for another year, the trustees secure, if possible, a distinct allowance for this department.

IS THE MANAGEMENT OF DUPLICATES JUDICIOUS? In a library of this character, duplicates are of two kinds, those needed for the shelves to meet the demand, and those not needed, and so held for sale or exchange.

The *shelf-duplicates* constitute one-quarter of the entire number of volumes in the *Lower Hall*, being mostly in fiction, though in other classes some books require, or have required them. Thus we have of

Kane's Arctic Explorations, in 2 vols.	22 volumes.
Livingstone's Africa	11 "
Different editions of Tennyson	12 "
" " Longfellow	44 "
" " Whittier	6 "
Froude's England, in 10 vols.	40 "
Motley's Histories, in 5 vols.	25 "
Prescott's " in 16 vols.	101 "
Bancroft's " in 9 vols.	67 "
Ecce Homo	4 "
Ecce Deus	4 "

Of the recent "Early Life of the Prince Consort," four copies were at once provided for the Lower Hall, and the English edition for the Bates Hall, and more will be added, if necessary.

It is evident that the demand for any book will slacken materially in time; but this fact, as well as what books require more duplicates, would not be satisfactorily ascertained, when it depended upon observation alone. The present registration of loans by slips brings together, at the year's end, the slips of each book, rendering it easy to determine, where duplicates are in excess of demand, and where more are needed. Furthermore, by the new "Indicator" it can be ascertained at shorter intervals, say weekly, when the duplicates of any book are exhausted, and when the same book is so reported week after week, more copies can be ordered, if the character of the book warrants it.

It ought not to be expected of a free Public Library, that in meeting the temporary demands for a fresh book, it will compete in the number of duplicates with a private circulating library established for that end. This institution is not a commercial speculation, and if five hundred copies of a popular novel are purchased, and in a month or two not four hundred of the copies are needed, any percentage on their prime cost, that could be received by selling them, would entail too great a pecuniary loss for having endeavored to meet the demands for an ephemeral book. Where a book is really good, even in fiction, the call for it may be measurably met, on the ground that a good novel will always maintain a fair circulation; but with the novels of the day it would be bad policy commercially, and demoralizing beside, for the city to undertake to cater to transient, though popular literary furors. The inevitable surplusage of stale fiction, which must follow the attempt, cannot be disposed of profitably except by subscription libraries, and even then the policy of smaller town and village libraries is to secure fresh fiction, and a book that has secured a month or two probation elsewhere, is so likely to be denominated musty, that this market for their sales is already too abundantly supplied. Your Committee are of the opinion that such a bartering business is no part of the duty of a library like this; and to follow it would entail a pecuniary loss altogether disproportionate to any gain that might accrue.

In the Bates Hall the duplicates are in very much less proportion. Some shelf-duplicates are desirable. Two copies of a valuable work will allow one to circulate, while the other may be restricted. A book with autographs or manuscript annotations may be of such distinct value as to require another copy for circulation. A different edition, as distinct from a different impression, has of course a separate bibliographical value.

The *sale-duplicates* are of another character, and naturally increase yearly in a collection which grows so much from casual gifts. In 1859, when the present building was first occupied, there were within it 1,804 such volumes, and now there are 5,146. Exchanges are constantly taking place with other libraries, but the process involves a good deal of labor, inasmuch as it is sought to make them book by book, so that the name of the original donor may be inscribed in a work of corresponding value. During the past year there were 714 duplicates added and 523 exchanged, increasing the aggregate by 191 volumes. During the war, by direction of the City Council, duplicates in considerable numbers were sent to the military hospitals, and some are still furnished occasionally to the City Hospital. If ever branch libraries are established in different parts of the city, use can be found for most of the present duplicates, and those yet to be acquired, by turning them over to these minor institutions. Meanwhile they cannot be other than the source of a good deal of labor. To sell them at auction, and to purchase new books with the proceeds, might seem to be the most desirable, as it would be the most expeditious way of managing them; but such a course is often considered ruthless by donors, and to preserve an equivalent for every gift by such a wholesale disposition would be far from easy. It is known that fifty years ago such a course cost the British Museum several valuable bequests; and since they stopped this selling in 1831, it is thought that the interests of that institution have been advanced beyond the drawback from their accumulation, which in twenty years was so large that they had 10,000 duplicates of the commoner kinds of books. Where the consent of a donor to an exchange has been withheld, it has been found desirable in some cases to exchange the earlier copy, if a purchased one, and this has been done to some extent in regard to the duplicates of the Parker collection.

III. CATALOGUES.

ARE THEY WELL DEVISED, IN GOOD ORDER, AND WELL KEPT UP? The question of cataloguing is one of vast importance, and it has become a very vexed one, though the decisiveness of a Panizzi is little warrant for a hasty judgment from less worthy hands. The difficulty increases disproportionately with the growth of a library. Success, passable perhaps at best, can only be serviceable by keeping the registration well up, which your Committee understand to be the case with this institution. The system here in use embodies the labor of many, and profits by the experience of other libraries, and has been adequately described in previous reports. The *card* system for an *unprinted catalogue* with full titles is more and more valued with experience. In all the subsidiary cataloguing the system of this Library seems to be as particular and diversified as is needful to cover all details, and to enable its officers to keep well in hand its literary forces. This reduplicated labor involves time and money, but if it is desirable—as it certainly is—to insure and have at command a perfect knowledge of the Library's condition, it is necessary. Large libraries are conducted oftentimes with but a part of this machinery, as is the case, we are informed, with the Astor Library, but its Superintendent must often be at a disadvantage where ours is not. Of course, with a free circulating library like this, these means of discovering irregularities, such as shelf-list, etc., are much more necessary than in a collection that does not leave the building.

The last voluminous Supplement to the *printed Index* of the *Bates Hall* is but a year old, and probably some years must pass before another of equal bulk will be required. In the mean time, new titles are entered promptly in an interleaved catalogue, accessible to the public, besides being given, as we have before stated, in a printed Bulletin, to be issued monthly, if required, and being enumerated—such of them as are current issues—in the order of accession in a "List of New Books received."

When the *Finding Lists* for the *Lower Hall*, which are printing, alcove by alcove, according to the classifications, are completed, it will be practicable to consolidate the titles in a new Index for that hall, thus dispensing with the present inconvenient Index, with its numerous Supplements.

The new *Indicator* is, also, an adjunct of the catalogues. There was a record made in 1860, for three days of the novel-seekers who went away without a book because every one on their cards was out, and they proved to be three per cent of the whole. This disappointment, as well as the need of some plan of expediting the delivery, led to the device, by the Superintendent, of this simple but effective instrument, which, if consulted, will prevent such uncertainties, while, from its facilitating the process of administration, it is hoped it will invite frequenters from the classes who could ill afford the time necessary to get a book under the old arrangement. The instrument seems liable to error only from the failure of the attendant to turn the pin, but this is guarded against at present by stated verifications; and in time it is expected its management will become almost automatic on the part of those in charge.

IV. ADMINISTRATION.

ARE THE RECORDS OF ALL KINDS IN GOOD ORDER? An institution conducted with so much machinery as a large library for popular use, must have a complete system of records, or its variety of detail does not afford the instruction for its better management that it should. Other than the catalogues, there is a variety of records connected with books, such as the book of invoices, record of "books asked for," of exchanges and of the statistics of circulation—all of which your Committee found in good order. The records of the Trustees have been kept with precision and neatness from the beginning, and are well cared for, with the files of reports and letter books. The books containing the signers for the use of the Library now occupy several large folios, and must be of interest at some future time as autographs of our generation. One book was of interest to your Committee, namely, that in which the officers and assistants of the institution enter their names, with the hour and minute (if after the regular time), in reporting for duty in the morning, and they were pleased to observe a commendable degree of promptness.

ARE THE EXPENDITURES PROPERLY CARED FOR? Your Committee learned that it is but two or three years since a set of monetary accounts, on a thorough system, was begun in the building, and they found them very creditably kept by the assistant in charge. Before that time there was much difficulty in apportioning the books brought, to the several Trust Funds, and there was no accurate knowledge of the general expenses of the institution to be attained except through the City Auditor. The amount of expenditures had become too large, not to have the means of scrutinizing the record, near at hand. There are eighteen permanent accounts opened, covering the twelve items of appropriations from the City Council, and the six Trust Funds, each book bought with the income of one or the other being carried to that fund. Besides these there is a great number of individual and minor accounts. In the Trust Funds' accounts for the year ending in May, we find an income of $5,760, mostly in gold, equivalent in currency to $6,874.21; and at that date, the whole of this had been appropriated for books, except $295.59; to cover which there was in the hands of Messrs. Baring $2,111.67, for the purchase of books.

It has been the policy of the Trustees, from the beginning, never to handle money, and all bills are payable to the holders on requisition of the President upon the City Treasury, after the items have been examined by the Superintendent, approved by the proper Committee, passed by the Committee on Finance, and confirmed by the full board. The only money received in the building is the small sums collected in fines, which last year amounted to $364.55, and which the Librarian is charged to pay into the City Treasury; besides the small amounts received from the sale of the catalogues, finding lists, etc., likewise disposed of in the same manner.

IS THE LIBRARY OPEN AS MUCH AS POSSIBLE? The Library proper has been open on an average for the last ten unbroken years, 276 days, and for the past year, 277 days. It has been kept open in one year (1860) for 297 days, which is one reason, probably, why the daily average delivery diminished materially for that year. The regulations close the Library on the fifty-two Sundays, and on six holidays, and if to these be added two days for any extraordinary occasions, and the month of August, we have left 278 days, which may be considered a fair average opening for a year. The month, that is now required for cleaning the building and verifying the shelf-lists, book by book, may not have been necessary in years past. The first year in this building, but eleven working days were required for this purpose, but then the building was new, and the shelves were much less filled. The task of seeing that every volume of a hundred and thirty-six thousand is in its proper place is no small one, and the recess is not by any means a season of relaxation to the attendants. It will be fortunate, if in coming years, this work can be kept within the month. In libraries that do not circulate, less time will be naturally required. At the British Museum, ten years ago, they kept open 293 days; any later account, since the completion of thier new reading hall, we have not seen. This number is ordinarily exceeded in the Reference Library at Manchester, and they adopt there the plan of three cleaning days each quarter; but in addition to not circulating the books, this Reference Library contains but a little more than one-third of our number of volumes.

During August of the present year, the Reading Room for the first time was not closed, (except for a brief interval while the periodicals were removed to another room, to allow the Reading Room to be newly painted.) It seems desirable that this should be the case hereafter.

The staff of assistants needs periods of relaxation, and the absence of any one regular attendant necessarily disorders somewhat the routine of the library business. This matter is regulated as well as is practicable by allowing as few as possible to be absent at any one time.

IS THE LIBRARY CONDUCTED SO AS TO BE AS USEFUL AS POSSIBLE TO ALL CLASSES? The institution was begun expressly on popular grounds. Mr. Everett, in his letter to the Mayor, in 1851, called it the completion of our public school system, and that has been a favorite designation of it ever since. In the preliminary report of 1852–the body of which was drawn by Mr. Ticknor–it was wisely recommended that a beginning should be made without any sharply defined plan, so that suggestions from experience could be made effectual; and it was not thought well to make it at once an imposing, learned or scientific collection, but rather to gather a library most fitted for the masses. Mr. Ticknor–whose contributions to the Library in time and experience cannot be overvalued–expressly says, in a letter accompanying a valuable donation of books in 1860, that he would "never have put his hand to the institution at all, but with the understanding that it should be made useful to the greatest possible number of citizens;" and he says that for eight years there had not been any *real* difference among the Trustees on that point, nor can we learn that there has been any since.

Up to 1856 the system of purchases had looked to supplying the most popular wants. The collection, which had then grown to near 30,000 volumes, was deemed large enough to satisfy the most reasonable demands of a general kind; and it began to be felt that there were particular classes of our citizens, apart from the general body, whose wants deserved recognition. So about that time we find that books in the foreign tongues began to be added, and the higher departments of literature more fully developed. The donations to the Trust Funds, now accruing, in being expended for books of solid and permanent value, served to strengthen very materially the upper classifications; while Mr. Bates's last munificent gift of books developed our weight in the same direction. The time was now come when it was very properly agreed that there was no department of learning, which some portion of the community was not interested in; and that every department should be cared for to meet such requirements. So the two distinct collections have been developed—the Lower Hall to meet the most ordinary demands of the people, and the Bates to serve the higher requirements of the studious classes, or of investigators in special matters—a scheme which your Committee can but think naturally evolved, and conducive to the satisfaction of every mental grade, and answering the requirements of all the intellectual demands of the community.

There is one feature connected with the methods of purchase, which your Committee can but consider almost unprecedented for its liberality, though it confers a privilege that comparatively few seem ready to take. It has always been the pleasure of the Trustees to order any book, if a proper one, when asked for, and not already in the collection. From 1854 to 1865, the number of requests of this kind annually made, greatly fluctuated between 18 and 221, and in one year (1860) several thousand notices were put in all the books delivered for a fortnight, but it secured only 25 applications, and the average for these twelve years was only 117. Latterly the plan has produced better results. Last year there were 306, and during that just past, 546, and in 95 cases the applicants had failed to discover the desired books were already in the Library, and of the remainder, 260 vols. have been received, leaving 191 still on the order-books of our agents. This privilege is an inestimable one to scholars, and indeed to all, and it is somewhat surprising to your Committee, that it is not more enjoyed. It is really an inducement for an inquirer in any department to make Boston his residence over any other city on this continent. It gives him, or any citizen in need of a particular book, facilities for searching the book-marts of the world, that the wealthiest can hardly command.

Your Committee also believe that in no other large library are readers more expeditiously served. The catalogues are well kept up and accessible. It can be at once known if book or pamphlet is in the collection, and the place of its deposit ascertained. In some other of the libraries about us, this is done only with delay. It takes from six to ten minutes to get a book at the British Museum, after the slip is handed in; so it will be seen that the extent of a collection must necessarily enhance the average delay, however well organized the delivery system may be. With some of the large libraries of the continents of Europe, we have a startling proof of the inconvenience of a less systematic process, in the hours that may be passed in waiting, which are sometimes so extended that a second day's pursuit becomes necessary.

Your Committee have heard occasional complaints from hasty people, that the Library can be of no use to them because they are debarred access to the alcoves, but they have forgotten, that with a printed catalogue of subjects as well as authors, the Boston Public Library is far more serviceable than another collection might be without this aid. Students have told your Committee that at this Library they can investigate a point with far greater expedition than they can in collections where their privileges give them the range of the alcoves, but where they have no assistance from similar catalogues.

Dr. Cogswell, of the Astor Library, has said, in one of his printed reports, that a free circulating library in New York was an impossibility, and that in less than five years any collection for that purpose in so large a city would be scattered to the winds. Such an opinion may be extravagant, but it is clear that no collection can maintain its usefulness unimpaired without due restrictions, and experience has shown in Boston, that, as you extend the privilege of such an institution, it is likely that those classes least accustomed to books, and least influenced by that reverence for books which is most wholesome, will be drawn in. Yet these are not the only people who commit depredations. Bibliomaniacs are proverbially notorious for some strangely lax notions, and, unfortunately, bibliomaniacs are fond of mousing in alcoves. To make class distinctions is not proper, since, instead of a free library, you have then a library for the elect. It is admitted that an hour's search in an alcove may in some cases satisfy an investigator better than a much longer time at the outside tables; and such access is always accorded to any one who has a determinate literary or other consistent purpose, in the presence of an attendant, if the request is properly made. It is not infrequently replied that all freedom and ease of investigation is out of the question, with such a looker-on to pass you the books. With some temperaments this is doubtless true, but it must be remembered that in allowing one reader a freedom from such restraint, the Library may be of diminished value to hundreds who come after him. Studious persons are not always the most orderly in obeying injunctions or in returning books to their exact place on the shelves, and their misplacements may remain undiscovered until the annual cleaning, so that every intervening inquirer for the misplaced book must be disappointed. This restraint, it seems clear, though sometimes irksome, is really preservative of the Library for the many to come.

Some exception is now and then taken to the rule which keeps from circulation rare or costly works, unless it be by the consent of the Superintendent or of two of the Trustees. This, doubtless, causes delays; but without these obstacles in the way of mere curiosity or amusement, valuable architectural works for instance would be a great deal of the time in the hands of idlers as picture-books, and when the student of that art required them it would be fortunate if he did not find them mutilated, or uncleanly, to a degree that might reasonably disturb his sense of propriety. Such restrictions are properly made, it seems to your Committee, for the preservation of the books *for the classes most interested in them*, and for whose benefit in part the Library has been gathered. A little reflection must convince those who have been most harassed in this respect of the truth of this.

DOES THE CITY ORDINANCE RELATIVE TO THE PUBLIC LIBRARY NEED AMENDMENT? The Trustees are charged with the management of the Library, and are properly allowed the appointment of their executive officers, inasmuch as their own good name is largely entrusted to the fidelity of such. In assigning duties to the various officers, they are not free to exercise fully their own judgment, until the apportionment of the salaries goes with the assignment. They have this liberty in all cases but with the Superintendent and Librarian, on whom the most responsibility falls, and upon whose trustworthiness they must depend before all others. It is eminently proper that the City Council should fix the limit in the aggregate of all salaries, but it seems to your Committee that it would be desirable to remove the restraint now existing, so that the Trustees may apportion the recompense, as well as define the duties, of all under them, within some aggregate limits.

The Ordinance of last year, re-organizing the Board of Trustees, opens the way to put five new members, or a majority, into the Board at any election—a conjunction of affairs that might work serious detriment to the institution in some season of temporary clamor—always to be provided against at times given to devising safeguards for the future—when the unseating of a majority of those most versed in the management of the Library may throw the control into the hands of the inexperienced, or of those chosen, in obedience to some passion of the hour, on other grounds than their peculiar fitness. It seems to your Committee most desirable that two successive elections should at least be required before the predominating influence in the Board can be changed, and this would give a portion of the final majority a year's experience before they shall decide the policy of the Board. A majority at a single election, if given to views gathered outside of the peculiar experience of the Library, might, it seems to your Committee, very likely act in a way prejudicial to its interests. It is most proper that a full representation of the City Council should remain, as at present, in the Board, and the change must accordingly be devised among the other members. It has been suggested, though some objections at once present themselves, that the term of service for those chosen from the citizens at large, should be six years, with one electable every year. This, with the annual three from the City Council, would secure a majority in two years.

V. CIRCULATION.

IS THE CIRCULATION SATISFACTORY? The number of signers from the beginning up to the opening of the present building was something short of 16,000. A new registration was then ordered, and an equal number signed in a little more than a year's time. Since then there has been a yearly increase of between four and five thousand, so that when the year closed on the first of August, something like 53,000 names stood on the books. It was known that a large proportion of this number, either from death, removal or want of inclination, did not use the Library; and new cards were given out last year, and including the new signers for that year, some twelve or thirteen thousand were taken, which number must, however, be in excess of the habitual frequenters of the Library, though probably below the number of readers, since in families a book may find several to read it besides the card-holder. At Manchester, for the same circulation as ours, in 1866 they had 7,339 cards in use.

The total number of books in use in *both halls* for the past year was 208,963, a daily average of 754, which is larger than ever before; while the greatest delivery in any single day was 1,813 (against 1,534, the largest previously, in 1863), and of this, 206 were in the Bates Hall, and 1,607 in the Lower Hall. This heavy work comes usually in February.

Lower Hall. The number of volumes taken from the Lower Hall, in 1859, was about 150,000; and the past year it was 183,714, which is very nearly the average of the last four years. There would, probably, the past year, have been a material increase over the previous year, but for the fact, that it was necessary in the preparation of the "Finding Lists" to keep two or three thousand volumes from circulation at once, and they were oftentimes of the most popular description. The daily average of loans the past year for the Lower Hall was 664. We can best understand the importance of the work we are doing by a comparison with other libraries, as far as statistics can be used, though any comparison is open to some qualifications. Three of the largest of the lending libraries of the Manchester institution had, in 1866, an aggregate of just about the number of volumes in our Lower Hall, or perhaps a thousand or two more. These circulated very nearly the same number of volumes, as with us for the same year, but as their libraries were open more days, it gives Boston the advantage in daily average of near forty, and it must be remembered Manchester has a population at least double that of Boston, and with its system of branch libraries brings its books much nearer to a larger number of households. Nevertheless, with those things in its favor, the circulation of the most prosperous of similar institutions in England varied so little from ours, as to be fairly considered identically the same.

The New York Mercantile Library has usually been considered the most flourishing of contemporary libraries with us. In 1866, it contained more than three times the volumes of our Lower Hall (to which it nearly corresponds in character), while its circulation for the same year fell more than 5,000 short of ours. The last yearly report of that institution (April, 1867) shows 90,000 volumes (to our 24,219), 206,120 issues of volumes (to our 183,714), taken by 12,274 subscribers, which indicates renewed exertions to extend its sphere, made effectual in large part by a vast preponderance of fiction among its 10,000 purchased volumes for that year. It should be remembered that more than one-third of the circulation of this New York institution (judging from the returns for 1866, not having seen this item in the last report) is through its two branch deliveries in different parts of the city, and also that, in a vastly larger population, it has no effective rival.

With a system of branch libraries with us, say one in Roxbury, one in South Boston, and one in East Boston, it seems probable that our popular circulation could be made far larger relatively, than it is even now to the most successful of such establishments at home and abroad. At Manchester, the system is well-established and works successfully. Their central collection, though considerably more popular in character than our Bates Hall, is a reference library, and does not circulate its books. A year ago, it contained 38,426 volumes. The five lending or branch libraries contained in the aggregate, 39,318 volumes. The accumulation of duplicates at a central library is always less burdensome, when there are supplemental institutions among which to share them.

Bates Hall. The total number of volumes lent from this hall for *home use* since 1862, when the collection was first open, is 53,920, and the past year it was 13,696, the largest number of any year.

It is not so easy to find the actual number of volumes, *used in the hall* for the year, there are so many not taken into account, as when any one by the consent of the Trustees is allowed to make protracted investigations in the alcoves; and, though record is kept of the consultations in the Patent Room, it is by hours and applicants and not by volumes; and, furthermore, no record is made of the use of the excellent reference collection, around the desk, to which the public have unrestrained access. Independent, then, of these classes, there have been used in the hall itself since 1862, 63,525 volumes, and the past year, 11,553 volumes, which was exceeded in 1865, when 13,090 were called for.

The largest number of books delivered in this hall for either use in any one day was 206. The average daily delivery has been 92 volumes.

Comparisons with the use to which other libraries of the solid character of our Bates Hall are put, must be made cautiously. As regards the Reference Library of Manchester, which is a little more than one-third as large as our Bates Hall collection, and shows about three times the number of users, it must be remembered that the population which sustains it is about twice as large, and that its only rival is the Chetham Library, one of those old monastic foundations, which is not of a character to interfere with the success of its upstart neighbor; while within much the same area, and with a far smaller population, the Boston Public Library must share this class of more or less cultivated frequenters, with the collections of Harvard College and the Boston Athenaeum. Beside this, we in this community are uncommonly well supplied with lesser collections, accessible to persons making investigations, like the libraries of the Historical Society, the Genealogical Society, State Library, the Academy Library, the Social Law Library, the old Boston Library, the General Theological Library, etc., so that in the aggregate there are at least half a million volumes in our community, accessible to the public, or reached with ease by any one desiring to use them.

There are two other considerations to be borne in mind in making the comparison with Manchester. First, that it does not appear that they omit to make record of the use in protracted investigations; and, second, that their Reference Library is not of the high character, relative to their lending libraries, that our Bates Hall bears in comparison with our Lower Hall. They put upon its shelves a great deal of contemporary English fiction, while our Bates Hall has little of this kind of literature, except what is classic from long-established fame. Bearing in mind that our upper collection is three times as large as their Reference Library, it will be seen how much more thorough, relatively, we are in the higher departments, if we take a few test authors, and put against each the number of titles in the respective catalogues, including both editions and commentaries.

Homer,	6 at Manchester	118 at Boston.
Dante,	4 "	93 "
Goethe,	11 "	38 "
Shakspeare,	40 "	175 "
Lessing,	1 "	44 "
Muiatori,	13(vols) "	92(vols) "

Turning to the Astor Library we find that, in 1860, it had about the same number of volumes that our Bates Hall at present possesses, but its number of volumes used was twice the number of those used in the Bates Hall the past year. Every qualification that we have used in regard to Manchester applies with greater force to the largest city of our country, and the most cosmopolitan perhaps of the world, excepting that in the Astor enumeration, they exclude, as with us, protracted investigations, and that in tone and quality its collection is much the same as our Bates Hall. It should always be remembered that since the Astor Library does not permit its books to leave the building, a considerable share of its frequenters (and very likely enough to reduce, if they were excluded, its delivery to the level of ours) is of the class that with us find their wants supplied in our Lower Hall.

Ten years ago the British Museum was six times larger than our present Bates Hall, and its daily use was twelve times ours to-day; but of course there are a multitude of reasons applicable to a collection which of itself draws many yearly to the greatest city of Europe.

Your Committee, then, have no reason to feel that the Bates Hall is not doing its proportionate good. As the Library grows and gets a national reputation it will, of course, draw investigators to the city, and swell the record beyond the present. It needs to be more generally known how excellent a *working* library, in character and machinery, we have got. The fact already mentioned, that it stands ready to provide any proper book, if it can be found in the book marts of the world, is warrant that it invites the largest use. If that privilege, or the collection itself, is not enjoyed to the highest possible limit, it is owing to the public wants being in part supplied in other directions, and not to the management of the institution, since, in all the collections with which we have compared it, *much more stringent regulations are in vogue.*

WHAT IS THE CHARACTER OF THE READING IN THE BATES HALL? This hall has been open five years, and the *average* yearly use of books in the several classifications is as follows:—

English History and Literature	17	per cent.
Useful and Fine Arts	10	"
American History and Literature	9	"
Theology, Metaphysics, Ethics, Education	8	"
Periodicals	7	"
Mathematics and Physics	7	"
Medicine	6	"
French History and Literature	6	"
General History and Literature	4	"
Italian History and Literature	4	"
Natural History	4	"
Transactions of Learned Societies	4	"
German History and Literature	3	"
Greek and Latin	3	"
Other (including Oriental) History and Literature	3	"
Bibliography	2	"
Law and Political Economy	2	"
Miscellaneous	1	"

The most marked annual variation has been in the classification, headed by Theology, which has fallen gradually from 11 per cent. in 1862 to 4 per cent. in 1867. This is owing, perhaps, to the fact, that, at the outset, special efforts were made to interest the clergy and educators in the Library; and possibly, also, to the fact, that the General Theological Library has been since established. American History and Literature have gradually gained, owing, perhaps, in some measure, in the historical part, to the late rebellion fostering an inclination to learn our own antecedent history, and possibly to the efforts which the Library has made to secure everything in any language relating to that rebellion. It will be seen that the use of books in this department is not much more than half what it is in English History and Literature, which is not so strange, perhaps, in view of the relative extent of the two departments. Nevertheless, there is doubtless a disproportionate inclination among readers for profit to go to books and themes of the the old world. Prof. Lowell, in a recent review of the Life of Josiah Quincy, gives a statement, which he was perhaps in as good a position as any one to make, to the effect that "it may safely be affirmed that for one cultivated man in this country, who studies American, there are fifty who study European history, ancient and modern."

The use of Transactions of Learned Societies has grown. The other departments have not much varied, except that of Useful and Fine Arts, which has greatly fluctuated.

We have no printed record of the use of books at the Astor Library, except in 1860, and by a comparison, as nearly as can be made, it seems apparent that with us the demand for books in the Useful and Fine Arts and for the Transactions is more, and for English, American and General History less, than at that New York institution. In Law and Political Economy, the Astor finds considerably more readers, and this is the department in least demand with us, owing, perhaps, to the existence of the State Library and the Social Law Library.

The records of our Patent Room collection are kept independently, and we have no means of knowing how the use of it compares with either of the other five sets in the United States. The past year 197 persons used them for 248 hours; being ten more persons than the previous year, and the same number of hours. The fact, that at Manchester the record is by volumes, and that the specifications are bound separately, while with us they are bound in groups, prevents any comparison between the two.

WHAT IS THE CHARACTER OF THE READING IN THE LOWER HALL? Your Committee have already shown that it was through the Lower Hall the mass of the people was sought in the beginning. The preliminary report of 1852 contended, that, if the habit of reading could be engendered, it would go on improving in character. In 1855, it was thought there was recognizable a demand for higher and higher classes of literature, and accordingly the next year the Trustees reported that they were buying fewer books of mere amusement and more of a higher kind, beginning at this time to add some in the foreign languages. In 1859, it was reported, that only the best of the lighter class of literature was bought. The next year there was a marked falling off in circulation, but such fluctuations are as inevitable as they sometimes are unaccountable. At Manchester they have experienced it in much wider range than with us, and our records generally show a steady increase. At Manchester their circulation in 1866 was no higher than it was ten years previously, yet in the interim it had been 50 per cent. more. The records of the British Museum show that an institution like that is by no means sure of a *steady* hold upon the class that consults its treasures. When our circulation fell off in 1860 (the average daily lendings dropping from 588 to 508) it was thought that this effort to raise the standard of reading, by buying fewer novels, together with the then recent opening of private circulating libraries, was the cause of it; but the next year's returns showed a gain equal to the previous loss.

In 1861, an attempt was made to ascertain what proportion of readers sought for fiction, and two days were selected for the test. On one there were 32 per cent. and on the other 50 per cent. of all borrowers. Not till the past year has it been possible to reach any exact conclusion in the matter, since the slips for the 183,000 volumes that circulated for the year, are now arranged so as to show how many times any book was out. The returns, as made, show what the various classifications were in this demand; but it must not be forgotten that this pertains *to the Lower Hall solely.*

Fiction and Juveniles	68 2/10	per cent.
Libraries, Collections, etc.	6 2/10	"
Sciences, Arts, Professions	6 6/10	"
Drama, Poetry, Rhetoric, Belles Lettres	4 7/10	"
Travels	4 8/10	"
History and Politics	2 9/10	"
Biography	3 9/10	"
Foreign Languages	2 7/10	"

The class, "Libraries, Collections, etc.," includes such sets as Bohn's Libraries and the like, and a good proportion of its 6 per cent. undoubtedly belongs to Fiction, so that roundly about 70 per cent. of the Lower Hall circulation is in the nature of English Fiction, including in this, however, it should always be remembered, a very large share of Juvenile books.

This large proportion for a class of literature that ordinarily includes so much that is morbid and even pernicious, may alarm some of the good friends of the institution, but the subject is not to be dismissed without examination from many points; and your Committee are of the opinion that although they might wish a different record, they must accept the conditions as arising from the mental tendency of the masses of the community; and they hope to show that the result with us is no worse than elsewhere, and even sometimes creditable by comparison.

A very competent authority in 1860 (Wm. Chambers) classed the cheap publications of Great Britain, as showing a *monthly* issue of these grades:

Improving books	843,000
Exciting but not positively immoral books	1,500,000
Immoral and irreligious	80,000

As these books are published for commercial speculation, it is fair to presume they hit the demand relatively, and it will be seen that in Great Britain the chance is about twice as good for selling an exciting but not positively immoral book, as it is for selling an improving book, when they are of the class of cheap publications. The exciting class will doubtless find more readers in the household than the improving, and it cannot be too much to say that three will read the exciting book to one the other. This, as we have seen, is above the proportion of our circulation between fiction and non-fiction, and our readers are doubtless of much the same average class that the cheap publications reach in England. It may then be taken as the normal intellectual taste of that class; but with us the exclusion of juveniles ought fairly to be made, before instituting a comparison, which would then be largely in our favor. The fact that the "Finding List" for fiction was the earliest printed the past year, thereby meeting that class of readers more openly, has also, doubtless, conduced in some degree to raise the percentage of the demand in this department.

Of course, as we rise into the more cultured classes, we find the proportion of novels dwindling, though the "Saturday Review" not long since, in giving its views on the demand for fiction, expresses the opinion that fifty novels are now read in England, for one that was read at the beginning of the century. With the class of our community depending on the Boston Athenaeum, for instance, it would not be surprising to find that their circulation of fiction is not equal to ours, yet it cannot be very greatly inferior. Richard Cumberland, in the "Observer," eighty or ninety years ago, testifies that it was the surfeit of novels then beginning, that led to the frequent establishment of circulating libraries, as a commercial specu- lation, though Ramsay, in Edinburgh, had begun one on a small scale a half century before. Yet, when these institutions are adapted to the higher classes, as is the case with Mudie's, in London, we find that novels, though still numerous, are not in the majority. Thus Mudie, in the ten years ending 1862, put upon his shelves 960,000 volumes, or seven times as many as this building now contains. We will compare, under a few prominent heads, the percentage of Mudie's purchases, with our Lower Hall collection (as it stood in 1860—not much changed relatively now), and with our circulation in that hall the past year; it being borne in mind, of course, that Mudie's purchases include a large share of such books as we would put in our Bates Hall.

Class.	Mudie.	Lower Hall.	Circulation.
Fiction	44 per cent.	37 per cent.	75 per cent.
History and Biography	22 "	21 "	6 "
Travels and Adventure	13 "	9 "	4 "
Others	21 "	33 "	15 "

It will be seen that our Trustees have catered less to the demand for fiction, than Mudie, in his commercial spirit, has shown the demand would bear, with his far higher class of readers; notwithstanding it is apparent that, with our Lower Hall readers, every volume of fiction will secure seventeen readers a year, while every volume, not of fiction will get only four, on an average.

It is not easy to get at any satisfactory apportionment of our frequenters by a social or intellectual gradation, other than as the books they take may be the measure of it. It was thought that possibly the slight restrictions put upon the applicants in the new registration now making, might serve to qualify the number already using cards, in such a way as to repre- sent a class more eager to enjoy its better privileges. With that idea, an examination was made of all the slips, showing the entire number of books out at the end of a fortnight, after the library opened in September, but the proportion was much the same, or even larger, for fic- tion and juveniles.

Mr. Edwards, when he had charge of the Manchester Library, after a careful enumera- tion, made out that three-fifths of its frequenters were of the class of artisans, mill-workers, operatives and their families, while the other two-fifths were shopkeepers, clerks, teachers, students, school-boys, etc. It is probable that, with our frequenters of the Lower Hall, much the same proportion is preserved among corresponding classes in our community. By the re- ports of the Manchester Library, it is not possible to say what proportion, year by year, fiction has held in their circulation, but Mr. Edwards determined, in 1857, that it was five-eighths of the whole, which is probably in excess of what ours is now, if our juveniles be thrown out; and they have, at Manchester, a subordinate department for such readers, which relieves of this class, in a measure, the general circulation.

It will be seen that, counting duplicates, over one-third of our Lower Library is fiction and juveniles; and if the Trustees were to make their purchases three-fourths of this class, ac- cording to the demand, thus multiplying the copies of popular fiction, they could much, and probably vastly, increase the aggregate circulation; but it would inevitably augment the fiction-readers out of all proportion to the other readers. It is in this way that the New York Mercantile Library has run up its large circulation, even among a class of subscription-readers, which must average on a social scale above ours at the Lower Hall, and which does not include readers of juveniles. They have latterly sought to make their purchases meet the demand, and the result has been that while in 1851, 27 per cent. of its purchases were novels, the proportion has been increasing so that it is now full 75 per cent. or somewhat more than our circulation is, including juveniles.

Your Committee, then, are not of the opinion that this large percentage of fiction with us, is anything that need surprise or alarm us. Good fiction is doubtless salutary, and the general character of juvenile literature is much improved over what it formerly was. That there are some books among the collection in our Lower Hall which are not of the wholesomest, may be allowed; but a conscientious effort is made to exclude rigorously everything that is of decidedly evil tendency, and of the half-morbid sort to allow but one, or at most but a very few copies. We may say that the best novels are seldom read in a way to do the most good; but that is a circumstance of course beyond any library's control, and there is a good deal to say in favor of supplying the masses with reading of even an inferior order rather than they should not read at all. Some are of the opinion that much reading of the lower grades will naturally conduce to over-satisfy such half-formed or vitiated tastes, and divert the reader into more wholesome ways. There are others who hold that excess only confirms the bad tendency. We will not judge between them. It needs must be that to most minds of a low intellectual culture, books must be of a character attractive in subject to that grade, or they will not be regarded at all. Once regarded, there is a fair chance of substituting for books attractive in subject, those attractive in manner, thus leading to a higher range of subjects. Take two instances: The Mühlbach novels have no great artistic or literary merit, but they make history attractive to an average order of minds, and the change from them to an attractive historian is not too abrupt to be easy. The Mayne Reid books—most of them—are exceedingly entertaining in matters of natural history, and show what an advance has been made within a half century in preparing science for the enlightenment of the young. The transition from such books to attractive works on science, say such as Hugh Miller's, is not uncommonly made. Your Committee look upon the passion for reading as formative, and, with such influences as is hoped may be at work in the public schools and in the family, capable of remunerative results even at the bottom of the scale. It is not to be expected, however, that this progressive betterment will show itself in our statistics, for every year a new influx of readers may take the place of those advancing, and preserve the old ratio. Indeed, it would not be strange, if as our circulation enlarges, there is a show of retrogression. The private circulating libraries are in the way of our greatly increasing the number of our frequenters in the Lower Hall from the higher classes; and we must descend lower and lower in the scale to increase at all beyond the natural growth of the classes ordinarily frequenting. Such a descent must inevitably tell upon the character of our circulation.

Your Committee were desirous of ascertaining by some test authors and test books, the general nature of this large demand for fiction, which included about 138,000 volumes for the year. They present first, a tabularization of some *juveniles*, showing the aggregate circulation of each in volumes.

Mayne Reid's Books	4,903
Abbott's Stories	3,521
Harpers' Story Books	2,219
Franconia Stories	932
Andersen's Tales	390
Grimm's Tales	311
Florence Stories	200
Carleton's "Winning His Way"	183
Oliver Optic's "All Aboard"	199
" " "Brave Old Salt"	120
" " "Young Lieutenant"	270
Every Boy's Book	156
Boy's Own Book	72
Swiss Family Robinson	70

Robinson Crusoe	55
Tanglewood Tales (Hawthorne)	50

We will next compare some popular *novelists*, showing the number of volumes to each, including duplicates, and the average circulation per volume.

Author.	No. of vols.	Aggregate circulation.	Circulation per vol.
Cooper	173	5,460	32
Marryat	116	3,730	32
Simms	104	2,345	22 1/2
Dickens	206	3,955	19
Thackeray	79	1,295	16 1/2
Charles Reade	57	923	16
Lever	126	2,146	17
Scott	200	2,663	13
Hawthorne	63	722	11
Tom Hughes	43	449	10
Theodore Winthrop	22	210	9
Mrs. Hentz	96	3,375	35
Mrs Grey	29	805	28
Mrs. Stowe	50	980	20
Miss Braddon	49	946	19
Mrs. Stephens	33	30	19
Miss Muloch	101	1,663	16 1/2
Miss Cummins	28	379	13
Miss Yonge	143	1,312	9
Mrs. Charles	40	350	9

Of course, this return must be taken cautiously, as showing the relative popularity of the several authors. To be accurate, it should be certain that the Library is supplied with copies of each relative to the demand; and regard must also be had to the fact, whether an author's works are in one or two volumes, since the return is by volumes and not by books; and with some of them, Miss Braddon, for instance, the number of copies was kept purposely less than the demand.

Some unexpected developments occur with regard to *separate books*. Thus, one of Cooper's least known novels ranks highest of all his, while the "Pioneers," which his publishers say sells the best, shows but little more than half the lendings to a volume.

Authors.	No. vols.	Total.	Average.
COOPER. Miles Wallingford	8	257	32 1/8
Stories of the Sea	7	258	37
Pioneers	10	258	25 1/8
MARRYAT. Midshipman Easy	5	385	77
Privateersman	2	70	35
SIMMS. Katharine Walton	9	207	23
Border Beagles	4	131	33
DICKENS. Pickwick	20	386	19
Nicholas Nickleby	31	344	11
LEVER. Charles O'Malley	12	273	22 3/4
SCOTT. Ivanhoe	22	144	13
Guy Mannering	13	259	19
Tales of the Crusaders	12	144	12
CHAS. READE. White Lies	2	60	30
Cloister and Hearth	10	136	13 1/2
Very Hard Cash	8	126	19

Authors.		No. vols.	Total.	Average.
	Never too Late, etc.	23	223	10
	Box Tunnel, etc.	1	26	26
	Christie Johnstone	4	126	31
	Peg Woffington	2	61	30
	Clouds and Sunshine	4	120	30
	Love me Little, etc.	3	43	14
TOM HUGHES.	Rugby	6	169	28
	Oxford	30	175	18
	White Horse	7	105	15
TOM HOOD.	Tales	1	20	20
	Tylney Hall	2	40	20
	Prose and Verse	1	13	13
HAWTHORNE.	Scarlet Letter	10	200	20
	Seven Gables	9	112	12
	Blithedale Romance	7	100	14
	Marble Faun	12	100	8
	Twice Told Tales	16	85	5
	Old Manse	1	75	75
D. G. MITCHELL.	Dr. Johns	4	56	14
	Other Books	16	107	6 11/12
LONGFELLOW.	Hyperion	8	70	8 3/4
	Kavenagh	5	36	7 1/5
THEO. WINTHROP.	Cecil Dreeme	9	88	10
	John Brent	9	60	7
	Canoe and Saddle	1	41	41
	Edwin Brothertoft	2	21	10
TROWBRIDGE.	Neighbor Jackwood	14	420	30
	Cudjo's Cave	6	212	35 1/3
MISS CUMMINS.	Mabel Vaughan	9	187	21
	El Fureidis	11	100	9
	Lamplighter	3	75	25
	Haunted Hearts	5	17	3
MRS. HENTZ.	Rena	9	279	31
	Planter's Northern Bride	14	400	29
	Ernest Linwood	13	371	28 7/13
MRS. GREY.	Flirt	2	182	91
MISS MULOCH.	John Halifax	12	241	20
	Christian's Mistake	8	184	23
MISS YONGE.	Heir of Redcliffe	19	205	11
	Daisy Chain	32	144	4 1/2
	Ben Sylvester	10	60	6

Take some single, *long-established works of fiction*:

Don Quixote	96
Gil Blas	58
Gulliver's Travels	92
Paul and Virginia	35
Tristram Shandy	21
Vicar of Wakefield	75
Miss Burney's Evelina, 9 vols.	245
Undine	43
Picciola	18

Take, now, a few good or popular books of recent years which may be presumed to have lost their freshness:

William Ware's Tales	160
Lavengro	22
Potiphar Papers	20
Elsie Venner	300
Caxtons	66
Lowell's New Priest	8
Pique	140
Amber Gods	18
Alton Locke	33
Vivian Grey	16
J. P. Kennedy's books	180
Typee	40
Charles Auchester	77
Naomi	46
Jane Eyre	181
Coningsby	12
Sam Slick	39
Out of His Head	35

A few of the more *ephemeral type*:

Dunn Browne	30
Artemas Ward	95
Verdant Green	45

We turn, now, to the remaining quarter of our circulation, covering other books than fiction. The circulation of *French, German and Italian* books was 5,064, and these authors are noted:

Dudevant (George Sand)	11
Victor Hugo	203
Goethe	338
Kotzebue	217
Schiller	262

Richter in English translations:

Campaner Thal	5
Levana	14
Titan	17
Walt and Vult	16

Poetry, Drama, Rhetoric and Belles Lettres circulated 8,750; and these are noted:

Tennyson, 12 vols.	124, or 10 each
Longfellow, 44 vols.	429, or 10 each
Whittier, 6 vols.	91, or 15 each
Clough	4
Shakespeare	545
Bell's Theatre	859
Minor Drama	757

Sciences, Arts, Professions, etc., circulated 12,250 vols.; and these are noted in Domestic Ecomony and Agriculture:

Mrs. Hale's Cook Book, 4 copies	4
Mrs. Putnam's Cook Book, 1 copy	12

Mackenzie's Receipts, 4 copies	50
Inquire Within, 2 copies	16
$600 a Year, 1 copy	4
How I Managed My Children, 4 copies	3
Copeland's Landscape Gardening, 2 copies	6
How to Get a Farm, 2 copies	8
How to Farm Profitably, 1 copy	3
Ten Acres Enough, 2 copies	17
Allen's Grape Culture, 3 copies	15
Rand's Parlor Gardener, 1 copy	16
Downing's Landscape, etc., 3 copies	25

Travels circulated 8,837; and these are noted:

Kane's Arctic Explorations, 23 vols.	205
Livingstone's Africa, 11 vols.	58
Burton's Travels, 8 vols.	16
Speke's Africa, 1 vol.	13
B. Taylor's books, 28 vols.	141
Eothen	7
Crescent and Cross	14
Fletcher's Brazil	20

History and Politics circulated 5,425; and there are noted:

Froude's England, 40 vols.	154
Motley's Histories, 24 vols.	125
Prescott's Histories, 101 vols.	323
Abbott's Histories, 10 vols.	64
Bancroft, 67 vols.	137
Headley's Histories, 2 vols.	14
Carlyle's Frederick, 10 vols.	21
Parkman's Pontiac	14
Parkman's Pioneers	2
Benton's Thirty Years, 2 vols.	12

These of *local* interest:

Frothingham's Siege of Boston	42
Drake's Boston	34
Barry's Massachusetts, 3 vols.	8
Wells' Samuel Adams, 3 vols.	2
Loring's Boston Orators	7

These connected with the *late war*:

Nichols' Great March	9
Miles O'Reilly	42
Semmes' Cruise	37
Coffin's Four Years' Fighting	8
Greeley's American Conflict, 2 vols.	22
Youth's History of the Rebellion	20
Barnard's Peninsular Campaign	22

These few *theological* or similar works:

Ecce Homo, 4 copies	34

Ecce Deus, 4 copies	15
Renan's Jesus, 4 copies	39
Cumming's books	85
Spurgeon's books, 5 copies	14
Ingraham's Pillar of Fire	10
Ingraham's House of David	15
Pilgrim's Progress	18
Essays and Reviews	13

These few *miscellaneous*:

Dana's Idle Man	20
Thoreau's Walden	54
Catlin's Indians	3
Webster's Works	32
John Adams' Works	9
Harper's Monthly, (bound volume)	2,737
Guerin's Journal	13
Oehlenschläger's Correggio, (Eng. transl.)	16

It should not be forgotten that these statistics pertain to the Lower Hall *solely*; and some of the works designated may also be found in the Bates Hall. Your Committee cannot but see that here are the means, through this record of slips, of apportioning supply in duplicates to demand, better than were at hand before this new system was put in practice.

IS THE READING ROOM WELL-MANAGED AND SUFFICIENTLY SUPPLIED? Until the past year there has never been any trustworthy record kept of the use of this department. The new system of delivering periodicals on application, while it debars some from a rapid survey of all as they lie upon tables, works advantageously for the greater number, secures order, and protects the property from mutilation and loss, to a degree not possible by any system of espionage. It has, accordingly, been safe to add duplicates freely, and of 13 periodicals we now have 53 copies, and 195 single copies of other periodicals, making 208 in all. The Reading Room was opened in 1859 with 140. The present number is divided by languages:

English	141
French	39
German	27
Italian	1

And by classes:

Scientific	85
Literary	68
Religious	18
Illustrated and foreign newspapers	12
Commercial	9
Fashions	6
Illustrated Magazine	3
Juveniles	3
Fine Arts	3
Diplomacy	1

During the past year there have been 91,832 readers of periodicals and reference books, and of this number 12,348 were females. It shows something of the different constitution of society, that of the 71,353 readers in the corresponding department at Manchester, but 288 were females. The average number of readers daily the past year was 254, and 283 magazines were read on an average daily for the 289 days the room was open. Some 60 persons, mostly strangers, enter the room daily, out of curiosity.

CAN ANYTHING MORE BE DONE TO GUARD THE BOOKS FROM MUTILATION AND LOSS? Mr. Ticknor, in the preliminary report of 1852, in sketching out a plan for the Library, novel in some important respects for a public institution, and which is substantially the basis upon which it is administered to-day, urged strongly the desirability and probable safety of circulating the books freely among certain classes of our community (where the class bore with it a kind of responsibility), without any surety but their personal recognizance; but contemplated that it *might* become necessary in ordinary cases to require some pecuniary guaranty. The free libraries in England, which were about that time starting, under the Parliamentary acts of 1850, were requiring this as a condition, before their privileges were accorded to a citizen; and they have retained it without any apparent check upon their usefulness, and with much greater security to their property, than we have enjoyed. Still, the experiment of a freer library than the world had ever known, was not, perhaps, an ill-timed one, and, for a while, it was thought to have been an unvarying success, and, to this day, no pecuniary voucher is demanded.

A few books were reported lost, at first, in Mason Street, and the number had increased, until the last year in that place, it was two hundred for the year. Still, it was thought there had been no wantonness. In 1857, we began to hear of mutilations, with hints at future stringency. The next year, it was thought some degree of wantonness was discoverable. The first year in the present building (1859), one hundred and thirty were reported lost; of these, forty-two were subsequently recovered, leaving eighty-eight unaccounted for. It increased yearly, until it had got to be annually between five and six hundred, when, at the beginning of last year, some check was put upon it by issuing new cards and recalling the old ones. Still, for the past year, four hundred and sixty volumes are reported missing, and of these, two hundred and ten are charged to borrowers, who cannot be found or traced at the addresses they gave, leaving the sad inference of premeditated fraud.

Nor is this a measure of the wanton damage to the books. Mutilations and defacements are becoming common. In 1862, the Superintendent reported, that, in his judgment, more was to be feared from this evil than from loss; and in successive reports it has been dwelt upon, and the time predicted when stricter supervision of the delivery would be necessary. There was formerly no adequate remedy for this kind of injury when discovered, and it was hardly possible with the force at command to collate a sixth part of the books returned. Last winter the necessary law to meet such cases of mutilation and defacement was passed by the Legislature; and the statutes of the Commonwealth now afford a wholesome remedy in discoverable cases.

The losses from wear and tear, if actually done in good service, excite no unpleasant inferences. Not a few books come into the library's possession partly worn. While in Mason Street 200 were reported worn out; and since the library has been in the present building, the number worn out must have averaged that yearly. The ratio will of course increase as the books are longer in use. During the past year over 4,800 volumes have been either rebound or had their bindings repaired, a small portion of which belonged to the Bates Hall. Your Committee cannot learn that this absolute wearing out of books is anything more than ought to be expected. Comparing our experience with that at Manchester, there seems to be something in our favor, provided, of course, the same degree of damage condemns a book in both libraries. Thus the aggregate circulation at Manchester for its first five years was about the same as ours for the first three years in the present building, and while at Manchester 800 volumes were reported worn out, with us it was less than 500. A popular novel usually wears out two or three strong bindings before it is condemned. Some estimates can be made of the wear, from the fact that one person is employed most of the time in renewing the paper covers on the Lower Hall books.

The total number of *missing and worn out books* has been about 6,700 volumes from the beginning; and this, on an aggregate circulation of 2,000,000, is only something over one-third of one per cent., which is not excessive certainly. This amount of loss is almost exactly the same that the records of the New York Mercantile Library show it to have sustained, on the same number of volumes, during its career.

What proportion of this number can be put down to absolute theft or books unaccounted for, it is not easy to ascertain; but your Committee see by the records that this most disgraceful kind of loss is increasing out of all proportion to the circulation, which is now only 30 per cent. more than it was in 1859, while the loss in unaccounted-for books, on the best data that can be found, is something like 300 per cent. more. This increase does not probably show a relative increase of offenders, since a *few*, by observing the impunity with which it could be done, would naturally enlarge their range of depredations. The reference books around the desks in the Bates Hall and the Reading Room are open to the inroads of a class of thieves, known to the police, to exist in fraternities, so that books stolen from libraries and shops in one large city, are transmitted to their fellows in another to be disposed of. These practices are in no small degree doing a work of demoralization, which every consideration of justice and well-being required to be checked.

To do this without temporarily curtailing the circulation were, perhaps, not easy. The example of Manchester showed, that where considerable restraint had been put at the start and consistently kept up, a large circulation could be maintained. Your Committee know that it is more difficult to impose restraints at a late day; but they believe it is never too late to do right; and the public will be sure to see that by right-doing their privileges are more fully protected than ever.

At Manchester they require two pecuniary vouchers among the rate-payers, renewed every five years, for each applicant. On the same circulation as ours in 1865-6, they lost but fifty-six volumes, and they were all replaced—thirty-three by the borrowers, and twenty-three by the guarantors. Beside this they enforce pecuniary satisfaction for mutilations and defacements.

Your Committee understand that in the new registration now in progress each applicant is required to give two referees, who can, if need be, verify his statements. By this means, several irregularities that might have caused confusion and loss, have been discovered and guarded against. Your Committee believe this restraint good as far as it goes, and trust that it will not be found necessary to go to the limit employed at Manchester; but they have no hesitation in saying, that this community should assert its right to be called quite as orderly as any other; and if that pre-eminence can only be secured by the pecuniary vouchers, they should be required.

In the *Bates Hall* the loss has not as yet been great. There were reported last year as lost since the opening in 1862, 43; and of these 10 have been recovered; and 18 have been added to this number during the past year, some of which will doubtless be found, so that the total now gone from the shelves is 51, beside 48 charged to borrowers and not yet returned.

In conclusion, your Committee would bespeak for the Public Library of the City of Boston, from all quarters, a continuation of that enlightened interest, which has in the past been bestowed upon it with a success, that is both gratifying to this community, and a source of admiration with strangers.

Respectfully submitted,

JUSTIN WINSOR.
ALFONSO BOWMAN.
CHAS. W. FREELAND.
C. D. HOMANS.
HERMAN J. WARNER.
R. C. WATERSTON.

PUBLIC LIBRARY, Nov. 11th, 1867.

2. REPORT OF THE SUPERINTENDENT [1877]

To the Trustees:—

The present report is the tenth of my administration as Superintendent, and the twenty-fifth from the foundation of the Library. The juncture seems a fitting one for an extended examination of the history of our institution, and such a one I intend to present to you at a later day. In this place I must confine myself to a synopsis of the progress of the Library during the last decade.

The death of Professor Jewett, my predecessor, left the Library in a flourishing condition. The foundations had long been laid, and his own exertions had done much to strengthen them. On the occupation of the present building in Boylston street, the executive charge of the Library devolved upon him, and for ten years, by his administrative faculties and bibliographical attainments, he proved himself worthy of an institution whose future seemed certain of eminence. During this period, the Library doubled both in its extent and its usefulness, and he left it with over one hundred and forty thousand volumes on its shelves, and with a record of annual issues of about two hundred thousand volumes. The institution had firmly established itself as a populat educational factor, and in this respect was without a peer in the country. The Boston Athenaeum had long been, with its excellent collection, the main dependence for reference and more scholarly uses to the inhabitants of Boston; but the Boston Public Library in this respect also was now about to eclipse its neighbor, and in the collection of Bates Hall it offered a Library for research quite the equivalent of both those of the Boston Athenaeum and of Harvard College, and surpassed only among the Libraries of the country in this respect by the Astor Library in New York, and by that of Congress, which, by the then recent purchase of the collection of Peter Force and by the engulfing of that of the Smithsonian Institution, had taken the first place.

Such was the position of this Library ten years ago, where the sudden loss of its Superintendent, and the ill-health of its next succeeding officer, the late Professor Jillson, caused a vacancy, which the Trustees chose to fill by the appointment of one of their own number. I found myself in a position congenial to my tastes, conscious both of the excellent condition in which the institution was placed for a career of development, and ambitious of enlarging its scope, in accordance with the principles which wise men had made its fundamental laws. It was a work worthy of any one's endeavors. With the countenance and encouragement of a Board of Trustees in sympathy with the project and largely instrumental in its success, and with a City Council responsive to demands for increased accommodations and resources, the results have been reached, which you will allow me briefly to set forth.

In 1867 our sphere of work widened from what is now called the Central Library; but in the report of the Examining Committee for that year attention was drawn to the success which had attended the branch system with the English Libraries, and as warranting its trial with us. The enabling acts of the Legislature of Massachusetts had early recognized the necessity, and had included Branches in the permission which they had afforded to cities and towns to establish Public Libraries; but this Library had been founded eighteen years before its first Branch was opened at East Boston, in 1870. It was ascertained at that time that the chance of a resident of that island using the Library in Boylston street was not a third of that of a resident of the city proper,—so important is the nearness of books to the homes of the people in developing a use of them. In 1872 the second Branch was opened, at South Boston; the third, in 1873, at Roxbury, under the favorable auspices attending a junction with the resources of the Fellowes Athenaeum, whose income opportunely became then for the first time available. With 1874, the acts of annexation, by which the City of Charlestown and the Town of Brighton became a part of our municipal territory, provided that their respective Libraries should become branches of ours. Early in 1875 our youngest dependency was opened in

Source: *Twenty-fifth Annual Report of the Trustees of the Public Library, 1877.* Boston: 1877, pp. 28-63.

Dorchester. This made the number of our Branches six in all, outlying like a cordon of posts, at distances from head-quarters varying from a mile and a quarter to four miles and a half.

A further development was begun in 1875 by the opening of a Delivery of the Dorchester Branch at the Lower Mills; and again, in 1876, by a similar outgrowth of the Roxbury Branch at Jamaica Plain. These Deliveries are maintained at comparatively small expense, and have proved so far capable each of adding ten or twelve thousand issues annually to our circulation. Brighton, our least-used Branch, scores about thirty thousand issues a year, and it may be well questioned if the villages dependent upon the Lower Mills Delivery, with the same facilities, would not patronize a Branch to an equal extent with Brighton. I am confident that at Jamaica Plain the circulation, by converting its Delivery to a Branch, could be carried far ahead, and that it would surpass even that of Dorchester, which now records about seventy thousand issues for the year; and there are regions still beyond, at Roslindale and West Roxbury, which, as Deliveries of a Branch at Jamaica Plain, would largely enhance the usefulness of the Library.

We have had abundant proof in our experience that the Branches, with the territorial extent which has been left between them, have not at all diminished the usefulness either of one another or of the Central Library. Some apprehension hazarding its chances of making the Library in Boylston street an important one for the country, and even for the world, in thus dissipating, as it was feared, the resources of the city among lesser projects, which would detract from the interest felt in the parent institution. The result has been just the reverse, as will appear from the following table: —

ANNUAL ISSUES.

DEPARTMENTS.	1868.	1869.	1870. (9 mos.)	1871.	1872.	1873.	1874.	1875.	1876.	1877.
Central Library Bates Hall	33,874	42,905	47,597	65,205	50,251	59,264	72,313	80,737	114,329	141,618
Lower Hall	141,853	175,772	163,366	231,110	254,246	238,057	253,097	272,834	348,842	405,732
East Boston Branch	. . .	. . .	. . .	26,130	75,846	68,212	81,091	85,548	90,987	102,627
South Boston Branch	. . .	. . .	. . .	. . .	. . .	102,322	108,566	112,525	115,530	135,179
Roxbury Branch	. . .	. . .	. . .	. . .	. . .	. . .	67,342	89,539	101,297	146,829
Charlestown Branch	. . .	. . .	. . .	. . .	. . .	. . .	33,391	79,375	85,815	106,816
Brighton Branch	. . .	. . .	. . .	. . .	. . .	. . .	9,642	21,842	24,805	29,792
Dorchester Branch	. . .	. . .	. . .	. . .	. . .	. . .	. . .	16,017	66,016	71,979
Totals	175,727	218,677	210,963	322,445	380,343	467,855	625,442	758,417	947,621	1,140,572

The check in the circulation in 1872-3 in the Central Library was owing to changes going on in the internal arrangements of the building. It should also be remembered that the first years of the Roxbury, Charlestown, Brighton and Dorchester Branches were not full years.

The table shows that, while the circulation of the entire Library has increased nearly seven times, the present aggregate is by no means wholly owing to the additional work of the Branches; since the use of the popular collection in the Lower Hall has nearly trebled, and that of the higher department of the Bates Hall has quadrupled. The Bates Hall delivers as many books now as the Lower Hall did ten years ago. Our experience has been that also of the principal English Libraries. Dr. Crestadoro writes to me from Manchester, that the successive establishment of the Branches of their Library has in no wise interrupted the constant appreciation in use of the pre-existing departments.

A system then so well established, and of so good record, must linger but little in further development. We need but a return of prosperity in the business affairs of the community for the Library to take a new departure with an acceleration all the greater for the present reservation of energy. A proposition now before the City Government for accepting the books of the Mercantile Library Association, using a part of them as the nucleus of a Branch at the South End, if agreed to, will give us a dependency, which must prove one of our most important.* The time cannot be far distant when Jamaica Plain will demand a Branch instead of a Delivery.† I think also one will be necessary somewhere between Beacon and Copp's Hills. An increase in our Deliveries I think inevitable.

As already indicated, a Branch at Jamaica Plain will lead to Deliveries at Roslindale and West Roxbury. The importance of the Dorchester Branch will be much increased by such natural dependencies at Neponset, Mount Bowdoin, Mattapan, and in the region lying between the Dorchester and Ashmont stations on the railroads. The Five Corners and Washington Village will perhaps more easily depend upon the South Boston Branch, if indeed the region they cover must not in time be advanced to the rank of a Branch district. South Boston Point and Bay View will also claim in time their partial if not entire independence of the same Branch. The remoter regions of Charlestown and East Boston will demand such accomodation. The Roxbury Branch must in time throw out Deliveries both in the direction of Upham's Corner to the south-east, and of Longwood on the north-west.

The possibilities of further annexations to the city are beyond our prescience. The Public Libraries of Brookline, Cambridge, Somerville, and Chelsea are at least well situated to add to the symmetry of our network, as delineated on the map.

Within the past year a sort of sub-delivery has been established at Deer Island, for the benefit of the City Institutions situated there, books being sent in boxes from the Central Library once a month, two or three hundred at a time. At the request of the Fire Commissioners, a similar service has been given to thirteen of the engine-houses in the City Proper, and to the fire-boat, for the benefit of the firemen; and it is probable that the Protective Department will come within the same rules.** Under a guaranty from the authorities of the Navy Yard, a like privilege has been granted to the reading-room within the walls of the yard, for the advantage of the enlisted men on the station; but the arrangement has not yet been put in force.

Such, then, is the extent of the circulating service of the institution compared with what it was ten years ago. The increase is great; but I think we find the condition of matters to-day as favorable for an equal increase during the next decade, and perhaps for a still greater one. I look for greater favor being accorded to the Branch system by devices for increasing the promptitude of the business by means of telegraphic wires for the transmission of messages, and not unlikely with telephonic attachments.

This enlargement of circulation from 200,000 to 1,200,000, or sixfold, has been in part brought about by other agencies than by a multiplication of points of delivery. It could have been increased still more largely had we consented to augment the accessions of fiction, and to

---

*This has since been determined upon.
†This has also since been determined upon.
**It has since been done. This Department has two houses.

duplicate to a great extent the copies of the last new book. I have heard my predecessor maintain that there was scarce a limit to the extent of circulation, should such a policy be persistently carried out. I am glad to say that this increase has been made without any corresponding augmentation of that class of reading; indeed, with a diminution of it; and this has been brought about through an improvement in our catalogues, which I may speak of a little later. Increased days and hours of access have also borne their share in the work. In 1869, for the first time in the experience of a large Library, it was not found necessary to close our doors for the cleaning of the shelves and for the taking an account of stock, and since that time the days on which the Library has been closed have been confined to the legal holidays, with an occasional exception of a general gala-day. This change was made through no neglect of stock-taking; but the newly adopted method of charging books on slips, which were arranged for the year's record numerically by the shelf-number of the book delivered, rendered it possible to account for books missing from the shelves and charged to borrowers, without an absolute inspection of the volumes. Under the previous ledger system, of charging loans in accounts with borrowers, the multitude of such accounts to be searched for a record of the book to be accounted for, made the business practically impossible.

Beside this increase of days, the aggregate of hours per week within which the books are delivered has been considerably extended; and it still remains a question of serious moment whether the most important department of the Library can be held to fulfil its perfect mission, until it can be as freely visited in the evening hours as it is now in the daytime. I think considerations of increased expense have only so far stood in the way of this change. The practicability of an evening service succeeding to the work of a day force has for some years been tested in our Lower Hall, and could be as well applied to the Bates Hall, for the delivery of books and for the answering of ordinary demands. Research of a curious and recondite order is increasing rapidly among the frequenters of the upper department, and requisitions are much more frequently made than formerly upon the time of its officers and the trained assistants for the evening hours; and the hours of this service at present are burdensome enough, with the mental strain accompanying them. Indeed, I may say that the skilled workers of the Library, though their labors require a breadth of knowledge and an acumen of the critical faculties rarely brought into requisition by the teachers of the schools, are subjected to greater application daily, with far less respite from vacation. They are, moreover, recompensed with salaries, which leave many of them to eke out a support by labors that impair their energies for the morrow's work. If the tax-payers of the city demand this sacrifice, the struggle must go on, and the harness must gall while the goal is reached. There is too much ambition to maintain the good name of the Library to allow any spirit of indifference to abate the labors imposed.

I think something, too, of the greater use made of the books is due to the changes which have been made in the methods of delivery, by which the average delay in finding books has been materially shortened. In the Lower Hall this has been partly accomplished by bringing the books, which were in galleries, all upon the main floor; but I am sorry that, owing to the faulty construction of the building, the awkwardness of obtaining books from shelves beyond the reach of the hand still exists, to the great detriment of the promptness of delivery. This blunder has not been repeated in the new additions of the Central Library, nor in the Branches. Our present method of making the public do their own charging, by filling out the slips which are left as a voucher for their loan, enables us to deliver in a busy season nine or ten thousand volumes a day with much less confusion and with more expedition than fifteen hundred volumes were delivered ten years ago. In our busiest days now, in the Lower Hall, when twenty-five hundred volumes are issued a day, the delivery clerk needs but the occasional assistance of the officer in charge, to accomplish a business that it took, under the old system of ten years ago, five or six people to meet, with less than half the number of issues. I do not deem that we have by any means reached the limit of circulation which the Lower Hall ought to maintain, though we are fast approaching the extent which is possible without an enlargement of the delivery hall. Among our branches, South Boston particularly finds its issues checked by the wants of larger space for the public in waiting; and it is to be hoped that the enlargement contemplated for that Branch will not be long delayed.

In the Bates Hall the time is also not far distant when want of space for the frequenters will interfere with its usefulness, as it clearly has on some days during the past winter. Ten years ago its aggregate annual issues were something over 25,000 volumes, or a daily average of less than a hundred, at a time when the space on the floor was given wholly to public use; but the case is far different when the issues per year are approaching 150,000, and the largest daily use is between nine hundred and a thousand volumes; and when, in addition, a considerable share of the open floor has been occupied by the cases of the Card Catalogue, with its attendant keepers. Furthermore, about fourteen months ago, it became necessary to enclose a larger space for a desk of delivery as well as of receipt, where one desk answered both purposes before, and to afford an additional counter for the consultation of reference books. The loss to the public floor has been in a measure compensated for by the new study-room in the rear of the main desk, where those requiring facilities of research and ink for writing are accomodated.

It will thus be seen that want of room is a serious obstacle to the Bates Hall doing all the work which it ought. You are aware that the City Architect and myself have been engaged upon plans for an extension of the building easterly, so to enlarge the Bates Hall in the direction of the Hotel Pelham, and to afford additional accommodation for books as well as for placing of reading tables for the use of the public. The plan also aims to provide fit storing rooms for our bound newspapers and duplicates, now disgracefully stacked in a basement, ill lighted and damp, and for an enlarged bindery; for additional book room to meet the growth of the Ticknor and Bowditch libraries, and of other parts of our collections; and for suitable convenience of a toilet nature, demanded by the physcial and moral good of the present large staff of both sexes. It also contemplates that enlargement of the public waiting rooms in connection with the popular Library in the lower story, now so necessary to the proper development of the advantages which ought to spring from the use of that hall. In the Periodical Reading-Room attached to this department the want of enlarged space is equally felt. While its issues now are nearly five times what they were a decade ago, for a year or two its use has not increased as it would have done with more ample space for readers. Its increase of use the past year over the previous year has fallen somewhat short of that of the Lower Hall Library, the former showing an increase of 13 per cent.; the latter of 16 per cent.; while the Bates Hall has increased in use nearly 24 per cent. At our most flourishing Branch, Roxbury, where the accommodation is ample, the increase over last year has been nearly 45 per cent., and during the winter has been over 60 per cent., while during the summer it was almost 23 per cent. With the Lower Hall, under the enforced restrictions of space, the reverse has been the case, and the percentage of gain in use in the summer months, when the accommodation is in better proportions to the number of frequenters, was thirty, which fell to less than twelve during the winter months.

There are one or two particular points which well express the relative interest of the public in the Library, to which I will further direct your attention. The system of inducing the public to recommend books not in the Library was begun with the organization of the Library, and it was looked upon as one of the best means of interesting the community in the Library's work. This belief was for several years trusted to in the hope that if results were not patent, they would become so in time. Every effort made to induce the public to recommend books produced little. During the decade preceding the last, one year fewer than twenty titles were handed in, and for the whole decade there was an annual average of no more than 223 titles recommended. This inertia, however, came to an end with that period, and in 1867 the number of titles derived from this source mounted to 546, from 300 the previous year. The annual number has been rising steadily since, and it is now about 2,500 titles, or about five times what it was ten years ago.

In 1867 the patent-room was visited by less than 200 persons, and the necessary oversight of it was given by any assistant from the other departments, who was detailed as occasion required. Now, it demands the constant attendance of one assistant, and the frequenters for the year have increased to over 2,600, or thirteen times.

In 1867 the registration of applicants for the right to use the Library, which had been begun in 1859, had reached about 53,000 names, showing an average of between six and seven thousand a year; and it was at that time, though a mistake, as I think, set aside, and a new one ordered. Beside causing additional labor, the new registration put extra formalities upon a public, always impatient of interpositions of such sort, and resulted in a temporary check of the circulation. The registration then begun reached 12,000 within a year, indicating the number of cards in the hands of the public at that time. It has gone on increasing, receiving extraordinary accessions in 1874, when the existing registrations of the Libraries at Charlestown and Brighton were assumed, until at the present time the number of cards liable to be presented for books amounts to 130,000. This shows ten times as many to be watched to-day as there were in 1867; and the yearly increase of this number is now about twelve or thirteen thousand, or double what it was then.

It is not likely, of course, that this full number of cards is in use to-day. Death and removal from the city have thrown out large numbers; but comparatively few have been presented for cancellation, and accordingly nearly this full number are under surveillance. When the *dead*, as we technically call them, bear so large a proportion to the *quick*, as they must do to-day, it is manifest that for facility of manipulating, some process of elimination must go on, if the whole is not periodically discarded for a new beginning. The process in lieu of the latter, which we now pursue, saying annoyance to the public, is to remove the record-slips from the general file to a subsidiary one, as we have evidence, through applications for new cards in place of those filled up, that the privileges of the Library are still availed of. In that way we establish a *quick* file, which answers the great bulk of demands, and which leaves but a few inquiries to be determined from the *dead* file. The *quick* file now contains four-fifths of the entire 130,000. leaving over 100,000 users in more or less active use of the Library.

One or two other items will clearly indicate the gain in the administrative work of the Library attendant upon the increase of its use. In 1867 something short of 16,000 notices were sent through the mail for books over-detained, and finable. While the circulation is now six times as large, this sort of delinquency has only increased four times, but this necessitates the sending of over 60,000 such notices a year. The Library has gained, with the rest of the community, in expedition and economy, from the use of postal cards, which now convey our notifications of all sorts. Before the government adopted the plan, the Library did, and for a year anterior to the appearance of the postal card in the mails the Library used its own, but with the necessity, of course, of two cents postage. The gain, nevertheless, was obvious. At present its mail service of all kinds on postal cards consumes nearly 70,000 a year,—no small item in our account of expenses.

With all the advantages of this augmentation, the most gratifying change of all is in the nature of a positive, as well as relative, reduction. In 1867 that portion of the community who were most regardless of their obligations to the Library, whether from wilfulness, or a culpable neglect bordering upon it, were increasing the losses of the Library to a degree, and with an accumulated proportion to the circulation, that boded a serious set-back to the good opinions which we were otherwise winning. One of the latest endeavors of my predecessor was to organize a system of following up delinquents, which has proved in the ten years since elapsed to have had the effect of reducing the percentage of loss in relation to the circulation, so that now the chance of a book's return is ten times as great as it was ten years ago. Not only the Library, but the community have gained, since the certainty of a delinquent being called to account has made the Library an important moral agent, and the sanctity of the mutual obligation of Library and patron has been so enforced that its rules and necessities command the respect and adherence of its patrons to a remarkable degree. With a circulation to-day of six times the extent, the number of books which require a messenger to recover them is but comparatively few more than ten years ago,—a little over 1,800 now, to 1,450 then. And of the books finally unrecovered, one in a thousand issues then is set against one in eight or ten thousand now. It has also been demonstrated that in the more confined localities supplied by our Branches, the issues can be made to reach more than 100,000 volumes, without the loss of a single one. I do not think the community is more honest now than then, but I do maintain it to be proved that the Library has added to its natural qualifications the credit of accomplishing a moral reform in enforcing a regard for the observance of its rules.

All these enlargements of the scope of the Library work have been brought about without a corresponding increase of the material which accomplished it. The collection of books has not grown in equivalent proportions. The number of volumes has increased from 136,000 to about 312,000, or about two and a quarter times; and while the popular departments, ten years ago, constituted a little more than a third of the whole, the congeries of such departments to-day embrace not far from a quarter of the aggregate volumes.

In some respects the most important work of the Library is that bestowed upon its Catalogues. Ten years ago the system of its printed indexes had already received a full development under Mr. Jewett. In the Bates Hall the two large volumes, probably the last instalments of a general *printed* Catalogue of that department, had been issued; and the first of a series of special Catalogues was in progress, covering the antiquarian and theological collection of the Prince Library. In the Lower Hall, the last of its general annual supplements had already rendered consultation difficult; and a series of divisionary Finding Lists had been begun, to serve a temporary purpose, while that department was undergoing thorough revision, rendered necessary by the wear and tear of a dozen or more years. There was no systematic organization of the Catalogue force; and the current accessions passing through the hands of those working on the Catalogue amounted to between five and six thousand volumes a year, the cards of which were acumulating in but a single set, with no proper arrangements for their consultation. A selection merely were entered by main title only in an interleaved copy of the first index, which was the sole accessible guide for the public.

The Cataloguing Department to-day is organized with an interdependence of service and methods, conducive to a regularity of work and efficiency for public use, that has become necessary with the enlarged scope of the operations. Four times as many volumes, or some twenty thousand a year, pass under its care, and among them is a much larger share of those, composed of many pamphlets, and which require an aggregation of work, often curiously disproportioned to their seeming value, as compared with books; but which, without such work, may as well have been kept altogether from the shelves. Instead of the laborious multiplication of references, rendered less irksome as well as less satisfactory by abridgement, a process not dreamed of at that time affords fac-similes of the transcriber's script, with a profusion that costs no time, with an accuracy that dispenses with revision, and with a fulness that preserves for the cross-references even more information than was given with the main entry before. A full record, both for public and official use, is kept up with a promptness that causes but a brief interval to elapse before the latest accession is known to be in the Library; and in a catalogue (so far as the public is concerned) which presents in one alphabet already the entire contents of the Bates Hall, and will, before long, embody those of the Lower Hall also. In the latter department, the temporary Finding Lists have become class- ·lists, which preserve their divisionary character for the convenience of new issues with less delay from time to time, while the additions are made accessible through subsidiary lists, maintained for the intervals between publication. The cataloguing for the Branches is added to the work of the Central Department, involving the printing of catalogues for each, the recording accessions between editions, both in the catalogue cases of the separate Branches, and in the consolidated record kept for all in the Central Department. At present, besides the work on the ordinary accessions, it devolves upon this force to carry through the press the Catalogue of the Spanish collection, bequeathed by Mr. Ticknor, which fell to the special care of the late head of this department, Mr. Wheeler, in the first instance, and now falls upon his successor, Mr. Whitney. The next of our special Catalogues following the Ticknor will be that of the Barton Library, the preparation of which is at present in the hands of the junior head of the department, Mr. Hubbard.

In 1873 the Library made an innovation in the bibliographical matter which was made an adjunct of its popular Catalogues. The new departure was a natural one, and followed as a matter of course in the development of the influence which it was the aim of the fathers of the Library to bestow upon the public. Mr. Everett, its first president, enunciated a sentiment that has never been lost sight of, when he claimed that its mission was to supplement the schools; and a happy embodiment of the idea has found shape of late in the phrase of "The People's College." With the growth of any collection the ease of consultation naturally gives way to an indecision in the face of accumulated titles on every subject, and without some guide to a choice of books discouragement is likely to ensue from any haphazard selection out of many, for any particular purpose. A consideration of these difficulties ripened the plan. As preliminary the thought occurred of alluring the pastime reader, of whom all Libraries, in any degree popular, have a large following, by easy steps, to become a reader of better purpose. I am too much a believer in the general straight-forwardness of ingrafted impulses ever violently to counter-act them. I believe men can be led rather than pushed. The implanting in mankind of the story-telling faculty, and the enjoyment of it in others, was not an idle creation; and the imagination has done too much for the amelioration of mankind not to deserve our acceptance of it, as a handmaid of virtue and a promoter of intellectual advancement. This assistance was accordingly invoked in a list of historical fiction, which was prepared in chronological grouping under countries, as calculated to instigate a study by comparison, and lead the mind to history and biography by the inciting of the inquisitive faculties. I have reason to believe that the idea was not a futile one, from the interest manifested in the movement, and the avidity with which more than one edition of it was taken up. This was but a trial. The next step was the more serious one of endeavoring to direct the ductile perceptions of the less learned among readers. The effort was not to propound positively any course of reading, for there is danger always in dogmatism, however right its foundation may be. The notes which were appended to the subject-references in the History, Biography, and Travel Catalogue of the Lower Hall, in 1873, served to render the ordinary reader more able to choose to his liking when an indistinguishable mass of equivalent titles perplexed him. That Catalogue was a year in passing through the press, a term lengthened by the destruction of part of the work on it in the great fire of November, 1872; and when it was published in August, 1873, I was able to record for the next year, month by month, a remarkable increase of the use of books from the Lower Hall, in history, biography, and travel, amounting in some months to two hundred per cent. At the end of the year we of course had to gain upon the work of its influence twelve months before, and the ratio of gain fell at once, though it still remained to give some testimony of its continued helpfulness. The files of the Library show the opinions upon these results entertained by many gentlemen interested in projects of popular education. A veteran in this sphere, Mr. George B. Emerson, said, "I have never seen anything so excellent; and hereafter no large Catalogue will be considered complete without something similar appended to it." From Europe like expressions of approval came. "I have shown it to some of the profession here," wrote one of the chief British librarians, "and they are as much astonished at the idea as at the execution of it. I do not think there will be many imitators. The labor of such a work must be enormous, and certainly beyond our resources and methods."

The expectation which was expressed by Mr. Emerson was soon realized in the adoption of many of its notes in the Catalogues of some of the smaller libraries, and in 1875, the Public Library of the town of Quincy full committed itself to the scheme, in the publication of an excellent Catalogue, which had the editorial supervision of Mr. Charles Francis Adams, Jr., the President of its Trustees. Somewhat similar work, particularly embodying references to the sources of study in periodical literature, which had been made a part of the scheme, appeared in the careful Catalogue of the Mercantile Library of Brooklyn; but the whole effort of its librarian, Mr. S. B. Noyes, cannot be appreciated until his work is completed. Similar notes, simplified to meet the wants of a smaller constituency, and improved in many respects, were repeated in a new edition of the Roxbury Branch Catalogue, issued last year. A set of references in elucidations of English history, printed in large type on broadside sheets, with spaces for the filling in of the shelf numbers, was perfected, with the numbers of each department inserted, and posted, with good effect, in the respective halls. The edition printed was small, and the demand for them from other places could not be met; but for the testing of its value in other communities copies were sent to various Libraries in this country and in England, and I have since observed, in their reports, several references to their value.

The latest attempt of a similar kind is the recently printed Fiction List of the Lower Hall. The system of class lists has its advantages, in enabling the Library to supply new editions of those sections most in demand, without involving a reprint of others, as a general Catalogue would require. An objection is often made to a separate Fiction List, that the searcher loses the chance of being attracted by other and perhaps more profitable books. It is certainly not without force. In the preparation of this new edition, this objection was met by the embodiment of the "Chronological Index to Historical Fiction," already mentioned, and by interpolating sections of "historical references" for pointing out the sources of the plots and delineations, and for marking the methods of parallel reading. It has been too recently issued to be able to draw any deductions as to its effect on the character of our issues; and the commingling of classes in it may render any statistical deductions difficult or impos-impossible.

Considerable labor of a like kind of bibliographical assistance will be found to have been bestowed upon the Ticknor Catalogue, a large portion of which is due to the care of Mr.

Whitney, the head of the Catalogue Department. It is a part of the plan of the Barton Catalogue, now in progress, to include much elucidatory matter, and, as far as the original issues of Shakespeare are concerned, notes of a tentative nature have already been submitted to Shakespearian scholars, through the medium of the Superintendent's Monthly Reports, and are still in progress in the same place.

In 1867 the Library issued its first Bulletin of new books, a meagre affair compared with its forty-page record of to-day. Every quarter, since the issue of the Catalogue of 1873, this Bulletin has been made the vehicle of communications, intended to convey to readers some comprehension of the position which important new books have taken in the literature of their subjects. Upon various matters of present interest more extensive research has been bestowed in various bibliographical essays. Subjects like art, in which interest has of late years been prominent, have thus been treated. A growing and studious class interested in philosophical studies have been thought of in another series of papers. In this way, also, the interest in the centennial period has induced a series of reviews of the literature appertaining to the events of a century ago, which have been carried along year by year with the recurrence of the anniversary, and will be continued till the period has passed. In order to make them component parts of a more comprehensive rendering of the historical study of the country from the earliest discovery, a series of notes has also been begun, which will in due time be brought down to the opening of the struggle for independence. If continued ultimately beyond the revolutionary war, into the present century, we shall have the material ready formed, subject of course to revision, for issuing, in the end, such a synoptical summary of the literature of our history as does not elsewhere exist, and which will be such a contribution to its study, for the benefit of the more thoughtful of our patrons, as seems worthy our endeavors.

The plan as thus developed, I am sorry to say, has given but comparatively little attention to the scientific side of knowledge; but I trust that the conditions of the staff will in the future be more favorable for a due presentation of this element.

Up to 1868 the Library had done but little in proportion to its destined importance in the gathering of pamphlet publications. The energies of the government had properly been devoted to the accumulation of the more substantial evidences of knowledge, somewhat arbitrarily called books, as distinguished from tracts or pamphlets. A great Library, it is conceded, cannot wisely neglect the preservation of all sorts of ephemera, and the destined value of the meanest printed production can never be anticipated. But such accumulations come with time and the opportunity; and in a Library confessedly governed for the greatest good of the greatest number, that time will come later in its development, and these opportunities will be sought when its first pamphlets had been secured, or an average of about 3,000 a year. The chief accessions in masses had come with the Parker Library, and with the divisions of the pamphlet collection of the late Edward Everett, when William Everett, Esq., gave a due share to the institution, upon whose career and good name his father had exercised so great an influence. Within the last nine years the claims of pamphlets for preservation have been fully recognized; and our efforts with our collection, first by assortment, then by binding and cataloguing, till we have acquired a collection which can hardly, in this country, be surpassed for serviceableness. In this nine years we have added an average of over 16,000 a year, or an aggregate of 150,000, which represents probably nearly as much work, in care and cataloguing, as the bound books shelved in the same interval.

The annual increase of the Library up to the establishment of the first Branch, in 1870, averaged, if the exceptional increase from the Bates donation and the Parker Library be thrown out, about 6,500 volumes a year. Since that period it has never been less than double that number; and one year, 1873-74, by the purchase of the Barton Library, and through the accession of the Libraries at Charlestown and Brighton, it ran up to over 50,000 volumes. The present year it is over 20,000 volumes. But the gross increase of books has had to be diminished for a net result of permanent addition, by the number of lost and of worn-out books, which, from accumulating wear and tear, is naturally increasing year by year. Ten years ago this loss was from 200 to 400 a year; now it is ten times as much.

It has always been a difficulty with the boys whom we employ as pages for the bringing of books, that their deficiencies of education unfit them for advancement; and it has always become a question of submitting to their spiritless performance of duty, when they have outgrown their work, or of discharging them upon the world to begin anew in some more profitable line of employment. During the past year one such page has been transferred to the bindery, as an apprentice, and if the experiment succeeds we shall not do amiss in providing for an increase of our force in the bindery from recruits of our own training.

The decade has also seen some important changes in the building of the Central Library, chiefly in increase of capacity, and in enlarging the official and working quarters, which were never even decently provided for in the original plan. The building can never become creditable, if adaptation to the purpose for which it was intended be considered the criterion of such approbation. Its defects are radical, and grew partly out of the inexperience of those, or rather a *majority* of the commission, superintending its erection, the records of that body showing a vote of four to three on all essential points concerned in arranging the plans, which induced an inability to comprehend the extent of work needful to be done in a rapidly growing Library, and partly from a sacrifice of fitness to a desire for ostentation. What has been done by alterations has, as far as possible, conduced to improve the building for its uses. In the Lower Hall the galleries have been converted into much-needed apartments for working and storing purposes; and the books transferred to cases on the main floor have been brought much nearer into connection with the points of delivery. In the Bates Hall the futile serrature of the lateral walls has been removed, and the alcoves, squared and subdivided, have been increased in capacity by nearly double the shelf-room, and have been lighted where they were before dark, by windows pierced in the walls. A large extension has been joined to the south-west angle of the building, affording enlarged accommodations for the bindery, and for some special collections, together with a capacious patent-room, and much-needed official quarters, catalogue-rooms and work-rooms.

The last extension is that of a two-story gallery, external to the rear of the building, which gives a room for students below, and an apartment for the work of the ordering and receiving of books above. It was calculated that the building would contain, as originally constructed, 240,000 volumes, 200,000 of which could be shelved in the Bates Hall. It is safe to say that as at present arranged its capacity is more than twice that, or about half a million volumes. It will be easily understood, however, that the limit of convenient storage for a classified library will be reached long before its full measure of capacity is filled.

From the statements which I have made it will appear that in most respects the work of the Library has apparently increased from five to ten fold. The work of detail naturally accruing to all processes which require handling of records of one kind or another is much larger, however, on each item, by reason of the larger masses to manipulate in a Library of 312,000 than in one of 136,000 volumes. Consequently the apparent increase of work, as shown by statistics of results, is not adequate to represent the positive enlargement of labor. Nevertheless, it can be shown that the expenses of the Library to-day are not one-half as much, relatively, as in 1867. At that time our expenditure was $52,658 for the year, while for the past year we had to expend the city appropriation of $111,500, with $6,300 income from our trust funds, making a total of $117,800, or not greatly in excess of twice the amount in 1867. If the annual expenditure be divided by the amount of circulation, it will show that the measure of the Library's usefulness, as indicated by such reckoning of the cost of issue per volume, has been reduced from twenty-five cents in 1867 to less than ten cents in 1877. I made an estimate of the cost for issuing a single volume in the Lower Hall and in all our Branches for the month of February last, reckoning from a division of salaries only, and I found it to range pretty evenly all around at about two cents. Of course the including of other expenses would somewhat increase the average; but it is apparent that the Library is delivering books quite as cheaply to its frequenters, at the expense of the city, as the private Circulating Libraries do, which require a fee of two cents *a day* for each book loaned, while the Library and its Catalogue offers scope for the advancement of the public education with which the Circulating Library affords no comparison. The returns to the City Treasury from fines and the sales of Catalogues is indeed small, but it has increased from $500 in 1867 to near $3,500 in 1877.

The year which has now closed has been probably the most important one yet passed for the Library interests of the entire country. The centennial fervor has extended its animation to librarians, who carried through successfully a convention of their number in Philadelphia, in October last. The desirability of such a gathering has been felt for some years, and when the only previous convention of the kind, presided over by my predecessor, in New York, above twenty years ago, and previous to his connection with this Library, adjourned, it was with the expectation of other meetings to follow. In the interval which elapsed, however, almost a new generation of librarians had grown up, and the Free Library system, then only in its infancy, has developed the most important Libraries of the country. The profession and all interested— and the public's interest is not too remote for consideration—owe it to the energy and hard work of Mr. Melvil Dewey, late librarian of Amherst College, that the movement was made, and carried so happily through. It gave three days' pleasant and profitable intercourse to over a hundred delegates, and has done much to make known the importance of the profession. Out of it has grown a National Association of Librarians, and of others interested in the work of Libraries, which has taken up the task of diminishing the cost of maintenance of Libraries, by inaugurating methods of co-operation, which it is hoped will secure in the department upon which money is too grudgingly bestowed, that of the catalogue, not only a diminished expense, but also uniformity in good methods, now so much desired. Measures are already in train for a new edition of Poole's Index to Periodical Literature, under a combination of labor, planned for some of the prinicpal libraries. Other work of a similar nature will in due time follow.

Whatever may have been the satisfaction to the members of this conference during the season of it, the procession of events already following upon it is likely to prove of much more importance. It has made known much to librarians in this country, by which their labors are lightened or rendered more effective. In Europe it has helped to make known the work which we are accomplishing here in a way so different from their own, and it has instigated movements for similar gatherings in England and Germany. In Great Britain the project bids fair to succeed; but in Germany the Libraries are largely under the charge of officers who divide the interest in their work with other duties, much to the loss of an effective emulation. In France there is more sympathy, and various recognitions of the advantages of our Free Library system have been made of late in their public press, in which this Library has more than once been pointed out as its exemplar. The destinies of Europe for the next decade may lucklessly be left to the arbitrament of war, but the season of the coming Exposition at Paris is likely, it is thought, to bring with it an international convention of librarians. It is somewhat significant that in a recent official document, laid before the Municipal Council of Paris, while a review is made of the budget for the ensuing year, the question is raised of the propriety of that city's establishing a great Public Library for popular use, and the system of our own is commented upon as the fitting one. I have been called upon for more details regarding it than our usual printed reports show, and a summary of such as I have given is now appearing serially in the *Journal Officiel*, under the supervision of Mons. Guillaume Depping, Librarian of the Bibliothéque Ste. Geneviève.

Growing out of the interest engendered with the Philadelphia conference, a new journal, devoted to the economy of libraries, has been set on foot, again largely through the efforts of Mr. Dewey, who secured the co-operation of the principal librarians of the country, and found in Mr. Leypoldt a publisher in sympathy with the cause. In it have been printed the proceedings of the Philadelphia convention; and month by month its readers are favored with matters and records of events that closely touch their professional interests.

Two or three years ago the Bureau of Education at Washington determined that their contribution to the records of the national anniversary should be an exposition of the Library development of the country. General Eaton confided the immediate direction of this work to two gentlemen; also sought the assistance of the chief librarians of the States; and the result of all their joint labors took shape in a ponderous volume, which must pass for a bibliothecal cyclopaedia, if the most varied and extensive gathering of knowledge and experience in Library economy ever made entitles it to that designation.

I have made mention in a former report of contributing a set of our catalogues, with scrap-books of our administration blanks, to the exposition at Vienna. The City of Boston receiving for its varied exhibition the highest award, we were denied the same, only under the rule which prevented the recognition of a department, when the city had been honored as a whole. For the exhibition of 1876 we entrusted a similar array of volumes, set forth in the handiwork of our own bindery, to the Board of Education of the State of Massachusetts, to become part of their exhibition. What we sent gave us a prominence that insured an award "for the extent and value of the work as shown by the reports, and especially for the great usefulness of the Catalogues, containing, as they do, bibliographical information, not only worthy the attention of scholars, but of the greatest use to the whole body of readers." The Honorable

Leverett Saltonstall, the Massachusetts Commissioner to the exhibition, said in his final Report to the Governor and Council: "The exhibits of the free Libraries of the State were especially good, and attracted much attention. That in Boston, the largest in the country, with its 300,000 volumes, and lending more than a million a year, at a loss of only 1/100 of one per cent., was represented by seventeen volumes, giving its history, catalogues, and an account of its administration." We shall endeavor to maintain our position at the Paris Exposition.

It remains to chronicle a few of the indicative manifestations in our experiences the past year; though I must refer you as heretofore to the records of the Appendix for the fullest particulars. At the date of the last report the new Card-Catalogue Room, with the students' room beneath, was in process of erection. Its completion and subsequent use have greatly facilitated an important department of the work, and with the crowded state of the Bates Hall, from the gathering of the ordinary takers of books, the lower apartment has afforded a much-needed room for the use of students, who require space and quiet for their studies. The shelving in the alcoves is hardly adapted to large volumes, particularly if expensive ones; and the cabinets which have contained such additions are approaching repletion. It will accordingly prove desirable, I think, to prepare the anteroom of this office, which was formerly the room of the Superintendent, for such accumulations, to be kept in locked cases. For protection against the danger of falling from the ladders in the galleries of the Bates Hall, iron bars have been put across the opening of the alcoves; and to equip the service with prompter aid in case of fire, a telegraphic wire, tested daily, now connects the Library with the nearest engine-house, and additional extinguishers have been placed about the building. The floor of the Bates Hall has been still further encroached upon by cases for the Card Catalogue, and it is only a question of time when its space must be entirely given up to such incumbrances, and a reading hall be found adjacent in a new extension.

The ventilation of the Lower Hall has always been excessively bad. Indeed, at times, according to the experiments of the late Dr. Derby, Secretary of the State Board of Health, the worst air prevailed there that he could find in the State. It is hoped, however, that an improvement has been effected by pipes, arranged to conduct the foul air from the floor into the flues, where a current is induced by hot air. The arrangement was suggested by Mr. Lewis, of the Board. The closed windows of another winter will test more thoroughly its efficiency than has been possible since it was put in operation, only a few weeks ago.

I have spoken already of the plan under consideration for the enlargement of the waiting-rooms of the Lower Hall. Its necessity was constantly apparent during the past winter; and on some days, at certain hours, the crowd was almost unmanageable for purposes of a prompt supply of books.

No definite arrangements have yet been made for the contemplated enlargement of the South Boston Branch, though I have long since submitted a plan to the City Architect. The need of action is pressing. At Charlestown it has become necessary to give more space to the public waiting for books by transferring to such purpose a portion of the space devoted to the reading-room. At Roxbury the Trustees of the Fellowes Athenaeum are now finishing a room in the upper part of one one of the towers of the Library building, which will give much needed accommodation for the accumulation of unbound newspapers, pamphlets, etc. It will probably be necessary during the year to shelve an additional wall-surface in the book-room to accommodate the rapidly growing collection of the Fellowes Athenaeum.

By the figures of Appendix I. it will be seen that the Library now holds about 313,000 volumes,—an enumeration probably in advance of that of any other Library in the country. The net increase of the year includes the collection of books relating to the West Indies, and to the immigration of poor into this country at an early period, which had been collected by the late Benjamin P. Hunt, of Philadelphia. The books as received numbered 612 bound volumes; but with them came a mass of manuscripts, maps, views, etc., which have now been arranged in other volumes, so that the collection at present numbers nearly 700 volumes. They are accompanied by a catalogue, annotated with care, which is likely to be of great service in the cataloguing of them under our own system. Among them are also some manuscript treatises, which are thus described in the catalogue:—

With this collection of books, manuscripts, maps, charts, etc., relating to the West Indies are included,—

First.—An unfinished account of "The Haytians," by Mr. B. P. Hunt, of Philadelphia, with their social, moral and political condition at the time of the author's residence in the island, from 1840 to 1857, making about 120 folio pages.

With this account of "The Haytians" are six note-books, of different sizes, filled with cuttings from newspapers, extracts from books, items of information, and incidents which came under Mr. Hunt's observation.

Second.—A History of Hayti, or the French part of the island of St. Domingo, from 1625 to 1695, consisting of 172½ folio pages in manuscript, written by Mr. B. P. Hunt, of Philadelphia, and by him left as a part of his bequest to the Public Library of the City of Boston, in the hope that at some future time sufficient interest would be taken in the subject to induce some student of the island's history to complete it.

Third.—"The Redemptioners; or, Some Account of the early Emigration of the Poor to America, and its Causes." By Mr. B. P. Hunt, of Philadelphia.

With this unfinished manuscript, consisting of about 112 4to pages, are eight volumes of MS. notes, comprising extracts from books, newspapers and records, all bearing upon the condition of the poor, from feudal times to the present, together with a small pocket note-book, containing a list of all the books and newspapers from which extracts have been made in the eight large note-books.

This history of "The Redemptioners," with the note-books which accompany it, was also given to the Public Library of the City of Boston, by its author, in the hope that some individual, studying this interesting subject, would be induced to complete it.

Our first knowledge of the bequest came through the following letter:—

PHILADELPHIA, Feb. 23, 1877.

To the President of the Boston Public Library:—

DEAR SIR,—Mr. Benjamin P. Hunt, formerly of Chelmsford, Massachusetts, but for many years a citizen of Philadelphia, died on the 2d inst. In his will (of which his widow and I are executors) it is thus contained:—

"I give and bequeath to the Public Library of the City of Boston, Massachusetts, of which Justin Winsor appears to have been on June 21st, 1871, the Superintendent, my collection of books, pamphlets, manuscripts, maps, charts and engravings relating to the West Indies, the titles and descriptions of which are contained in a catalogue marked on the cover 'Special Catalogue of Books, etc., relating to the West Indies,' and I direct that this catalogue, now deposited on my Library table, shall accompany the said collection, which shall be delivered within three months after my death."

And by codicil the testator further directs:—

"I give to the Public Library of the City of Boston, to which I have given my West India books and papers, all my manuscripts, notes and collections relating to the Emigration of the Poor and to Hayti, which shall not be otherwise disposed of at the time of my death."

I have no special knowledge of the value of the bequest, but am informed that the late Mr. Hunt (whose interest in and study of the subject entitled him to an opinion) considered this collection to be second only to one now in Paris.

In pursuance of my duty, I make this formal notification, and will only add that the executors will, of course, comply with the directions of the will as to time of delivery. When the necessary formalities of inventory, etc., are completed, I will write you again.

Very truly,

JOSEPH PARRISH,

Executor.

A sketch of the life of Mr. Hunt has been furnished by his executor, at my request, and may be found, with other accounts of the bequest, in Appendix XXIX.

The accessions for the year as reported do not include nearly a hundred volumes, which are now in the bindery, and illustrate the history and character of the Philadelphia Exhibition. They embrace pamphlets, circulars, advertisements, maps, prints, photographs, etc., etc., pertaining thereto, which were gathered for us, and transmitted monthly by an agent, who was in Philadelphia during the continuance of the exhibition. The labor of arranging and scrapping has been chiefly done by the Assistant Office Secretary. In addition to this, the exhibition is illustrated on our shelves probably by as many more volumes, which were either issued as books or disposed of as such on receipt.

We have aimed to gather all local historical tracts and other publications which the Centennial year has called forth; and, had it not been for the thoughtful care of the Rev. Dr. Tuttle, President of Wabash College, we should not have been able to trace a large number, particularly relating to the local records of parishes of the Presbyterian Church.

The tariff seriously interferes with the promptness with which we can put new and popular foreign books before the public of our Branches. Only two copies of a book are allowed to be imported at one time under the clause of exemption from duty; and we have consequently been obliged to make a succession of importations by twos. A letter to the Secretary of the Treasury, calling attention to the peculiar constitution of our institution, as a congeries of libraries, but under one direction, was duly considered, but no way was found to change the interpretation of the law. A statement of the case was entrusted to our Representative in Congress, the Hon. Henry L. Pierce, who kindly brought the difficulty to the attention of the Committee on Ways and Means, but without as yet any result.

It will be remembered that when the Prince Library came into our custody it contained but two of the five copies of the Bay Psalm-book which originally belonged to it. The others had been parted with for a consideration, and were respectively in the keeping of the late Dr. N. B. Shurtleff, of the late George Brinley, of Hartford (who had received it from the estate of the late Edward A. Crowninshield), and of the late George Livermore, of Cambridge. After the death of Dr. Shurtleff, the copy which had been in his possession, and which was the most interesting of them all, as it had belonged to Richard Mather, one of its compilers, was offered for sale at public auction, December 2d, 1875, and an injunction was served to prevent the sale, at the instance of the Deacons of the Old South Church, who are the legal owners of the property, as trustees, the Boston Public Library holding under a contract by them with the city as sub-trustees. The claim of the counsel of the Deacons was, that the sale of the book to Dr. Shurtleff was illegal, because of the want of authority in them as Trustees to alienate any part of the trust; and evidence was adduced, showing that it was known at the time that the books given by Dr. Shurtleff in payment were not equivalent in value, and that it was the understanding of all parties to the transaction that the book would in due time be returned to its proper repository. The defence claimed a notorious possession of the book for fifteen years, and plead the statute of limitations. The court sustained the latter point. The volume was afterwards sold by auction, October 12th, 1876, to Mr. C. Fiske Harris, of Providence, for $1,025, to whose collection of American poetry, the finest in the country, it proved an important contribution, as the first book and first collection of verse printed in British America. This decision removes all chance of successful claim to the other two copies, both of which are now, or may hereafter be, offered for sale as parts of their respective collections.

In 1858 the kindly appreciation of this Library entertained by the family of the late Dr. Nathaniel Bowditch induced them to place with us his collection of books, which is known as the Bowditch Library, and it has added largely to the value of our mathematical department. The eldest son of that family, J. Ingersoll Bowditch, Esq., has within the year handed in his check for $500, to be expended on works in pure mathematics, to be added to his father's collection, and placed under the same conditions. Communication has been opened with Prof. J. M. Peirce, of Cambridge, with President Runkle, of the Institute of Technology, and with Mr. Seaver, the head-master of the English High School, for their assistance in a selection of titles.

Early in the year the balance of money, amounting to $335.13, as due the Library under the agreement of the previous year, by which the Lower Mills Delivery was established, and the books of the Dorchester and Milton Circulating Library were turned over to the city, was received and paid into the treasury, where it is hoped it will become the nucleus of a fund to be held for the benefit of the Dorchester Branch.

The figures in Appendix XII. will show that the circulation of the year has increased nearly 20 per cent. on that of the previous year, the gain in the several departments being independently as follows: —

Bates Hall,	24 per cent.	South Boston,	17 per cent.
Lower Hall,	16 "	Roxbury,	45 "
East Boston,	13 "	Charlestown,	24 "
Brighton,	20 "	Dorchester,	9 "

The aggregate of issues shows a change in the relative business of some of the Branches. South Boston, which has been first, yields that position to Roxbury, which gains it doubtless in part from the help that the Delivery at Jamaica Plain and the circulation of the books of the Fellowes Athenaeum afford, and partly from the impetus naturally following upon a new edition of its Catalogue. In the third and fourth places, East Boston has given place to Charlestown without so apparent reasons. The circulation of both of these Branches suffers doubtless from the interval that has passed since their respective Catalogues were printed. The discouragement arising from the use of old Catalogues in a Library of great use, with a consequent displacement of books, from wear and tear, will be understood from the results of an examination of 53 unsuccessful calls for books not fiction in the Lower Hall, one day in March last, which disclosed that 28, or over half, no longer existed, though still standing in the printed catalogues.

The large demand for books shown during the year has been partly due no doubt to the large number of people out of employ. This is shown in part in the great increase of books issued for use in the buildings. The gain over last year in this particular is five times that of the home issues. There has been a great difference in the increase of such use in the several departments, as follows:—

Dorchester,	388 per cent.	Brighton,	54 per cent.
South Boston,	224 "	Charlestown,	36 "
Roxbury,	126 "	Bates Hall,	28 "
East Boston,	55 "	Lower Hall,	23 "

The calls for books have been so much in excess of the supply that users of the Library suggested, what seemed pertinent, that some plan be devised for insuring a prompter return of books loaned, so that a larger number of people could have the perusal of the same books in a given time. Investigations showed that scarcely more than one-third of the books were kept over a week, and that the porportion could well be reduced without more hardship to present readers than might reasonably be endured out of regard to expectant ones. Accordingly, on the first of November, a change of the rules was made, by which books were allowed to the same borrower for no longer period than one week, with the right to renewal for a fortnight longer in the case of books not newly added. The operation of this rule can be seen from the following table, which shows the gain in percentage of issues over the corresponding month of the previous year:

DEPARTMENTS.	May.	June.	July.	August.	September.	October.	November.	December.	January.	February.	March.	April.	Average for 1st 6 mos.	Average for 2d 6 mos.
Bates Hall	42	16	. .	11	21	17	29	25	30	20	25	18	18	24
Lower Hall	44	26	23	30	31	12	23	14	9	3	8	3	27	10
East Boston	9	. .	2	12	20	8	11	17	16	9	20	9	8	14
South Boston	7	. .	. .	9	23	10	29	33	22	13	29	18	8	24
Roxbury	13	11	20	30	43	37	60	64	60	53	64	45	26	58
Charlestown	24	23	16	30	31	13	31	31	31	6	27	11	23	23
Brighton	11	10	17	20	36	9	60	35	14	17	19	3	17	25
Dorchester	12	9	6	16	25	6	29	16	. .	. .	9	. .	12	9
Total	. .	. .	. .	. .	. .	. .	. .	. .	. .	. .	. .	. .	139	187

These figures show a clear gain of about one-third for the entire Library under the new rule. In the Bates Hall, where it was apprehended, on account of the character of the books, that rule might work a detriment to the circulation, the gain has been 33 per cent. In the Lower Hall the decline—though there is still an absolute gain of issues—has been equally marked; but it is chiefly to be accounted for from the crowded state of its Delivery Hall in the winter months, compared with the summer. In fact, the capacity of that department for an increase of use is about reached, except in the months of lighter service. Of the Branches, Dorchester alone shows a gain diminished by 25 per cent.

The various catalogue work of the Library has gone forward as usual, under the general charge of Mr. Whitney, who has specially cared for the progress through the press of the Ticknor Catalogue, which is likely to be completed during the coming year; at the present writing, the letter M being in the printer's hands. An additional value will be given to it, by including all Spanish books in other sections of the Library; and by references in the notes to works elucidating the principal subjects, where the resources of the general Library amplify the facilities of the Ticknor Library. The publication of the Memoirs of Mr. Ticknor during the year has augmented the interest in the collection; and in those memoirs the public has again been able to judge of the important part which Mr. Ticknor played in forming the Library, and in shaping its policy. The cataloguing of the Barton Collection has been in the immediate charge of Mr. Hubbard, and is progressing at a rate which may warrant the printing of the Shakespearian section of it during the year. Meanwhile, the books have been made accessible to the public by the insertion of brief main entries, for a temporary purpose, in the Public Card Catalogue. The Superintendent's Monthly Reports have continued the Shakespearian notes; and through the favor of Wm. F. Fowle, Esq., formerly of Boston, now of London, the wealth of the British Museum in the early quartos of Shakespeare, with collations and descriptions, have been put in print for the purpose of comparison with the resources of the collections of this country. A brief tentative essay, on the bibliographical contributions of America to Shakespearian knowledge, was prepared early in the year from the Barton shelves, by Mr. Carl Knortz, and published in Boston, as preliminary to a contribution on Shakespearian Study in America, which that gentleman intends to make to the Shakespeare-Gesellschaft of Germany.

The Quarterly Bulletins have been made, as heretofore, the vehicle of bibliographical communications, which may be of interest to studious classes; and efforts have been made by sending them to such for the purpose of enlarging the circle of our patrons. It is hoped that in this way the considerable class who are interested in the study and progress of mental philosophy may have profited by the work of Mr. F. B. Perkins, the office secretary, on that topic; and the numerous classes, whose perceptions of artistic beauty have been awakened of late years, through the Art Club, the Bric-a-brac Club, the schools of art, and the beneficent influence of the Museum of Fine Arts, have derived, it is apparent, not a little assistance from the paper on "Pottery and Porcelain," which was prepared by Col. Ware, the keeper of the Bates Hall. In the address which was made by the Mayor, at the formal opening of the Art Museum, on the 3d of July last, he spoke of the Library and that institution as the crown of our educational system. There is every chance for the two to work in harmony, with the President of our Trustees, *ex-officio*, a member of the Board of Trustees of the Museum.

I have spoken in the earlier part of this report of other subjects which the Bulletins have followed, and of the characteristic features which were given to the new editions of the Catalogues of the Roxbury Branch, and of prose fiction in the Lower Hall. Following an example which was set by Mr. Poole, of the Chicago Library, five hundred copies of the forty-five hundred which constituted the edition of the Fiction List were printed on a Manilla paper, of the same weight to the ream, forty pounds, with the ordinary white paper on which the rest were printed. The Manilla costs 8½ cents per pound, against 11¼ for the white. The experience of Mr. Poole, and of our own use of the sheets during the printing, is, that with the copies for public use the duration of wear is increased by at least a third. As the appearance is agreeable to the eye, there seems no reason why Manilla should not become a favorite paper for catalogues, and indeed for school-books, and works of reference requiring much handling. The printers soon learn that it must be put on the press dry.

The usual broadside-sheets of the gelatine process have been continued, and 338, of 20 titles each, have been prepared, and cut up and inserted in the various Card Catalogues, against 260 for last year. In addition, an increased extent of cataloguing has been done in manuscript, where the use is temporary, pending the printing of volumes, and where the requirements for cross-references have been small. The work of transcribing, inscribing, and assorting may be judged from a record of nearly 107,000 cards being put in the several Card Catalogues, against 70,000 for last year.

The indexing of the United States documents has been completed, consolidated and revised by Mrs. Eastman. As the work approached completion, a petition of the Trustees, joined in by the principal libraries and literary societies of the country, was presented to Congress, through the Hon. Henry L. Pierce, asking that the work which had been done for our own community should be made available for others by being printed. The matter was referred to the Committee on the Library of Congress; and some correspondence ensued, by which it appeared that a consolidated index, not only of the regular documents of Congress, but also of the Congressional Globe and the Journals of the Houses, was in preparation, under the charge of the Librarian of Congress. The committee further expressed a wish that the Index of the Documents, as prepared by this Library, should be intrusted to Mr. Spofford, to be embodied in his general index. In this way the matter has been for the present left.

I have already mentioned, as one of the results of the Philadelphia conference, that, under the co-operation of various Libraries, a new edition of Poole's Index to Periodicals is to be prepared and printed. As the work is likely to be for a considerable period in hand, and as the references to current periodical literature is one of the growing uses to which our Library is put, it was arranged, some months since, that about fifty of the chief periodicals of this and other countries should be immediately, on receipt of the successive numbers, distributed to certain of the principal officers, and indexed on uniform slips of paper. These slips are handed in to the keeper of the Bates Hall, and are kept by him in an alphabetical order for consultation.

The Appendix contains the usual tables recording the proportions of the various classes of books as sent into circulation. It will be seen that there is little change in these ratios. The most significant and gratifying is a marked diminution, since 1873, of the use of fiction in the Lower Hall; but it is apparent that the change has been brought about by the methods of instruction which we employ. The natural craving of the masses is for story-telling. It cannot be eradicated. The attempt would only drive the frequenters of the Library away in large numbers. I look upon the dominating taste in reading, as Kant regarded the general tendencies of mankind,—to accept it and to strive to better it. The wise course is to regulate it, and to use the instinct as a means of its own improvement. I selected one Saturday in the height of our season, and directed that all slips, handed in at the Lower Hall counter, which failed to secure a book, should be saved. They numbered nearly 5,000, showing that twice as many slips failed of their purpose as succeeded. An analysis of these requests shows that 404, or about a twelfth part, only were non-fiction; more than two-twelfths were a miscellaneous assemblage of novels, each asked for once, twice, or perhaps thrice, but not sufficiently characteristic to signify any marked intent. Over 500, or more than a tenth part, were calls for dime novels, but few of which are now left in the Library,—the remnants of a set which were, some years ago, experimentally put into use, but which at this time still stood in the printed Catalogues which were on hand. The single author most in request was Horatio Alger, jr., a writer for youths, whose books were marked on 390 slips. Mrs. Southworth came next, 301 times; then Oliver Optic, 292; Dumas, 189; Mrs. Stephens, 158; Miss Braddon, 154; Mrs. Holmes, 146; Fosdick, a writer for boys, 125; Fleming, 87; Kingston, a boys' writer, 83; Ainsworth, 69; Mrs. Wood, 60; Grant, 59; Lever, 58; Mrs. Grey, 54. The most sought-for single book was Alger's "Timothy Crump's Ward,"—64 times. Almost a quarter of the entire number may be called juvenile books. Over a third certainly would class among the lower grades of popular novelists, without counting such as were not popular and of this grade. About a sixth of the whole may be considered from fair to first class at to literary merits. Out of this 4,875 total, some of the well-known names in literature stand low in the scale of demand, as, for instance, Don Quixote, 2; Jane Austen, 2; Goldsmith, 2; Swift, 3; Goethe, 4; George Sand, 4; Scott, 5; Thackeray, 5; George Eliot, 9; Hawthorne, 10; Bulwer, 10; Charles Reade, 10; Miss Muloch, 10; Dickens, 25; Wilkie Collins, 27; Cooper, 34; Marryat, 44; James, 44.

This record should not afford the foundation for off-hand conclusions. The hours during which the slips were saved were the busiest of the week, and which the better readers shun. Duplicates of the higher class of novels being supplied on less urgency than those of inferior position, the exhaustion or such books signifies a relatively greater demand than is the case with the lower classes. It should always be further borne in mind that in public Libraries the demand for the better books is considerabley lessened, from the fact that such books are brought more commonly for the family book shelf than the inferior ones. It is for this reason that reputable authors of popular fame, like Irving and Hawthorne, never represent, in the circulation of public Libraries, their hold upon readers.

On the other hand there is compensation in the growing circulation of the Bates Hall, representing the highest reading. Fifty-two per cent. of its issues are for reference in the building. A seventh part of the books recommended for purchase are in foreign languages.

A scrutiny was made in April of 200 issues to the firemen in one day, as indicating the average demands of adults. Only one-third was fiction, and the proportion of the lower grades was low. Of the remainder the selections indicated a wide range of interests, and exhibited a very creditable standard of intellectual requirements for a responsible arm of our municipal service.

The large circulation for the year has been maintained with the same satisfactory immunity from loss as before. Out of nearly 1,200,000 issues only 129 are unrecovered, or one in eight or nine thousand. The Central Library sustains the burden of this loss. In the Branches it has proved possible to deliver at Roxbury 146,829, with no loss whatever; at South Boston, 135,179, with a loss of two; at Charlestown, 106,816, with a loss of three; at East Boston, 102,607, with a loss of four; at Brighton, 29,792, with a loss of one; and at Dorchester, 71,979, with no loss at all. That is, an aggregate Branch delivery has amounted to 593,202, with a total loss of ten, or one in nearly 60,000 issues. The heavier loss of the Central Library arises, as I have several times before explained, from the greater difficulty of tracing delinquents in the larger masses of the City Proper. It is one in 4,599 for this year, against one in 4,824 for last year, and in 5,124 for the year before. One kind of loss, which swells the aggregate at the Central Library, arises from the delivery of books for hall use from the Lower Hall. Green slips for drawing such books used to be exposed, to be taken at will; but for two or three years past they have only been given to special applicants, each of whom comes under an officer's eye. Nearly 13,000 volumes are thus given out in the Lower Hall during the year, and of them nine were not returned, or one in 1,400 or 1,500. The proportion is a good deal larger than the loss from books delivered for home use, and may not yet have become alarming; but it proves the value of our method of establishing identity, as is required for the issue of a card to those who draw books for home use. It may possibly be necessary to establish some further checks. It is not the fault of the system, for 74,786 such issues were made in the Bates Hall, without any loss; but the difficulty lies in the lessened supervision of the crowds which fill the lower halls.

Late in the year a considerable increase of the force in the bindery was made, as it was apparent that the accumulation of books needing binding or repairs increased beyond our power to dispose of them. Notwithstanding this strengthening of that service, the balance of work and accomplishment is not yet reached, and I am fearful that we shall fall still further behind the coming year. The wear and tear of the books naturally increases year by year; and with the constantly growing accessions the ability of the bindery to meet our requirements is severely taxed. We have introduced during the year an expeditious way of binding pamphlets. Covers of various sizes, half bound in leather, are kept in stock, and from one to three pamphlets, as their importance may determine, being in the first place stitched with stout thread, are attached to guards within the covers. The style is serviceable for the purpose, and not only relieves the bindery, but expedites the accessibility of such publications. Notices of the discussions on binding at the Philadelphia conference elicited statements in the English journals regarding the use of buckram instead of leather; and I learned from Mr. Nicholson, the Librarian of the London Institution, that ten years' use had satisfied them of its excellent qualities for durability, while gas-lighted and heated apartments may render it much more permanent than any leather. The article is a stout linen cloth, of various colors, highly glazed, and may be used with a leather lettering piece, or it will take tooling of itself. The samples which have been produced in our bindery, with loose joints, such as are used in parchment or blank work, and dressed with varnish on completion, present a satisfactory appearance. The article has never been introduced into this country, but I have brought it to the attention of importers of Scotch linens, who will introduce it at once. As the duty is 40 per cent. *ad valorem*, its cost compared with American skins may be increased to make it more nearly equal to that of leather than it is in England.

The pressure of the times caused us to figure so closely at the beginning of the year on the anticipated cost of maintenance for the year, that I expressed in my last report an apprehension of the result. We were with difficulty enabled to compass our outlay with the funds at disposal, and it would have been impossible without the balances abroad with which we opened the year. I feel under the same difficulties regarding the allowance for the coming year. It certainly will not permit us to extend our usefulness to meet all the demands upon us, and the amount to our credit in Europe will not compare with that of last year. For the several items we can depend as follows: —

Binding. — City appropriation		$5,500 00
Books and Periodicals.	City appropriation	15,000 00
	Balance with Barings, London	2,192 78
	Balance with Flügel, Leipzig	382 77
	Balance with Riaño, Madrid	197 34
	Bowditch deposit	500 00
	Income from funds	6,300 00
Catalogue. — City appropriation		6,000 00
Fuel. " "		4,000 00
Furniture. " "		2,000 00
Gas. " "		5,000 00
Expense, etc. — City appropriation		3,000 00
Printing and Stationery. — City appropriation,		6,000 00
Salaries (including binders) " "		70,626 00
Transportation, postage, etc. " "		3,000 00
Total		$129,698 89

Of the above sum $120,126 is the regular appropriation of the City Council. The total available for books and periodicals is $24,572.89, and if binding and the salaries of binders is included, $40,224.89. Besides this there is the income of the Fellowes Fund, for the benefit of the Roxbury Branch, on account of which $1,833 has been spent the past year. There has been no change in the investment of our funds (see Appendix XXIV.); and the financial statement for the year is given in Appendix XXIV.

I cannot close this statement of the year's work, and this review of a ten years' service, without reference to the general good feeling and spirit of emulation in fidelity which has on the whole characterized the staff. I think the Library owes much to an *esprit de corps* among its servants, who have felt that they were sharers in the advantages of its good name. Barely ten of the hundred and forty names of the regular and extra service now on our rolls were on it when it fell to my lot to direct their labors. Of the important officers, who have been associated with me, the name of one must show the asterisk of death. The late Assistant Superintendent, Mr. William A. Wheeler, entered the service only a few months after my own appointment, and until his death, in October, 1874, he was my coadjutor and friend,—two terms mutually suggestive, and which I will not here qualify with a redundance, that can avail nothing. In the Board of Trustees the term of service of their President now embraces more than a score of years, and his recollections of the Library's career extend beyond that of any one in the Board or on the staff. Only one other member of the Board, Mr. Weston Lewis, can date his acquaintance with the Library as far back as my own. The Chief Janitor of the institution, Mr. William E. Ford, leads in seniority on the staff, his entrance into the service dating back to 1858.

Finally, let me say, that if much has been done, a great deal remains to do. The same spirit of mutual accommodation and common endeavor, which has brought the Library where it is, can but carry it onward towards a goal continually receding, only because one step of development opens the way to another.

Respectfully submitted,
JUSTIN WINSOR,
Superintendent.

PUBLIC LIBRARY, May 1st, 1877.

3. FREE LIBRARIES AND READERS

The modern institution of free libraries is barely five-and-twenty years old. In England and Massachusetts (which took the lead in America) they date back to acts of Parliament and legislature of nearly even dates.

The career of a free library runs naturally on by stages, and is at the best self-developing, or but partially aided from the outside. The old adage that "work begun is half done" is, perhaps, true in some sense. There are struggles in a community over the appropriation, or to secure the raising, of funds, but it is merely initial work. The future of a library depends on what is done next. In the formation of a collection of books there will be much scattered and aimless action, unless the problem of correspondences between the library and its constituency is studied, solved, and the corollary obeyed. In a committee this will come in conflict with individual positivism, having a love of domination irrespective of consequences. A little bookishness in a committee-man may be as dangerous as a sip from the poet's Pierian spring, particularly if there is no deeper learning in any of his associates. He knows just enough of books not to know he knows nothing of libraries. He does not comprehend that a large part of his duty is to reach down to those who are reaching up, and he is deluded with the fancy that crowds will cling to his coat-tails as he struggles to mount higher. The result shows him that his caudal artifice stands no rivalship with his neighbors' friendly grasp over the verge. It is fellowship, shoulder-to-shoulder ignorance, a beckoning hand, a child among children, ploughmen and ploughman, a signpost for the way — that constitutes your committee-man above others. If he can be all these, and is entrusted with the selection of books for the shelves, he may have as much book-learning as he pleases, and it will not hurt him. It is only when bookishness becomes exclusiveness and prevents sympathy, that it injures. The books that are provided become the librarian's tools to accomplish his work, and as the work of moulding readers is multiform, his tools must be as various — some coarse, some fine. Either quality alone is insufficient, or rather positively bad.

There is a good deal of misconception as to what constitutes a well-selected library. It is a problem of fitness, adaptation to the end desired, and there can be no such thing as a model collection so long as communities differ and individuality survives. That library alone is well selected which is best able to answer reasonable expectations, and these differ according to circumstances. And yet your committee-man knows all the books "no gentleman's library should be without," as the advertisers say, and if they do not suit, they ought to, and that is enough. Just there is the difficulty. It is the difference between tact and perversity. It is the very exceptional man who by force of mere will can succeed. Most successful men are full of tact — it is the fitting time they seek, the fitting influences they ply, the fitting goals they aim at. They never drag, they push. If they would inure, they give graduated exposures. If they would carry up a height, they cut their footholds as they go. This is all worldly experience, and this makes successful libraries, as it makes successful manufactories. A community of three thousand souls is a complex one, no matter how rural. If they are true to their American blood, they can not be driven either in their reading or in their politics. Wrong will turn them, and promises will coax them.

The fact is, a library must reach the summit of its usefulness naturally, as most agencies do. It fails as a hot-bed. Transplantings from it wither, unless they can stand the new soil that receives them. There must be growth before there can be grafting. You must have the sturdy root before you can train the branches. In other words, you must foster the instinct for reading, and then apply the agencies for directing it. You can allure, you can imperceptibly guide, but you make poor headway if you try to compel. Beware of homilies: they run into cant, and cant is always cheap, and often bogus. Do not try what is called "discreet counsel," unless you have to deal with a mind naturally receptive; but let the attention be guided, as unwittingly as possible, from the poor to the indifferent, from this to the good, and so on to the best, and let it not be forgotten that there are as many kinds of best as there are people, and what is *best* for one is but fair, or indifferent, or poor for another.

Source: *Library Journal* 1 (1876): 63-67.

The mistake in forming a collection of books according to some conventional notion of what a library should be, is a common one; it is a mistake that has disheartened many a librarian, who finds his borrowers drop off as the first interest declines. There is no excuse for letting this first interest decline; and the library will, if it has a chance, right itself in spite of all such unfavorable conditions. If it can not, it languishes and dies. Fortunately few do die of this untimely paralysis. They assert gradually their natural development, and in the long run succeed. The conditions of success in libraries are much the same as in all practical affairs. A factory does not insist on putting unsalable goods upon the market. It alters its machinery to suit the new conditions, and the new stuff makes equally good coats and petticoats with the old, and, what is more important, there is a demand for it. The fabric may be worse, but *then* you may be sure the preference for it will not last long. The style may be less tasteful, but then the wearer must encompass the difficulties by his individual skill in making up.

There is a fashion in books that can not be ignored. I am by no means an advocate of a slavish subjection to it; but I know you have got to pay some deference to it, or the spirit of fashion will flout at you, and you will become utterly helpless. Your life as a guardian of a library is one of constant wariness and struggle. In fashion, in low tastes, in unformed minds, you have an enemy who must be made to surrender. You must not despise him; if you do, you will give him an advantage that will result in your surrender to him.

In one important particular the librarian wields a power far superior to that of the schoolmaster. The one great defect of our American educational systems is that of assorting humanity into lengths that do not correspond—into classes in which all kinds are mixed up together, with little chance for mutual assimilation, and with individuality repressed and obliterated. Our schools will never reach their full fruition until the undeniable advantage of personal contact among pupils is presented together with the development of individual training, securing the natural bent in study and character. The problem is difficult of solution with inherited notions such as ours; but the great educational director will yet arise, who, by force of fitness for command, will accomplish it.

Here the library has the advantage. It appeals to and nurtures every idiosyncrasy. Like the soil, it imparts this quality to that grain, and others to the different fruits. The law of nature rules, and each crop draws what it needs and leaves the rest.

It follows, then, that with a public of many instincts and yearnings, your books must be as various and many-sided, if you would have them do their work. Nor only that. There must be every degree in the variety and a due preponderance of the low degrees. In fact, a popular library begins as a school does, with pastime pursuits of the kindergarten sort.

In a *literary* sense—mark my adjective, for I shun disrespect—in a *literary* sense the average town community has very little elevation through culture, and it is governed in these matters by impulses or badly-reasoned syllogisms. A story,—and artistically a poor story it may be,—a wordy style, a flabby tissue of thoughts, are the qualities that often commend themselves to even shrewd people—people whose natural business-talk is terse, whose companionable interchange of thought at the village post-office is by no means devoid of sense, and whom a plausible rogue will not delude. But it seems natural for most people to think the ideal excellence is extraneous to every-day life, and, by a simple law, what is extraneous they consider excellent. You will accordingly find very poor novels—artistically considered—the staple holiday reading of many really sinewy-minded people, whose fortune has not placed them among people of culture. This condition, however, is a stage, not a goal, and the librarian must never forget that the object of a goal is that it should be reached.

Accordingly a library, to be "well selected," as the phrase goes, must have all the variety needed by all the variety of people who frequent it. It must aim to amuse as well as to instruct. It must be remembered that a large proportion of the readers of a general community need books for recreation as much as for edification. It is not reasonable—it is not wise—to expect that the weary artisan will, in most cases, give his winter evenings to study. He yearns for the life and manners which he is not used to, and is not critical according to a standard that has your respect. The lawyer, even after a week with his causes and his reports, finds recreation for mind and body in the last new novel of George Eliot. Some of the most presistent novel-readers I know are learned judges and doctors of divinity. The hostler of the tavern stable sits between his labors in the breezy avenue of the open doors, and though he may look upon the inland mountain without, he pictures rather the Spanish Main in the sea-stories of Marryat. It is as legitimate a function of the public library to afford this gratification as it is for the schools to begin the education of life by providing blocks to build houses with, or clay to mould rabbits out of. "The child is father to the man" in this as in many other things. Grown-up people can not all be antiquaries, or mathematicians, or Darwinians, or financiers.

I have said there are three stages in the progress of a free public library. The first one is the gathering of the books,—and this is often a committee's work, and not always wisely done, as the librarian will discover.

The second is in securing the reading of the books, and this can only be done by providing the books in due proportions that are wanted—the exclusion of vicious books being assured.

The third follows in inducing an improvement in the kind of reading; and in these latter days this is a prime test of the librarian's quality. It is not a crusade that he is to lead. People who read for recreation are not to be borne apart from it; but they can be induced to pass from weak to strong even in this department—from the inane to those of historical bearing; from the mishaps of the dejected swain to the trial of Effie Deans; from the lover's straits to the exploits of Amyas Leigh.

If the web of the weird romancer has meshed a curious reader, take him at the time, and show him the pleasure of disentangling it in the light of history and biography. A young man's asking me one day in which of Scott's novels he could find Cromwell figuring, led me to the classification of historical novels, by epochs and episodes, as the cataloguer would arrange the titles of his history list, and with manifest advantage, as stepping-stones from fiction to history, travel, and biography.

Let me warn you, however, that though the way is clear, the work is one of patience, equalling that of an admirable Waltonian by the brook-side. The most confirmed novel-reader will present himself some time with the spell weakened, and half longing for your guidance. With those having the instinct for knowledge you may be more readily successful. But for your own sake, dull acquiescence is not so fascinating as the conquest of the gamey scoffer at your mission.

But, I pray you, do not be discouraged with the seeming small results. It will be long before your statistics will show much, and then not constantly. Every propulsion into the higher planes leaves a vacuum which the new generations of readers rush in to fill, and so keep the percentage tolerably constant. But the work well begun may be trusted for its own development.

In conclusion let me say that the day is passed when librarianships should be filled with teachers who have failed in discipline, or with clergymen whose only merit is that bronchitis was a demerit in their original calling. The place wants pluck, energy, and a will to find and make a way. We are but just beginning to see the possibilities of the free library system; and the progress of the last score years must be taken as an earnest for the future. Hand in hand with the home and the college, the free library with its more ductile agencies, with its more adaptable qualities, must go on to assert the dominion that belongs to it, if librarians are faithful to their trust and recompense the people as they ought.

4. READING IN POPULAR LIBRARIES

Character of Reading Considered—Pastime Readers—Natural Tendencies of Reading towards Elevation of Taste—Opportunities of Librarians—Youthful Readers.

People who look wise, and shake their heads, and talk about public libraries being after all not an unmixed good, are the greatest encomiasts which the system has, because they imply that they differ from most people, and that the practice of imputing unqualified good to libraries prevails, when nobody thinks of assigning such a condition to the pulpit, the bar, or trade.

These censorious flatterers refer to the character of the reading that is put into such libraries and is drawn from them by the mass of readers, and they estimate the value of that reading wholly from their own wants and predilections, and without any regard to the immense variety of minds and character which fortunately makes up communities.

If the good influences largely predominate, most advocates of libraries will be content, and they are not altogether strenuous that the good should be positive in all cases, being quite happy if a negative benefit is brought about.

It is a very easy matter to form a library to suit the wants of specific conditions of people; but it is not so easy to gather such books as will afford the greatest and most varied interest to all sorts of readers. What will harm some will work no harm to others, though it may do them no more good than to grant them a pastime, and it is with this object that three quarters of the reading of people not professedly bookish is carried on; and whether it be desirable or not, the pastime readers are the most of the people to whose wants public libraries of the popular sort minister.

Books can neither instruct nor amuse if they are not within the comprehension, or it is perhaps better to say, within the literary sense of their readers. One may understand a book, but it does not allure him from other things, unless it responds to his intellectual wants, or runs upon the plane of his mental training. When we consider the vast multitudes of people who are destitute of literary culture—and they may be none the worse citizens, and many even may be bright thinkers—we need not be disappointed that so many read what, in a literary sense, are poor books; and that so few read for other reasons than to refresh themselves after sterner work.

It is not very considerate to establish anything like a fixed standard of good for all people, whether in dietetics or literature. There is doubtless a universal goodness in literature as bread is in diet; but no one wants to live on bread solely, and it is the variety, and to a considerable extent, condiments and relishes in food and in books, that give health to the appetite and vigor to the digestion. These critics cannot understand why the epicure eats the trail with the woodcock. They call what is unpalatable to them or mawkish to their ideas trash, forgetting that this much abused word represents a quality which is not positive, but only relative, and is like the freezing point, which depends upon the substance to be frozen. Water is useful and iron is useful, but they solidify at such different temperatures that they are not equally useful in the stomach.

This doctrine of the average mind and procrustean lengths in education, is unfortunately one that cannot easily be discarded in our schools, where a few teachers are to instruct many scholars; but in libraries, where the teachers are dumb, and are not annoyed by whispering, each reader can have his own mentor, and there is not a little gratification in the emancipation from rule which is thus produced. There is also some significance in the up and down traveling of the trash point according to the quality of the pupil.

Thus it is: A spurns as trash what elevates B, who looks down on the highest reading C is capable of, and so on till you get down to the mere jingle that amuses a half idiot, who is happy because he can understand something above the caterwauling of the roofs. If this principle is understood, the whole question lightens up. It is by no means to be inferred that, however we take things, we must leave them as we find them. Librarians do not do their whole duty unless

Source: *Public Libraries in the United States of America: Their History, Condition, and Management, Special Report, Part 1*. Washington: Gov. Print. Off., 1876. pp. 431-33.

they strive to elevate the taste of their readers, and this they can do, not by refusing to put within their reach the books which the masses of readers want, but by inducing a habit of frequenting the library, by giving readers such books as they ask for and then helping them in the choice of books, conducting them, say from the ordinary society novel to the historical novel, and then to the proofs and illustrations of the events or periods commemorated in the more readable of the historians. Multitudes of readers need only to be put in this path to follow it. This can be satisfactorily proved by statistics in any well administered library where the records of circulation are kept in a way to be a guidance rather than an obstacle to the librarian.

But the proofs do not show all, and only the librarian knows what allowance must be made for several interfering influences. Most of the frequenters of a popular library drop off when you have begun to have the most effect upon them, because they have attained an age when business first begins to engross their attention, and they confine their reading to a newspaper on week days and to a chance number of a periodical on Sundays. Librarians know that if these influences can be resisted, and the young man can continue to frequent the library, he can be helpfully advanced in his reading. Again, every year many young readers begin their experiences with the library. They find all the instructive reading they ought to have in their school books, and frequent the library for story books. These swell the issues of fiction, but they prevent the statistics of that better reading into which you have allured the older ones, from telling as they should in the average. A reasonable conclusion, then, is, that the mass of readers in popular libraries crave pastime only; but they can be made to glide into what is commonly called instructive reading quite as early as it is good for them.

5. LIBRARY BUILDINGS

Site—Design—Economy of Space—Furniture—Numbering of Cases—Labor Saving Devices—Stations of Officers—Unpacking Room—Catalogue Room—Bindery—Extra Work Rooms—Branch Libraries—Room for Growth—Newspaper and Duplicate Room—Room for Patent Specifications—Cabinets—Students' Room—Pamphlet Room—Stock Room—Janitor's Quarters—Toilet Rooms—Plans and Description.

To have a good library building, a sufficient area should be secured to leave it detached on all sides, and to provide for future additions. Its plan of administration should be decided upon, and in accordance with that its book rooms, public waiting rooms, official and service quarters should be planned to fall into the most convenient relations one to the other. Describe this to the architect, and ask him if he can build his edifice around these quarters without disturbing size or relative position. If he complains that the public apartments do not give sight of the books, and that he must fail of half his effects if he cannot have handsome bindings and vistas of shelving, tell him to fail; that the public wants books to read, not to look at. If he says that your $100,000 will not build anything but an ordinary building, and that he cannot elevate the aesthetic conceptions of people who look at it unless he can spend $200,000, tell him that $7,000 worth of books annually purchased with the income of that extra $100,000 will be more than a match in the long run for his flutings and bas-reliefs in the production of aesthetic effects. We have too many of these architectural enormities in library structures already. Witness the public libraries of Boston and Cincinnati, the Astor in New York, and among the smaller ones that of Springfield, Mass.

Men do not erect a building and decide afterward whether it shall be a playhouse or a hospital; and yet these two are not more awkwardly interchangeable than the two kinds of library buildings needed, say by an antiquarian society and a municipality; still committees go on and build a building, leaving the question an open one whether their library shall be of one sort or another.

The traditional form of a large library, of which we have examples in all the libraries named above, has come down to us with other old monastic ideas, when the monks were the only users of books, and when the seclusion of alcoves comported with their literary habits, and gave convenient access to the books shelved about the recluse. The alcove system, arranged about a central area, where the books are also to be used, is to this day the most convenient plan where a collection is devoted to a small or solely scholarly use, and where, as is the case with scientific societies or other bodies of specialists, their members are allowed unrestricted access to the shelves. The alcoves being at the end of radial lines from the central tables, and each alcove carrying out the same principle in relation to its own central table, the service of the library, whether performed by one's self or by deputy, requires the minimum of time and strength.

A like economical principle needs to be preserved, when we come to change the character of the library to that of a great collection to which multitudes have access, and but few are personally known to the librarians. Such a state of affairs, it needs no argument to show, involves the shutting out of the public from the shelves. Rapid intercommunication has brought users of books to focal points in the world, where great libraries exist. The spread of literature has enlarged the bookish classes among stationary populations. Hence the new development of enormous use which great free libraries are making. Masses are impatient of delay and need to be served quickly in order to be kept happy; and to accomplish it the page who goes for a book must not be obliged to scan titles along a shelf, or series of shelves, but must find a book at once by its number in its proper place. Thus to insure a certainty of the book being in its place, it is necessary to exclude the public from the shelves for the reason that most prowlers among shelves do not restore books they have taken down to the exact place from which they took them.

Source: *Public Libraries in the United States of America: Their History, Condition, and Management, Special Report, Part 1.* Washington: Gov. Print. Off., 1876. pp. 465-75.

These facts indicate the conditions which should be imposed upon an architect in building a great modern library: viz, that the service cannot be performed by the readers, but must be performed by officials; that there is one point of contact between the readers and officials, which is the delivery desk, where the books are charged to the borrowers; and that this delivery desk must be placed in the most convenient relations both to the reading tables and to the books, or, in other words, between them.

In the plan of a central area for the readers, with surrounding alcoves shut off from public approach, this is not the case; for the pages who fetch the books travel around the public and make the average distance to be run and the delay consequent fully double what it would be if the point of delivery were midway between the public and the books.

The main idea of the modern public library building is, then, compact stowage to save space, and short distances to save time. This has been carried out in the new building in Roxbury, which is one of the branches of the Boston Public Library. Here we have a book room 27 feet wide by 55 feet long and 24 feet high; the desk of delivery being midway on one of the longer sides, just without a door which opens into a waiting apartment. In the first place, the bottoms of the windows are 8 feet from the floor, giving an unbroken wall shelving around the room. Then two rows of ten double-faced cases, each 8 feet high, are placed, standing crosswise, in the room, leaving a middle passage and two side passages 2 feet 6 inches wide along the length of the room. The passages across the room between the faces of the cases are at present 3 feet 6 inches wide. When required, lay a Hyatt light floor on top of these cases, after having moved them together till your 3 feet 6 inches cross passages are reduced to 2 feet 10 inches, except the one just back of the delivery, which is thus widened to receive the stairs. Repeat the same cases and shelving (only the windows will break the wall surface) on this floor, and again on a third floor, when required, deriving now additional light from a lantern on the roof.

In this way your room (27 x 55 x 24) will give you three stories of 8 feet each, less the thickness of two glass floors, and will hold a hundred thousand volumes, all within a shorter distance of the delivery by far than any hundred thousand volumes are placed in any other library.

The cases are divided into sections not over 3 feet long. There are no lengthwise partitions separating the two faces, but a bead on the uprights keeps the shelves from touching at the back by its thickness, allows a passage down for dust, and makes a current of air, which is necessary to leather bindings, since they deteriorate in a stagnant and foul atmosphere. The shelves are supported by common ring-head screws, such as are used for "picture eyes," which are easily moved as required. In cases 8 feet high, including base and cornice, you can get nine shelves, including that formed by the base, but all of these will not ordinarily be required, unless the shelves below the breast-level are kept so near together that the books must be pushed in on their fore edges, which does not hurt small books, gives better stowage, and enables the pages to read the shelf numbers on the bottom of the backs without stooping or kneeling. If the books are kept in this way, it is better that the shelves, from the base up to the level of the breast, should recede, one by one, an inch each, counting upon having the shelves on which the books stand upright 8 or 9 inches wide.

The cheapest and most easily adjusted arrangement for making books stand perpendicular on the shelf, is a block of hard wood; two of which can be made out of a cube of 6 inches each way by dividing it diagonally. They should be shellacked, when first made, to prevent checking.

For numbering, give a number from 1 upwards to each face of the cases, and paint this number in large figures over the middle of the case; put secondary numbers, 1, 2, 3, &c., over the tops of the ranges, (or spaces between uprights.) Then number your shelves from the bottom up, 1, 2, 3, 4, 5, 6, 7, 8 –painting the proper figure on each shelf edge, range by range. Your shelves are now easily designated: 3825, for instance, meaning the 38th case, the 2d range, and the 5th shelf; and it has the advantage that shelves 1725, 2325, etc., will always be in the same relative position in the 17th, 23d, cases, etc. Next number your books on the shelf in the order in which they stand, and book No. 5, so marked, will be designated 3825.5, which means 5th book, of the 5th shelf, of the 2d range, of the 38th case; and if the 5th book (or title) has several volumes, any particular volume will be designated by its proper figure after a second dot; as, for instance, for a third volume of the above book, 3825.5.3. A number arranged in this way conveys to the attendant the exact position of the book before he leaves to fetch it, and he can almost find it in the dark; he certainly could if all the books on the shelf were in their places, and none had more than one volume.

This is on the supposition that all the cases are uniform, which is desirable, as thus the contents of two cases can be transposed bodily, without alteration of numbers, except so far as transposing the case numbers on the cases themselves. This is sometimes of importance, since the books in a case near the delivery may in time cease to be much used, while the fresher books in a more distant case take their place in common demand. If a transposition takes place, then much time will be saved in the service. It may break temporarily the order of position, but as other classification requires a similar change, the change of all becomes, in the end, like that of the rear ranks of a platoon stepping to the front, while the foremost fall back, and order is re-established.

Of course there will be books of exceptional sizes which must be accommodated with cases and shelving to fit.

In the case of very large libraries, some partially automatic system of fetching books will naturally follow. The number of the book can be struck by the desk attendant on a keyboard, and be shown in a signal frame, within sight of all the stations of the pages. The proper page will find the book, deposit it in one of a succession of boxes journeying on an endless band towards the delivery, where, as it goes around the barrel to return below, it will throw out upon a cushion the volume in question or a card containing its number, which indicates that the book is not in its place. These same boxes are used for returning the books to the shelves after assortment, their procession being reversed. If this latter service needs to be supplemented, trucks should be used of two or three stories each, resting on four wheels, one at each end and two at the center, which, being a trifle larger than the end ones, serve as a pivot, on which the truck can be easily guided through the narrow passages.

The Boston Public Library, for many years before the establishment of its six branches, (at distances of from one to five miles from the central building,) consisted of two separate libraries in one edifice; and they still exist, one having the higher classifications of books, and the other the more popular literature. This dual system has the disadvantage of making the habitual frequenter of one of the departments prone to overlook the other, for the two of necessity somewhat overlap, and both need to be examined in many instances of inquiry; but its great advantage is that it separates in large measure the mere pastime readers from the studious ones, and insures such order and quiet in the higher department as would not be possible if the two were made one, beside collecting and putting under better observation the borrowers of the more expensive books.

But in order not to repel from the lower department adults and girls, by reason of the contact they must have with crowds of boys, particularly at hours between schools, it would be well to confine the boys in their approach to the desk merely to one side of a rail, as they need to be dealt with by the same officials, since as messengers of adults the record of the loans they need to cancel or make afresh must be made at the same desk. This could not be satisfactorily arranged if they were confined to a separate waiting hall and used an entirely separate delivery.

The official headquarters of a library should be situated as nearly as possible in the center of the system, so that the controlling power shall come with the shortest possible delay into relations with every part, whether devoted to the staff or the public; and there should be every convenience of dumb-waiter and speaking tube to bring all parts into easy communication.

In enumerating further the variety of apartments necessary to the thorough appointing of a great library, mention must be made of many that can be dispensed with or embodied with others in lesser institutions.

Books received in cases should be unpacked in an apartment adjoining an elevator by which they are raised to the catalogue room. This should be a large hall, with stalls about the circumference, the head of this department being situated on a raised platform in the middle, where he can control every section. These stalls should be occupied in succession by the different attendants through whose hands the books successively pass in their processes of fitting them finally for the shelves. Trucks on tramways, or some other means of passing quantities of books on from stage to stage, should be provided.

The order of these stalls (and in large libraries each will be occupied by several attendants under one head) will fall more conveniently in a sequence which shall assign H (see plan[1] of main story) to the ordering clerk, who makes out the lists of books to be ordered, dispatching these lists to the library agents, keeping records of them, and who watches the publication of all serials to see that successive numbers are promptly supplied. This stall should have room for a small bibliographical apparatus, and be provided with ample room for pigeon-holes, and other conveniences for assorting, as the details of the work are numerous. To this department all books received are first committed, so that the order lists may be checked and the books marked for their proper destination.

In G the work collation should be done, and the collator of each book should be required to put his initials in a given place in it.

In F the accession catalogue is kept and each book is entered, and acquires a consecutive number, which is attached to it, with the date.

In E such as need to be bound are arranged for the bindery, entered on schedules, and dispatched to the binder, and, when received back, are pushed on with the rest.

In D the pasting in of the proper book plates, (showing purchase by fund, acquisition by gift, etc.,) and impressing the library stamp, take place.

In C (and B, A, M, L, etc., according as the space is required, and the different departments of the library have the cataloguing assigned to different attendants) the books are catalogued. These stalls, as well as H, should be in convenient proximity to an adjacent apartment devoted to the working bibliographical apparatus and to the cases of the official card catalogue; or these may be arranged in the middle of the hall, as in the plan.

In K (if that comes next) the custodian of the shelves should determine the position of the books on the shelves, give them shelf numbers accordingly, and enter them in the shelf lists, which are used in the periodic examination of the shelves by this officer, and which constitute in some degree a classed catalogue of the library. This officer takes from the books the cards which come in them from the cataloguers, and marks both on them and on the book the shelf number which he has given the book. He delivers the cards to the alphabetizers, who put them in their proper places in the official and public card catalogues, (they are made in duplicate,) and the books to boys, who on trucks wheel them away to their shelves.

If the cards are printed, as is the case in the Boston Public Library, other work intervenes growing out of such substitution for manuscript which need not be described here.

There should also be an extra workroom, where any work of unusual extent, such as a large donation or extraordinary purchase, can be managed without interrupting the processes of the ordinary service in the catalogue room.

If the library has branches, communicating daily with the central department, the business of receiving and dispatching the boxes that go between, answering the branch librarians' requisitions and transmitting the books and periodicals designed for the branches, should be in charge of an officer, who will need considerable space for the details of his work, conveniently situated for the access of the expressmen. This officer will also attend to the express-service of the library, which grows with the collection, and pertains to the distribution of catalogues the receiving of exchanges, and all other packages, other than from the library's agents.

Every great library will find it of importance to have a considerable area reserved for contingent growth, in which large collections, bought or received as gifts, may be kept separately when desirable; and the possibility of giving them such seclusion from the bulk of the library will often decide the question of benefaction, when the claims of other libraries, which cannot so provide a separate space, are under consideration.

The officer in charge of the circulation of the library should have his station separated only by a rail or counter from the public whose serving he is to look after, and with whom he can thus more readily hold the necessary communication. It would be well that the public card catalogue should also be under his immediate supervision, as he will need constant access to it, in assisting readers in finding or choosing books.

[1] The plans here referred to will be found on pages [115, 116, 117].

A newspaper room and duplicate room can profitably be made one and the same, reserving the lower spaces for newspapers, and the upper spaces, where from their distance from the floor large volumes like newspapers will be conveniently shelved, for duplicates. This room should have conveniences for the attendant to do the work of assorting and collating newspapers for the binder, and should have tables for consulting them. Newspapers are best kept on their sides, not over three volumes on a shelf; but if kept on end, the uprights should not be over 18 inches apart, and then jacks should be used for holding the volumes up, if the spaces are not nearly full. If a library is going to make a newspaper collection, it should be remembered to make the space for it ample.

If the library is furnished with the patent specifications of Great Britain, France, and the United States, an apartment at least 30 feet square should be provided for the present extent of these collections, and for the next ten years' growth, which amounts to about one hundred and fifty large volumes annually. A counter shelf, for consulting the volumes for brief examination, should run in front of the shelves, while tables are provided for the centre of the apartment.

Cabinets for holding the rarities of the collection, large volumes, and portfolios of engravings, and maps, should be kept in an apartment where they can have the constant supervision of a custodian.

A large room with stalls, or a series of small apartments with tables and shelf conveniences, should be provided for students making protracted investigations, and wishing to keep the books they use at their desks from day to day. The officer in charge of this room should see that in such cases dummies are put on the shelf in the place of the books thus appropriated, to show where they are, if wanted by others.

A large room, with tables and shelf conveniences, should be appropriated to the assorting of pamphlets, and making up volumes of them for the bindery. These volumes, when bound and catalogued, pass into the general catalogue, so that this room should be conveniently near the catalogue room and the official card catalogue, as the curator must have constant recourse to these apartments in his work.

In connection with the reading room for periodicals there should be an ante-room, in which the back numbers of magazines are pigeon-holed until they are prepared for the binder, and when bound they are passed on, like other books, to stall H of the catalogue room.

The circulating department should have a room where the work of inspecting books needing repairs or rebinding, (and the covering, if practiced,) can be done, and where they can be scheduled for the bindery, and received and manipulated when returned from the binder.

A stock room will also be necessary for storing catalogues and documents of the library, blanks, stationery, etc.

The janitor will need living quarters and store rooms for his supplies, etc.

It is desirable in a large library to have a bindery in the building, which should be amply provided for.

Appropriate toilet rooms, with washing arrangements, water closets, and wardrobes should be provided; and for each sex, if women are also employed on the staff.

PLANS FOR A LIBRARY OF ONE MILLION VOLUMES' CAPACITY.[1]

The main Book Room, marked A, is to have seven stories, with glass floors between and a glass roof, each story 8 feet in the clear; the walls to be shelved; the cases, double faced, to stand on each floor in rows, with passage 2 feet 10 inches between; spiral stairs to connect the floors; dumb-waiters and inclined planes, with stations on each floor, to deliver the books at the space marked F, whence pages are to take them to the Delivery Counter at C.

The section for Popular Books, B, is to be similarly arranged, but of only two stories, while the five stories above B, extend over the Popular Delivery Room as shown in K, (second floor plan,) and so connect also with the room A on each story, forming a component part of the same. A spiral staircase somewhere near the passage D should render these upper stories

[1] The accompanying plans are the joint production of Mr. Winsor and the architects Sturgis and Brigham, of Boston, Mass.–EDITORS.

readily accessible from the Delivery C, while additional staircases will render the second story accessible to the pages attending the Delivery G. The Students' Room is intended for tables for such as make protracted investigations, and need to have the books they use kept from day to day. A side entrance is arranged for such as visit the library for popular books only, and the noise attending the larger concourse of such readers is kept apart from the greater quiet of the more studious frequenters of the General Delivery Room. An attendant at E would have oversight of the rooms on either hand, the popular reading room being given to the more commonly used of the magazines of the day for old and young. The General Delivery Room is the main consulting room of the more permanent collection of the books, and should have tables for readers and the cases for the public catalogues. Additional light should be provided by wells in the floor above. These wells could be made circular, with reading shelves on their rails.

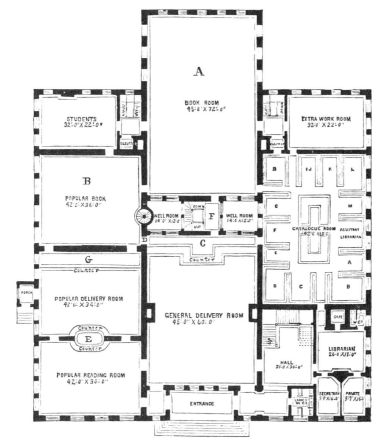

PLAN OF MAIN STORY.

The Catalogue Room is developed to the requirements of a larger working force. It should, however, have connection with the space C by a door. The stall H should open on the elevator, so that books can be directly received from the Unpacking Room below. They then pass from stall to stall round the room, a separate process being gone through with in each, until they are at last put upon trucks to be wheeled to their destined shelves. A Librarian's Room is ordinarily placed to best advantage in the center of the system, but a sub-executive officer stationed in the center of the Catalogue Room will exercise the needful personal supervision of the whole establishment, leaving the head of so large a library the greater freedom for superior direction. It would be well to connect his secretary's office with his own without necessitating passage through a public hall. The Reading Room on the second floor is for the higher and less popular periodicals, which are delivered at the counter, while the back volumes, which have been shelved as books, are reached by the passage N in the Book Room L. There should also be a door at O for access to the upper floors of K. A door at P should give access to the Newspaper Room. Bound volumes of newspapers can be delivered through the door P over the counter in this room, for use on the tables in the Reading Room. With this arrangement there will be no occasion for the public use of the space adjacent to the Newspaper Room, (marked Hall,) which could be converted into another contingent apartment. The elevator should also open into the Newspaper Room. A door for official use should open from the Patent Specifications room to the Book Room K. In the basement plan the Transmitting Room is intended for the express

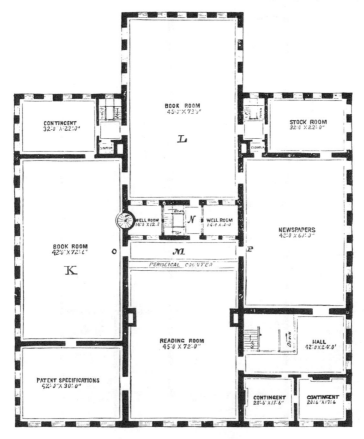

PLAN OF SECOND STORY.

service of the library, which, if it has a system of branches, needs considerable space. This work could, however, be done in the Unpacking Room if the bindery should require, as it probably would, the space. The apartment marked Pamphlets would probably have to be extended over the adjacent Cellar, and the whole building should stand high enough on its foundations to give the basement both light and dryness throughout. It is not unlikely that the range of rooms on the other side of the building will be needed for library purposes, and there would still be room enough in the Boiler Room and under the entrance steps for fuel. There needs to be distinct accomodation for wardrobe and toilet use for the two sexes of the library service. The Storage Rooms X and W might be devoted to this use in connection with the adjoining water-closets, if they are light enough. Otherwise, such arrangements could be made on the side of the porch, that entrance being made the official entrance of the library staff.

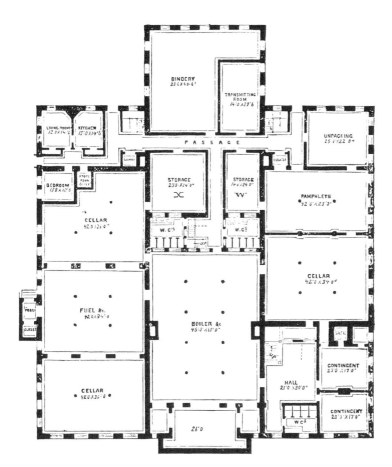

PLAN OF BASEMENT.

Ephemera—Binding—Reference Books—Library Statistics.

EPHEMERA.

The librarian of a great library largely escapes that choosing between books necessarily imposed on those in charge of smaller collections. The larger the available income for the purchase of books, the less distracted he is in making choice of them. Everything will come in use sooner or later in a large collection, as everybody expects to find everything on the shelves. No selection can, therefore, be wholly amiss. But the perplexity most commonly arising with the lesser libraries is that of the preservation and storing of what are usually denominated *ephemera*. For a given bulk the labor which must be bestowed on pamphlets, broadsides, scraps, etc., to render them of any use in a library—assorting, cataloguing, binding, etc.—is vastly greater than for books; and, as labor is money, and as money should be made to go as far possible in a library, there is no reason why ordinary libraries should give any of their resources to this end, except so far as the matters to be preserved are of local interest. These they should care for by all means, as the community which they serve, presently and prospectively, has a right to expect of them. A few great libraries in the country, the chief one in each principal geographical section, should do this work, and they should open an exchange account with each other, say, in our country, the Boston Public Library for New England; the State Library at Albany perhaps for the Middle States, or the Library Company at Philadelphia; the Library of Congress for the whole country, and particularly for those remoter sections where there is no large library to look out for their preservation; the public libraries of Cincinnati or Chicago for the West; and the San Francisco Mercantile for the Pacific Coast. The lesser collections will do the best thing for the future historical investigator if they will make regular contributions into the larger repository of all such grist as may come to their mill, so that it can there be cared for and rendered available for use by indexing of one kind or another. The cost of this work is large, and the chief libraries should by all means provide for it. A great mistake would be made if the present outlay is compared with the present advantage. The experience of the Old World libraries shows how material of this sort, which would have cost little to accumulate at the time, is now beyond recovery, or is obtained at prices that are appalling; and these prices are given because of the real value of this material for history. Ephemera are the best reflex of the times which saw their first issue, and we cannot read Macaulay, for instance, without seeing the legitimate use which an historian can make of them. It should be remembered that unless the chief libraries make it a part of their business to preserve these things, the work is not done at all. Societies notoriously neglect the preservation of their annual reports. The United States Government and its departments are without complete files of their important documents. Perhaps not a State in the Union can show a full collection of its own printed records. Cities and towns are almost always deficient in this way, and what collections they have are often at the hazard of a fire in the town clerk's sitting room. The States should compel by law the sending of every town document to the State libraries and to one other large library in their section of the country. Librarians cannot do better than make occasional collections illustrating important anniversaries in their neighborhood, preserving for such purpose everything that has passed through the press—books, pamphlets, newspapers, broadsides, prints, and also manuscripts, the originals of addresses, poems, etc., photographs, music—in fact everything which at the next recurring anniversary will have interest; and there is little that a hundred years will not enhance in value.

Source: *Public Libraries in the United States of America: Their History, Condition, and Management, Special Report, Part 1*. Washington: Gov. Print. Off., 1876. pp. 711-14.

BINDING.

In the matter of binding, it cannot be too strongly impressed upon a librarian's notice that he should acquire something of an expert's knowledge of the binder's art. There are a great many tricks in all trades, and a binder's has its full share of them. There are mud-board, and sham leather, and false gold, gluing instead of sewing, and twenty other devices that can be practiced upon a librarian ignorant of such matters, so that his books will not last and future cost will be incurred. Cheap binding is often dear binding. Strong sewing, real leather, and solid board are worth paying for.

By all means let large libraries bind in with their periodicals, as well as with pamphlets, their original covers. Matter of real importance is preserved in this way, and the color of the covers forms convenient marks on the book's edge for clearly indicating the successive numbers. Books issued in parts should have the covers for the parts bound at the end, preserving all of them if they vary. Many an important question has been settled by such covers. It increases the expense somewhat, but the large libraries should incur it. It is not worth while for the smaller libraries to do it.

In binding pamphlets, bind important ones singly; but the general mass can be bound in groups, either subjects or authors. Never bind them in miscellaneous collections.

Foul air and an air heated and vitiated by gas light are very detrimental to binding, but genuine morocco stands the best. Calf is handsome for a private collection, but unsuited for a public library; it dries and cracks very easily. There is no propriety in a public library of putting on full binding, except in rare instances nor much tooling on the backs. If books are found by shelf numbers, the lettering on the back should be as brief as possible; put the author's name at the top and the title below it, with a dash between.

The cost of labor and material makes binding in this country at the present time very costly, and orders should be given to European agents to bind all books before shipment. If the time might be spared, books could, indeed, be sent to Europe for binding at less cost by one-half than they can be bound for here, and yet pay freight and insurance both ways.

If binders can be found who understand the working of it, half parchment binding gives variety to the shelves, costs less than morocco, is very durable, and answers every purpose for books not much in use. At all events, see that the binder protects and strengthens the corners of all the books with a bit of parchment wrapped about the angle beneath the paper. For this purpose parchment scraps can be bought by the pound from the principle stationers.

Remember, also, that money is saved by rebinding before the book gets so far gone that the inner edge of the leaves has become torn or worn and cannot be properly sewed over.

It is always best for a public library that books which are issued in loose sheets in covers or portfolios should be bound. Much risk of loss of parts is thereby avoided.

REFERENCE BOOKS.

In the matter of reference books, all libraries should be well supplied, and no hesitancy should be felt in repeating the book in newer editions, as issued. Ask librarians who have had experience what the selection is that they have found best. An important library should have all the great encyclopedias; a library with restricted means is compelled to choose. Every library should afford Chambers's, and if it can get another, let it be Appleton's. The latter, without Chambers's, strengthens the references to American subjects; but Chambers's is by no means a superfluity alongside of Appleton's (new edition) large work. Webster's Unabridged is the best dictionary, even for Worcesterians, in orthography—since it offers the user his choice in this respect, and is much superior in all others. Guides to courses of reading are inadequate, since the wants of no two people are alike; but of helps of this kind an intelligent reader will avail himself in his own way; consequently provide them, and also a sufficiency of maps and tables of statistics.

LIBRARY STATISTICS.

There is no branch of library economy more important, or so little understood by a librarian as helps to himself, as the daily statistics which he can preserve of the growth, loss, and use (both in extent and character) of the collection under his care. The librarian who watches these things closely, and records them, always understands what he is about, and what he accomplishes or fails to accomplish. The patrons to whom he presents these statistics will comprehend better the machinery of the library, and be more indulgent toward its defects. The methods employed in the library, of course, determine in large measure what kinds of statistics are desirable and what are possible. Some systems, like a slip system for recording loans, for instance, will yield results, and important ones, which it is impossible to get under a ledger system, or if gotten are attainable only by labor which costs too much. It is all important that the nature and future of a library should be well understood at the beginning, and that its system should be devised to yield the desirable statistical results. If it is not so devised, it is very difficult to engraft a change upon its radical methods at a subsequent period. For this reason, however desirable it would be to procure uniformity in library statistics throughout the country, there is little chance of its ever being accomplished.

"We have no schools of bibliographical and bibliothecal training whose graduates can guide the formation of, and assume management within, the fast increasing libraries of our country; and the demand may perhaps never warrant their establishment: but every library with a fair experience can afford inestimable instruction to another in its novitiate; and there have been no duties of my office to which I have given more hearty attention than those that have led to the granting of what we could from our experience to the representatives of other libraries, whether coming with inquiries fitting a collection as large as Cincinnati is to establish, or merely seeking such matters as concern the establishment of a village library."—Justin Winsor.

7. A WORD TO STARTERS OF LIBRARIES

Every well-established librarian occasionally or even frequently receives letters of which the following is a fair sample:

"PUNKEYVILLE, July 10, 1876.

"DEAR SIR: The Honorable Hezekiah Jones, of our town, has donated [by the way, *given* has dropped out of the dictionary with such people] $—— to found a library in this his native place, and we wish the library to reflect honor on him and credit on Punkeyville. Accordingly we would be obliged for any information you can give to enable us to establish this trust on a correct basis.

"Very respectfully,
"For the Committee,
"JOHN BROWN.

"P.S.—I hope you will send us your catalogues, your charter, and your rules."

Mr. Brown is very likely an estimable person, whom the benefactor has designated as suitable for the head of the trust. Perhaps he is a clergyman, and if you should ask him to tell you the way in which to run a church and take care of a parish, he would remind you that, if it were not for writing the next Sunday's sermon, he might find time to enlighten you. Perhaps he is a physician, beloved of the people, and trusted above all by the Honorable Mr. Jones; but if you asked him something about the theory and practice of medicine, he would refer you to the journals of his profession or recommend a course of study in the schools. Perhaps Brown is the lawyer of the place who has the most business in the County Court, and if you should ask his professional opinion, he would charge you for it according to the time he takes for it, and according to the number of letters he has written you about it. Perhaps he is a teacher of the academy, which is another of Jones's benefactions, and he finds all the spare time he can get from teaching valuable to him in preparing an annotated text of Nepos, which through Jones's influence he hopes to get introduced into schools by the State Board of Education, and to profit thereby enough to lay aside a beginning of a competency for a rainy day.

And yet—

Brown the clergyman has written a letter without a firstly and so on to lastly in it, and evidently with the expectation that the librarian can answer in a sentence more points than he ever ventured to put into half a dozen sermons.

And yet—

Brown the physician has asked a diagnosis without giving you a symptom to go by, without the slightest intimation of any of the conditions, in gift or community, to be met.

Source: *Library Journal* 1 (1876): 1-3.

And yet—

Brown the lawyer has written a letter which will require another in return to learn what is really wanted, knowing very well that librarians never send bills with "letters" charged at so much.

And yet—

Brown the teacher thinks the librarian has no time outside of his prescribed duties that can profitably be spent in laying in his store for a day when he can labor no more.

I hope those who are laboring to advance the library interests of the country will understand that I am not aiming to abridge the useful advice which an experienced librarian can bestow outside of his own sphere, and can bestow gratuitously, but I would inculcate upon all having occasion to avail themselves of such experience, that it is the result of application that is never ceasing, and that it is only fair to such librarians that they should not be called upon to spend time on cases until the cases are well made up. There is no disposition on the part of librarians to shun a general duty which they owe as citizens, if the propositions which are made to them are put with understanding and in such a way as to show that the seekers have fairly tried to help themselves.

Now, how can this be done? In the first place, procure what is in print—such volumes, for instance, as the new publication of the Educational Bureau at Washington. Send to any library which is a fit exemplar, and ask for its rules and reports, and do not forget to enclose stamps for postage; but do not ask of a great library to have its catalogue sent till you have learned something of what you are asking for, a little later in your progress. I think you will never, or rarely, get a rebuff to such a request. Take time to study all these documents and when you have got a clear idea of what a library is, and how it should be administered, consider closely the fitness of this or that library to this or that kind of community, or to these or those conditions under which you are to work. Do not think you have no time for this. If you have not, resign your trust to some one who has, and who has a correct appreciation of the old adage that those who help themselves are soonest helped by others.

Now, after this, if you find there are still points on which you are in doubt, and questions which your study has not given you solutions of, you may bother an old librarian. You can now write him understandingly. He will discover it at once, and will be propitiated. Ask him your questions concisely, and come to your points at once. Avoid all irrelevant twaddle. The librarian will not understand Brown's quandary any better from learning that Jones married Brown's wife's sister, or that Jones's endowment is invested in the Punkeyville Mining Company, which pays good dividends. There is no busier man than the librarian of a large library; for his work is never done, and he is one of those people who find the more expected of them the more they do. There is one thing more. You must not be surprised to find some diversity of views among experts. They arise from different experiences and because of the varying conditions under which a library may be administered. The processes of one library can rarely be transplanted to another without desirable modifications, arising from some change of conditions. This accounts for a great deal of variance in the opinions of librarians; but it by no means follows that each of two systems under proper conditions may not be equally good, when both are understood and an equal familiarity has been acquired with each. Choose that which you naturally take to; run it, and do not decide that the other is not perfectly satisfactory to him who chose that. Whichever you have chosen, study to improve it, and you will probably do so, in so far as it becomes fitted more closely to the individuality of yourself and your library.

Justin Winsor.

8. THE PRESIDENT'S ADDRESS [1877]

FELLOW MEMBERS OF THE ASSOCIATION: I think we meet with a confidence greater than last year, and with the feeling that a good work has been begun, and well begun. Our purpose then was undefined as compared with our present aims. We have fostered a fellow-feeling that has been helpful to each other, and convinced those not *of* us that they can well be *with* us, in spirit if not in brotherhood. We have vindicated the profession before the ordinary working-day world, and have brought those who by training can best affiliate with us to a better conception of the work a librarian can do. There are still corporators and civic councillors who conceive that the extent of a librarian's duties is to pass books over a counter, and who fancy there is no special training necessary to administer a library. They say of us, we have nothing to do and are fully equal to it. We must expect to find such people using authority vested in them on general principles to control purposes of which they have no conception; upon whom popular suffrage has bestowed the right to an opinion, but upon which nature has put a veto. Fortunately we shall find side by side with them at the same board those who have modesty and comprehension. It is well that we encounter foes as well as friends: the conflict will sharpen our wits; and I know of no profession whose followers have greater need to know men as they are, since a mission that is to ameliorate mankind must have its base of operations in a thorough knowledge of it.

I must say, however, that scholarly attainments do not always make a broad or circumspect mind. I have sometimes found as supreme ignorance of our work in the man of cultivation as in the man of affairs; with this difference, that you can impress the scholar with the scholarly elements, but it is by no means so easy to impress the mercantile perceptions with what our profession calls for of their equivalent. Scholarship affiliates with scholarship, whatever the diversity of range; but the money-makers are apt to think that a knowledge of books precludes of necessity the business habit, which is in fact an instinct often independent of training. The man of trade knows too well that competition has engrossed his time to the exclusion, in many instances, of almost all the culture of mind beyond the range of business methods; but this last is undeniably a culture. He reckons success by palpable figures on the credit side of accounts. He sees no objection to giving the manager of a corporation with a capital of a million a salary which, in his judgment, would adequately pay two or three librarians, each with an equal amount of invested capital in his charge, because it yields an income of mental rather than of creature comforts.

We must expect this judgment; but it is in our power gradually to change it. As long as the average standard of librarianships is low, we shall have estimates formed on such average. Until the profession itself can educate its successors in numbers equal to the growth of libraries, we must expect that men who have failed in the shop, in the school-room, and in the pulpit will successfully urge their claims upon easy-going committees. The body of librarians, I know, is not accountable for these accessions. Our members gravitate to us by the choice of others. But the remedy is nevertheless in ourselves. We must draw to us by personal acts of kindness, by the help which we can bestow, by the ill-directed labor which we can prevent, such a body of the rising generation whose gratitude will ally itself with appreciation, that we shall not in the end have to ask for consideration, because it will become a debt that good sense will pay.

There is no doubt that individual librarians here and there will accomplish this of themselves, for strength of purpose and a determination to succeed always grow in the face of obstacles; and, paradox as it may seem, energy is often expended only to be stored.

But the benefit to the individual should be the gain to the class; and as the profession gains the public is recompensed proportionately. Such is the object of this Association. Its members are to have the stimulus of common endeavor and a share in common advantages, and the public is to reap the harvest.

We need not seek far for the argument of our being. You remember the wit's five reasons for drinking—

Source: *Library Journal* 2 (1877): 5-7.

"Good wine, a friend, or being dry,
Or lest you should be by and by,
Or any other reason why."

It is never difficult to find excuses for the inevitable. To us they may be as satisfactory as our wit's comprehensiveness; but to others they will be superfluous unless we justify expectation.

The efforts with which we signalized our national Centennial have already begun to show results. We owe thanks to one of the departments of the general government that, in making a report on the libraries of the country, they made a cyclopaedia of our science that has given wider views of it, and opened new avenues to enterprise and munificence.

We owe it to the Secretary of this Association that we are banded together in a common cause, and that we have a journal for the interchange of views and for the advancement of library economy.

Finally, we owe it to our own example that a general spirit of emulation has risen in Europe, and that some of us, next month in London, can meet our brothers and impart and derive benefit and encouragement. I will not now enlarge upon our work during the past year; that is to be the subject of discussion to-day and to-morrow. We shall learn that methods of co-operation have been and can be applied to the work of libraries, as they are now applied in so many other directions. If affiliations of this sort work much good, they can likewise be abused, as recent events have shown. Banding together for mutual assistance and the common weal may, if we are unwary, present a ready organization to be used for unworthy purposes. We cannot be too cautious in order to prevent such abuse. It should not be overlooked that an association of librarians exists primarily for the benefit of the libraries, which they represent and which they hold in trust for the public, which supports them, directly or indirectly.

I think we may rest assured that the kind greeting which our new Association has received, and the interest with which its proceedings have been regarded, is an evidence that our work is thought by others to be in the right direction. Hope, you know, has been called the dream of those who are *awake*. I trust that the aspirations of a vitality of spirit are ours, and that we may find incentives in such dreams. Above all, let us conceive we have raised expectations that we are bound to fulfil. To that end we are here; to that end we shall separate; to that end let us live our lives.

9. THE PRESIDENT'S ADDRESS [1879]

LADIES AND GENTLEMEN:— Boston receives this association with quick sympathy. Three years ago we first gathered in Philadelphia, drawn to that city by the patriotic impulse then pervading the country. We were filled with a desire to signalize that Centennial year by an effort to put the library system of the country upon a basis of reciprocal endeavor, of united interests and of mutual understanding. While we recognized that libraries had always been powerful instruments of human enlightenment and of social progress, we could but feel that they were too often but types of stubborn conservatism. We came together at that time largely pervaded with the idea that a library was in essentials a missionary influence; that the power which belonged to it needed consolidating and directing, and that the first step in such work was for librarians to become acquainted with one another. To that end, and almost without any definite plan of coöperation, we first met; sealed our friendships; proclaimed our existence; measured our strength, and planned to set about our work. Exchange of sentiments among ourselves encouraged us. We put forth some phrases of our purposes, and we found them kindly responded to. A journal was founded for us. Our example was followed in Europe; and some of us, after our meeting in New York, went to London and participated in that international conference of which you have had the record. We were received kindly, even affectionately, and gratifying tributes were paid to us for the lead we had taken. Thus has the ball been set in motion. After another interval we have met again, this time in Boston,—and, perhaps, it is no arrogance for me to say it,—the recognized centre of our American library interests. In no other city, certainly, is there so great a public library, thrown open without stint to multitudes, and with amost entire immunity from loss. In no other community is there a larger or more powerful associated library, accomplishing so much to render our American bibliography a credit to us all. Here, too, we have the pioneer of our historical libraries. In no other neighborhood is there so large and productive a college library.

I am not unmindful of the claims of the great commercial metropolis, and I well know that through the richness of her private libraries, almost unsurpassed as a whole in any part of the world, that city has perhaps taken the lead from Boston in some of the most difficult fields of research. Her Lenox library, when it shall be thrown open to the public, will be found the richest mine of rare and recondite learning that the country possesses. With this exception, in a comparatively narrow sphere, New York must still be content, though not perhaps for long, to hold a secondary place for her *public* collections of books. In Philadelphia you know what new developments are going on.

We all look to Washington with a hopefulness that the long-delayed justice to the national library may in time arrive, when the treasures of that collection may be housed as they should be, and well filled shelves and a busy staff, adequate to its work, may make manifest the reason of its being, and disclose its inevitable leadership in the future, if legislators be but wise, and the example of its master-librarian be perennial. In the West we all know what has been accomplished, but rather as an earnest of what is to be.

If the outlook for our new library philosophy be an encouraging one, we must not fall into the error of over-estimating it. The old philosophy was not so bad. Great libraries have grown under it, and great librarians have stamped their individuality on their work in a way that our later coöperative methods, if perfected, may have a tendency, not altogether satisfactory, to repress. What we may do by organization, important as it will doubtless prove. must not lead us to forget that isolation of endeavor has its advantages also; and that the librarian who merges his action in a union of forces loses in some ways while he gains in others. Should we succeed in working out a symmetrical biblothecal science, there will be a tendency, in subscribing to its canons, to depart from that freedom of action which indicates character and accomplishes great ends. These results we must, then, aim to accomplish in spite of, rather than by virtue of, such science.

The time was ripe for this combining of ours. The changed conditions of our later social economy called for it. Schemes of coöperation, union of forces, barriers of distance overcome,

Source: *Library Journal* 4 (1879): 223-25.

all the new developments acting upon the daily life of communities, could not long be resisted. If libraries and their management are to fall into the line of progress—or change if you prefer so to call it—it is the part of wisdom to establish that control which gives power to intelligence, and maintain the circumspection that avoids pitfalls. I shall leave the Secretary in his report to trace the work in the new direction that the last year has added to its forerunners; and you will pardon me if, in the few remaining words I have to offer, I point out rather what, with all our enthusiasm, we may fail to do and what we may be inclined to overdo.

We claim—and it is not for me to gainsay it—that the libraries of the country are a great engine in our hands. It may be a commonplace of rhetoric to say that books, singly or in battalions, awaking responsive sensibilities in every kind of nature, at times marshalled, as it were, into aggressive ranks and assaulting strongholds of beliefs, are a power that may be both relied on and feared. A single library, adroitly managed, throws out its forces into a community with something of the discipline of an invading army, with its foraging parties, with its engineers to bridge streams and its pioneers to break the way. The generalship that directs all this may be humane, sacrificing some good in one direction for much gain in another; or demoralization may take the place of constancy, and what should be our defenders may become our covert enemies. I will not discuss now—what you will have ample witnesses to in one of the sessions of another day—the power for good or evil of public libraries among the great masses of the people. It is a pet phrase with us, that the public library is the people's university; and it is a mooted question among economists and educators, whether it is wise for the people to instruct themselves out of the common purse much beyond the elementary stage. That it will be attempted, so far as libraries go, seems to be inevitable. But if there is evil to come of this widened scheme of education, in libraries at least, the danger is not in the use upon the higher, but upon the lower, plane of intelligence. There will always be a tendency to score large figures of circulation, and, in so far as it signifies sympathy with the people in the management of a library, it is commendable. But the true librarian will value this power of increment of use only as a force to be directed. He understands that he holds a brake upon it, working through the increase or diminution of popular prose fiction. He is not wise who applies the brake severely, nor yet he who lets it wholly off. The love of fiction, so ineradicable,—let us remember *that*,—is in a large measure the very power that renders a library a beneficence at all. Its very existence enables the librarian to work deep at the centre and to push wide through all the dark purlieus of city life. But it is at the same time a dangerous power, fruitful of evil, no doubt, under some circumstances—as every ordinary good is—but ductile under restraint, and capable of confinement in channels that lead to happiness.

We may disagree about the best ways of control, but let us not forget that abstinence in the readers of fiction, as in all else, loses all the moral beauty of temperance, and that all of life is not instruction, and that pastime is often the best nurse of virtue and promoter of health. There is a conservation of energy in saving the waste that comes of ten doing what one can do as well, and it augments power; but it may not be all gain. The photograph is inexorably common. The pencil sketch is vitalized with a spiritual life that only the human agency can give. It is futile to question their comparative value: each has its importance. If we are going to act widely, and render the *large* use of *many* books *inexpensive*, we must take our measure in the same inexorably common way; but we shall still have room enough for that individually alert, cunning and impulsive librarian, who gathers his books about him as his family, and who sends them out each almost in his own likeness. The time is not yet come for the racy, self-centred librarian to die. Coöperation will not kill him, fortunately.

But a few months ago word came to us of the loss of such a librarian, out of harness, to be sure, but to the last his was an influence shaping the character of many a follower. The world has perhaps never seen a greater librarian than Panizzi. He had to overcome stolid content, the hardest of tasks. He had to vivify virtues that were dormant, like the vital principle of the grain in mummies. But he did more. He made the respectable *well-enoughs* understand that there was a work to do; and THEY did it. While their national exchequer was shuddering at the cost of additional Bloomsbury lands, for their great museum library, he made the little sketch that dropped that magnificent dome from the skies, right amidst the pile, and showed how power evolves from its own centre! Upon this very table he sketched that historic plan; and this seat, so long the throne of ANTONIO PANIZZI, becomes to-day the *chair* of this transatlantic assemblage of librarians.

10. THE PRESIDENT'S ADDRESS [1881]

LADIES AND GENTLEMEN:—We are to be congratulated on coming together in Washington; and we come here opportunely. We are glad to draw nearer at last to the National Bureau of Education, remembering how it signalized the centennial year for us by the publication of that encyclopaedic report about the institutions we represent.

We are glad to find ourselves face to face with that ardent friend of bibliography, the librarian of the Surgeon-General's office, who has shown, not only us, but the experts of the older world, how the highest results of that science can be reached by a rare intelligence and a comprehensive energy.

We are proud to be, as it were, the guests of the Librarian of Congress. We come in full recognition of a merit that well befits his official dominance among us. We hope the cheer he gives us only foreruns the pleasure which is due to him, when he shall see the treasures of a national library spread in all their amplitude through a spacious depository, worthy of a great nation and worthy of him.

Before our sessions are over we shall have opporutnity to inspect the plans which have been proposed for this great national library. Whatever the disposition to make it every way worthy of our needs and worthy of our resources, there must still be, in the construction of it, errors to be escaped as well as merits to be embodied. The problem, it must be confessed, is not an easy one. It will not solve itself, like some political ones. This is to be confronted successfully only by a thorough understanding of the possibilities of the future. The mechanical devices for annihilating time and space present, in these days, the question of library construction in a changed light.

The new significance of libraries as the necessity of the many, as well as the essential home, as it may be, of the few, widens the field of observation, and makes the institution both a monument and an empire. The library has grown to have eminently a practical bearing upon our general education and upon our training as citizens. I think of it sometimes as a derrick, lifting the inert masses and swinging them round to the sure foundations upon which the national character shall rise. You who have had daily dealings with the work of libraries know this to be something more than a piece of rhetoric. We may discuss the many recurring mooted points in our economy,— the fiction question, or any other,—assuming that we tread upon a vantage ground; we may peer through vistas of our own making, and think we see the universe; we may be uncircumspect; we may go on floundering, without lead or compass, and while we are doing it the library has grown; men and women have come up to it, and taken something better than homilies. The beneficence of the world of books has been spread about, and the wheat has choked the tares.

I would not be blinded to the fact that mischief, and enough of it, may lurk in books. It will do its work in spite of us; but, if we would keep it at its minimum, we do not wisely make this mischief prominent. Our emphasis should be upon the wholesome, and upon that which healthfully stimulates. I would put more trust in one such educational catalogue—as the term is—like that, for instance, of the Brooklyn Library,—an admirable boon to all of us,—than in scores of narrow visionaries, who do not know that it is the motes in their own eyes which become the blotches on the playful page. I must decidedly differ from those who, for the common good, take to the method of magnifying an evil the better to eradicate it. I believe that under cultivation the weeds succumb.

Source: *Library Journal* 6 (1881): 63-64.

11. ANNUAL ADDRESS [1882]

LADIES AND GENTLEMEN OF THE ASSOCIATION:—We pay to-day our first visit as an Association to the Valley of the Mississippi. Since our initial meeting in 1876 the principal sea-board cities have welcomed us. We have now moved somewhere near the centre of our American population, and I cannot but hope it augurs an increased library development in the Western, or, I should rather say, in the middle regions, of our country. It is, I am afraid, true, that with all its wealth of books, for the student and the people, the seaboard seems still to develop more conspicuously. Within a half year we have seen—you will allow me to say it—a native of Massachusetts lay the foundation in a Southern State of a great popular library to supplement the scholarly collection given to it by another native of that same State; and these two merchants—never so much princes as when patrons of learning and instruction—have caused the city of Baltimore long to remember the names of Peabody and Pratt. It is to be hoped that the time is not far distant when Chicago will associate with the name of Newberry an active work equally shining and equally or even more munificent in its inception. And what shall be the name which Cincinnati is to honor? Its excellent free library, nobly sustained by the people themselves,—always, it must be confessed, the best resource for such an institution,—could, I doubt not, to the advantage of learning, lend its organization to the creation of some special department should such become opportunely the foster-child of any of its liberal citizens. For while it is true that the generalizing of libraries best fits them for the work of popular instruction, it is equally certain that conspicuous strength in one direction gives a collection rank in the community of libraries; and rank of this sort is not a mere vain-glorious pretension,—it means substantial scholarship, the pushing of the bounds of knowledge, and upon this follows fellowship with the great collections and repute among scholars, wherever they are. It makes the library, which has such strength, the Mecca of devotees. It makes it friends wherever there is learning. It gives it a fame that tells for its advantage in many ways. I cannot too strenuously impress upon all whose lot it is to control the development of libraries, the great desirability of giving a part of their energies in making their libraries noteworthy in some way. Of course it is only the large libraries that can hope to take one of the great departments of knowledge and make it an exemplar; but every library can find some minor topic of local interests, like the history of its neighborhood, like the growth of some controlling thought or power which sprung from a brain nurtured in its clustering homes. I must confess I take pleasure in looking at that alcove in the little library of the town of Concord, in Massachusetts, which contains the works and biographies of its own towns-people. It is most true that it is not given to every village to have its Emerson, its Hawthorne, and its Thoreau. But there is no village but sooner or later develops some index-mind, which creates, it may be, a calling, invents a machine, or writes a book, which stands for something in the history of the world.

It may be left for the library of Harvard College to form a matchless collection of folk-lore; for that of Cornell to honor the name of Petrarch; for the Public Library of Boston to be unsurpassed in this country, at least, in the wealth of Shakespearian literature; for the Lenox Library to amass the most wonderful gathering of bibliographical nuggets, indeed, in various directions; for the Library of Congress, as it ought, to widen into all the recesses of American history; but the town that gave birth, say, to Elias Howe, can well gather the literature of the sewing-machine, and no one can do it with more grace.

In the bibliographical work of our libraries the year since we met has been signalized, not to speak of minor work, by the completion of Mr. Cutter's admirable Catalogue of the Boston Athenaeum, and by progress in the great authors' Catalogue of the Library of Congress, and in the general Catalogue of the Peabody Institute at Baltimore.

And I must not fail to mention the work of printing, now well begun and rapidly going on, of the "Index to Periodical Literature," of which we must learn later from Mr. Poole, and of the speed of the Cambridge presses, which are likely to gratify our eyes with a sight of it before the year is over.

Source: *Library Journal* 7 (1882): 123-24.

Nor can we but be gratified with the notes of progress in Europe. The greater of our libraries are welcoming with warmth the gradual putting of the enormous Catalogue of the British Museum Library into print. The Catalogue of the Advocate's Library at Edinburgh is now complete. On the Continent some of that recognition of our suggestions in cataloguing, which have been so kindly noted in England, are beginning to have their effect. Dr. Petzholdt, who has so laboriously chronicled what we do in his Anzeiger, has never quite understood how we make a business of library management. He has recently, however, praised a new German catalogue, for adopting the American dictionary system, which, in his own words, "presents to the user the titles in the way easiest to find." The Germans have just begun to wonder at the American practice of analyzing the contents of books, and of making subject-references to parts of works; but to wonder succeeds use in due time. In Italy it is somewhat amusing to find a Roman librarian announce and describe our well-known fashion of cataloguing as his own invention, which is the best unintentional compliment yet paid to the American so-called dictionary rules, of which Mr. Cutter has given us the standard code.

But with all this gratulation let us not forget that an honored and veteran chief among us has passed from his earthly labors. I regret that brief must be the tribute which, in passing, I pay to the estimable personal qualities, the untiring devotion, the wise mind, and the well-balanced learning of Samuel Foster Haven, the late Librarian of the American Antiquarian Society. His name is fitly commemorated here, in company with those eminent British librarians whose deaths were not long since announced. In the urbane Henry O. Coxe, the Bodleian lost a loving and lovable fellow of our craft. In John Winter Jones, the British Museum lost one, though not to the last in its service, who had, by long and varied labors, united his name with the history of that great institution. They have all gone over to that majority to which librarians as well as all other laborers for human development must accede. May we emulate their example!

12. ADDRESS OF THE PRESIDENT [1883]

Our sixth annual meeting finds us for the first time on the frontiers of our country, whence we can easily extend a hand of welcome to our neighbors of the Dominion. We are glad to find that later in the session some of our Canadian brothers will accept it. However tariffs and fealty may separate us, there is nothing alien in libraries; and why may not *American*, in a bibliothecal sense at least, include the whole brotherhood of the New World? We need attrition. Nothing has so much improved the standard of library management as this very commingling of librarians every year. Those who are familiar with the history of libraries in this country know that the advance in all that makes our work a system, and gives our calling an influence, has been vastly greater since librarians have acquired a neighborly habit.

The inquiry is sometimes made, "What do you find to do and say at these meetings of librarians? Don't you get talked out?"–"Yes," we reply, "but we can go home and recuperate for another bout; and we take home with us, too, a kindly interest in one another; a tincture of other ideas than our own, wider sympathies, broader views, and deeper meanings than are deducible from the experiences of our little autonomies. Such are the uses, such the fruits of these annual gatherings."

As I look over the topics of reports and papers in the programme before us, and recall the discussions which these topics have elicited at previous meetings, I am sensible of the varied points of view which our isolation from one another at home and the circle of our separate experiences have given us. It is an argument in itself for an occasional segregation. Nor must we expect that this social and mental contact is going to unify all our ways. It would be a pity if it did. Our national motto touches us as deeply as librarians as it does as patriots, for we are one in our diversities,–none the less united because each finds his own way the best. The ideal rule or system does not imply bondage to an idea. As long as mental action is various and experience is different, that system is best which we best assimilate. Time and locality, and more particularly that element which it is the fashion to term our personal equation, establish variety in our ideals. The folly of dogmatism is one that these meetings make us the better to understand.

Custom has defined the scope of your president's address to be the recognition of what is important in the shaping of the general library interests of the year gone by. First in that respect is the established fact of your coöperative labor brought to a definite result. It was a favorite thought of the elder Agassiz that what our civilization most needed was a reserve of money, to be applied with wise discrimination to paying the cost of publication of contributions to knowledge which could not be expected to pay for themselves. The sum of human knowledge is but as the transit of a minor planet across the illimitable disk of light; no one knows that better than a librarian; and, with the true scientific instinct, Agassiz recognized the duty of preserving, as well as studying, the knowledge which does not stand for money in the world's traffic. From the inability of the investigators to put in the costly shape of type the result of their observations, Agassiz reckoned that the loss to mankind was incalculable; and in the first instance as pure science, or what can be known, and secondly as applied science, or what embellishes or elevates our living,–a loss which is incalculable in not only not preserving what has absolutely been found, but which also diminishes effort because of the absence of that incentive which makes us work the better under the promise of a permanent record.

At our very first meeting in Philadelphia we were possessed of a similar thought. We had all felt the want which Mr. Poole thirty years ago had shown could be supplied by labor. Since that time the burden–I use the word advisedly–of periodical literature in a library had become well-nigh intolerable, as all wastes without finger-posts are. Years before, I had urged on the secretary of the Smithsonian Institution the undertaking of this work as preeminently one of the diffusion of knowledge. I got excuses of preoccupation. I had suggested to the librarian of Congress to take the lead in some movement; but he was always overburdened, as I was in my own definite province.

Source: *Library Journal* 8 (1883): 163-65.

But at Philadelphia the work was done, and community of labor established the fund that Agassiz had dreamed of.

Its first fruits is the great index, which properly associates with it the name of our brother of Chicago; and of the value of that first fruit I need not tell you. (Applause.) Important as it is, the principle which it has made manifest is more important still,—namely, that it is within our power as a body of librarians to create, in our combined efforts, just such a fund as Agassiz longed for. Further consideration of other schemes of a like import are, I perceive, set down for us on the programme.

We must still regret the failure of Congress to cancel the debt which it owes to good scholarship and the largest learning. The national library is still without adequate housing, and the prospect of Congressional attention is not encouraging. What Congress fails to do in its sphere, individuals and municipalities are not backward in accomplishing elsewhere. The Pratt library in Baltimore approaches completion; and a new building for the public library of Boston is assured by ample appropriations. These are conspicuous examples of the needs of our great municipal libraries being handsomely met. Chicago, too, I believe, is in a commotion that we may hope "presages some joyful news at hand."

The new building of Columbia College, and of the library of the University of Michigan, almost ready for its dedication, and the planning of a new building to be erected by private munificence, fitly to hold the library of the University of Vermont, with its recent accession of the collection of the late George P. Marsh,—that accomplished scholar in more than one department,—are instances of the watchful interest bestowed upon what is more and more recognized as the central force of our college life, the college library.

There is no phase of our recent library management more striking and more suggestive than the growth of what may be called a practical bibliography. This science, long the sign of recondite scholarship, is shown to be adaptable to the wants of the less erudite. It is becoming more and more recognized as an indispensable help in every department of intellectual activity. There are many reasons for this change. It arises in part from a clearing of the perception that it is a waste of time for one to attempt to tread a subject by the first way which opens, when a full survey of the literature of it will point him out the better avenue. The student is otherwise in much the same position with the inventor who attempts the combination of mechanical movements to a given end, before he has examined the records of the patent office. The past year has seen some admirable helps in this respect in the little manuals which Mr. Leypoldt has published, and which indicate effectively the devoted labors of our brothers, Green, of Worcester, and Foster, of Providence.

Men now living may remember the beginning of what may be called the missionary career of libraries. It may be said to have begun in this country in the foundation of social, apprentices', and mercantile libraries. There was indeed a start as long ago as Benjamin Franklin founded the Philadelphia library, still doing its good work to-day; but nothing like general interest was taken in the movement till the second quarter of the present century.

Thereupon followed, in due time, what we now understand by the free library system, which, without any concert of action, also began in England about the same time; but with us it moved more rapidly, and even here it is confined for the most part to narrow geographical limits.

At about even date with this development in its earlier stages, a question of library purpose was brought to an issue in New York. Mr. Astor had left what was, in those days, a very large endowment for a library. He had not himself been disposed to that form of munificence, and had rather preferred to signify his regard for his adopted country in a huge monument to Washington; but Dr. Cogswell, who was his adviser, prevailed upon him to endow a library. The question to be decided was, whether that library should assist in the education of the people directly or indirectly, and this was a proposition on the decision of which there was no doubt in Dr. Cogswell's mind. He held some views regarding the public relations of libraries which were proper, and some which time has not justified. He argued that for the diffusion of knowledge the initiative might well be left to the people, who knew how to take care of themselves. In that he was right. He also expressed his confidence that a free public library could not be maintained and protected in a large city. In this he was wrong; as the experiment tried in Boston and elsewhere has shown. With such views there was of course but one scheme for a library which he could accept, and so he made his argument thus: "There is no way so effectual to diffuse knowledge through a community as by elevating the standard and creating the greatest possible number of highly educated men. They become (he says) the living teachers, diffusing and disseminating knowledge much more widely and judiciously than is ever done by books."

One hardly wishes to quarrel with such a conclusion, for, in some respects, it is a prudent one; but in other respects it is a survival of a feeling which has its tap-root in the cloudy past.

The truth is, no exclusive or vicarious system of library nourishment is sufficient. The student certainly needs the incitement of the personal contact of the teacher. The librarian in his office sees the effect he can have upon those who seek his counsel. Mr. Poole, in his occasional and friendly talks to his constituents at Chicago, and the same sort of work which has been done at the public library at Melbourne for some years, and which, under many different phases, is the mission of many other librarians, is certainly giving a new power to librarianship. But for all this the reader needs the personal contact of the books themselves quite as much. The two schemes are fitly reciprocal, as we are every day showing at Cambridge, and are by no means alone in doing so.

The issue which Dr. Cogswell sought to make (and as he seemed to think in the interests of scholarship) was an Old-World issue, which had always, among old civilization, been decided one way.

The argument was simply an excuse—the traditionary excuse—of a habit which had been accustomed to regard libraries simply as book-piles whence writers and scholars could replenish their intellectual fires, and not as agencies for the making of books useful to the many. The idea of the missionary character of a library has a certain repulsiveness in the minds of those who have had charge of the great libraries of Europe up to a very recent period, for the break of a dawn has hardly yet mellowed into a universal light. In this venerable estimate libraries are institutions to be sought by those who have a definite search, and they do not stand, as they ought, for allurements and invitations. It is something that American librarians may well take a pride in, that they have signalized themselves as leaders in this new and healthy cause.

13. FIRST REPORT (1878) OF JUSTIN WINSOR, LIBRARIAN OF HARVARD UNIVERSITY

TO THE PRESIDENT OF THE UNIVERSITY:—

SIR,—I make what is properly my first report,—a brief memorandum furnished last year having been preliminary in character. A year's service has established my knowledge of the Library and of its sphere of usefulness. In making what I held to be improvements in the administration of the Library, I have not acted without due deliberation; and the changes made have been kindly accepted by the staff, and by those whose servants we are. I have at all times aimed to enlarge the Library's importance in the eyes of our academic community. I wish to see it become, not merely in complimentary phrase, the centre of the University system, but, in actual working, indispensable and attractive to all. The new methods of teaching in the University must necessarily render the Library more and more important among the various agencies of instruction. I think that in the higher education the methods which science so successfully adopts must in the future be more closely applied to instruction in arts. The controlling influence of text-books in higher methods is, I judge, waning, and happily so. They have their usefulness; but it is one subsidiary to work in a broader field.

American libraries are growing far beyond the most sanguine expectations. When Gore Hall was erected, forty years ago, it was considered large enough for the accumulations of the rest of the century; but in twenty years there were calls for more space, and the least confident of us hardly expect that the century will go out without showing a capacity of shelves four or five times what was then contemplated filled to repletion. But the mere accumulation of books is not in itself sufficient: a great library should be a workshop as well as a repository. It should teach the methods of thorough research, and cultivate in readers the habit of seeking the original sources of learning.

The usefulness of any library depends largely on the character of its catalogue. I found a catalogue system in use here, devised by Professor Abbot, when he was an officer of the Library. It was a composite of two well-defined plans.

The first is the so-called dictionary system,—such as is exemplified, with differences, in the catalogues of the Boston Athenaeum and of the Boston Public Library,—in which one alphabet is employed for author and subject entries mingled together. The simplicity of this method is its great advantage. From such a single alphabetical index, provided with abundant cross-references between synonymous titles and between general and specific headings, even an unpractised person can obtain a clue to the book he is seeking. But with these aids the single alphabet becomes cumbersome under countries and large municipalities and widely ramifying associations, when these are considered to be the authors of their publications, and also when groups of topics having geographical relations are placed under the names of countries, instead of being classed under the respective divisions of knowledge. The growth of libraries may compel some changes in the scheme as devised by the late Professor Jewett, and enforce further transfers of such entries to topical heads. This system also ordinarily omits groupings of kinds of literature, as classed by their forms, like poetry, drama, &c.; though lists of this sort can readily be made by way of supplements to the main catalogue, and are undoubtedly useful in popular libraries. Even in higher libraries, certain form-lists, when the extent of the literature embraced does not carry them to too great extent, become desirable, as with periodicals, serials, and publications of learned societies; and there is nothing in the fundamental arrangement of a dictionary catalogue to preclude these additions. With such helps, that form of catalogue is, in my judgment, best

Source: *First Report (1878) of Justin Winsor, Librarian of Harvard University*. Cambridge, MA; 1878.

calculated to secure the greatest general use of a library, and to economize the time of the larger number of people. It is also rapidly becoming the system most in vogue.

The second system is the classified gathering of titles, according to some scheme of dividing all knowledge into sections and divisions which stand in some intelligible relation to each other, through absolute or supposed affinity. While all dictionary catalogues closely resemble each other, classified catalogues vary widely; and, as a general rule, no one can use a classified catalogue until he becomes familiar with it, and even those most accustomed to it are not infrequently at a loss, inasmuch as such relations as the classifications are based upon are not at all times viewed in the same light by the same person. With the inevitable changes in the accepted relations between different branches of knowledge, particularly in natural science, a classified catalogue is necessarily liable to become antiquated. Such a catalogue may, therefore, be rather an obstacle than an aid to the casual or infrequent user of a general library; and the bulk of those who resort to libraries are rather of this sort. For the adept, the classified system has undeniable advantages; and for the library of a union of scientists or other specialists, constantly invoking the aid of the catalogue, no other system is as good.

In the catalogue of this Library it was Professor Abbot's aim to preserve, in the main, the chief advantage, and to avoid the chief disadvantage, of each of the two systems. A prominent feature of his scheme was also the division of books not only with reference to subjects, but to form of literature, as Ballads, Drama, Fiction, Poetry, &c. In his plan, the arrangement of classes or subjects is throughout alphabetical, not scientific; but it differs from the simple dictionary system in this, that the natural subdivisions of many subjects, instead of being scattered through the general alphabet in the order of their names, appear in a secondary alphabetical series under the general head. If these subdivisions are comprehensive, the names of the particular topics which they embrace form another alphabetical series under them. No acquaintance with any scientific system of classification is needed in order to use the catalogue, the arrangement being everywhere alphabetical; but the student of any branch of knowledge must know its subdivisions, and then he has the advantage of finding the general treatises and the specific monographs all brought together. Under CHEMISTRY, for example, after the general works, the monographs on particular topics appear in one alphabetical series in the order of their names, as in a Dictionary of Chemistry; so under ZOÖLOGY–*Insects*, all the monographs relating to insects appear in one alphabetical series in the order of the names of their subjects. In the simple dictionary catalogue, all these would be scattered through the general alphabet. To many users of the catalogue, these alphabets within alphabets have an appearance of complication; and without cross-references, which have hitherto been very imperfectly supplied in the catalogue, the seeker will not always know under what general head in the alphabet some specific subject is to be looked for. I find that even the officers of the Library cannot always use the catalogue with facility, while many of those who frequent the Library are more or less perplexed by it. It must be admitted, however, that when its plan is understood and well fixed in the memory, it offers advantages for scientific or scholarly research to be derived only with much greater labor from the common dictionary catalogue.

Dr. Abbot's connection with the Library, as officer, ceased before he had perfected the details of his system. The scheme developed and grew upon his hands, and the work of the numerous assistants employed from time to time upon it was somewhat differently directed in the earlier and in recent years. Hence there are inconsistencies in the catalogue,—and inconsistencies are always stumbling-blocks in index-searching,—which, however, can in time be rectified. In a catalogue which does not, like a dictionary catalogue, carry its own key, finger-posts or guides, to mark the changes from groups to sections and branches, are very essential. But in Dr. Abbot's catalogue such supplemental aids, although originally intended and proposed as parts of the system, had been only to a small extent actually provided.

The problem presented to me by the state of this catalogue was a difficult one. My experience taught me that the catalogue as it was could not afford all the help which a catalogue should, in increasing the usefulness of a library like this. The alternatives were, either to remodel the catalogue, or to throw some permanent light on its arrangement. The first plan involved a reassortment of a million of cards, more or less; the interruption of the use of the catalogue in some measure, great at times, and always annoying, even if small; the disturbance of the habits of those who had become accustomed to its use, as a whole or in some of its parts; and the disappointment of those who appreciated its peculiar merits, and who would not willingly see it cast aside, until the details of the system as originally designed had all been carried out.

The second plan called for brief, printed explanations, conspicuous labelling and indexing of the drawers on their exterior, and the marking of the ramifications of the arrangement by guide-boards; this to be followed by printing a pamphlet to show the system by tabulation, with an index of it by subject-headings in one alphabetical list. The obstacles in carrying out the plan of remodeling were so great, that it seemed wiser to give the catalogue the advantage of all the elucidation just described; and to that end much of the work indicated has already been done, although the pamphlet still awaits the completion of the earlier labor. To prevent loss and misplacement of cards, from which the catalogue had suffered, a wire has been run through a perforation in the lower part of the cards, which serves also to support them so that the blocks for support formerly used with loss of space can be dispensed with.

I have confidence that the catalogue—so admirable in some of its features—can be made a valuable coadjutor in the important work of improving methods of study.

The Bulletin, or quarterly list of accessions, has been changed, to cover not only the additions to the College Library, but also those made to the departmental libraries. The specialists of the departments and the users of the central collection gain in this way knowledge of the resources of the whole University; and the record further serves to define and make known the respective limits of purchases in the several libraries.

In several respects, more intimate relations between the different libraries belonging to the University would be advantageous to all parties. Some method of concerted action in the purchase of books seems necessary, if the University's resources for that purpose are to be prudently used. As the purchases made for the Museum of Comparative Zoölogy cover to an appreciable degree the range of the purchases for the College Library, it seemed important that a record of the Museum's orders should be preserved at the College Library; and this has been done, with manifest advantage. To some extent, cataloguing is already done at the College Library for the Observatory Library, upon such books as chance to come under cover to Gore Hall. These are, I trust, but the beginnings of a perfected system of partially united administration.

Some change has also been made in the method of printing the Bulletin. Titles are sent to the printer as they accumulate, instead of at the expiration of the quarter. Proofs are returned in galleys; and these proofs are posted, as lists of the freshest accessions, not only here, but at the departmental libraries, the marks against the titles signifying in which library the books may be found. The proofs are also cut into strips by titles, and the printed titles thus obtained are pasted, in alphabetical order, into a large blank-book. This book has now become the most convenient key for all books added within the last two years, provided the name of the author is known, for it is much easier to consult than the cards in the drawers. At the expiration of the quarter, the titles are all in type in these successive galleys; so that the redistribution of the titles into one alphabet, and then the press-work, are the only impediments to a prompt issue of the Bulletin,—a delay rarely carried beyond a fortnight.

There needed, as I thought, to be added to the authors' list of the Bulletin something analogous to the subject part of the card catalogue; and with this view a Supplement was planned, the purpose of which was to give bibliographical information regarding current accessions and topics of interest. I hoped, also, that the officers of instruction would use it as a means of printing, in permanent form, the advice they give their classes concerning authorities and collateral reading in their respective subjects; and that they would work out the bibliography of subjects within the range of their instruction. I wished, also, by timely announcements of the progress of the Library, to supply data of interest to other libraries and to the friends of the University. In this work I needed the sympathy and co-operation of the professors and other instructors; and this support has been abundantly given me. I soon found that the work done was too elaborate and excellent to be left scattered through successive numbers of a periodical, which, by its nature, served rather a temporary than a permanent purpose. As the pages were stereotyped for the printer's convenience, it was an easy matter to arrange that the plates should serve for issuing these bibliographical contributions as monographs, on their completion as serials. I think that the publication made in this way will be welcomed beyond the limits of the University. The change in the character of the Bulletin has created a demand for it, elsewhere in this country and in Europe, among other libraries, and with teachers and specialists, whose wants were met by particular articles, so that it has become necessary to increase the edition largely. The demand is still rapidly growing.

In connection with this bulletin work may be considered two other publications, the second of which has been carried on by the contributions and pecuniary assistance of other libraries in Boston. The first is the printing—now in progress—of Mr. Samuel H. Scudder's Catalogue of Scientific Serials, which embraces all periodicals and serial publications of learned societies in the field of pure science the world over, whether existent or defunct,—a list never before attempted with equal fulness. Its publication was conditioned upon the obtaining of subscriptions sufficient to cover the cost; these have been secured. A small surplus of copies will inure to the Library's advantage by way of exchange for other publications. There seems every reason why the Library should undertake, under like conditions of security, the publication of other bibliographical works, which will be useful to scholars, and, at the same time, serve to enhance the usefulness of the Library.

The other publication is less extensive,—a list of all periodicals and serials now currently received by the several libraries of the University and by the principal libraries of Boston, with the designation of such libraries against each title, so far as the separate serials are taken at these libraries. It will serve as a guide to all users of this kind of literature, and will be the means of better providing against the taking in of a larger number of copies among the libraries of these adjoining communities than the demand for them warrants. In this connection, let me add that I see no good reason why, in regard to books not in common demand, there cannot be greater reciprocity of use among these neighboring libraries. With an express at our service, I have found no unwillingness in my *confrères* of other institutions to engage in some interchanging of this sort during the past year, and have even extended the service to remoter libraries. I try never to forget that the prime purpose of a book is to be much read; though it is equally true that we are under obligations to posterity to preserve books whose loss might be irreparable, and that the passing generation cannot always decide correctly which books are the most precious.

This community of use has already been established in some degree between this central collection and those of the departments.

I consider nothing of more importance than the provision of large classes of books to which unrestricted access can be had. At present, the inspection of the shelves is permitted to the officers of the University alone. The students can handle—this absolute contact with books is, in my judgment, humanizing—the newer books, as they stand on certain shelves, for a while after their accession; and alcoves, with tables, are also given to an ever-changing collection of books, designated by the several professors as collateral reading for their classes. These latter books, now conspicuously labelled with a different color for each professor, are retained from circulation, except at hours when the Library is not open. I mention later the extent of this limited home-use of these books.

When the rearrangement of the Library is completed, so far as the sections destined for the new book-room are concerned, and the original Gore Hall can be remodelled, I hope to see a wider latitude than this. I have sketched a plan for the reshelving of the gallery and the walls of the central area,—then to become the main reading-hall,—with a general disposition which is the counterpart of the new stack, and with a single unit of shelving space, as security that the least possible confusion shall ensue upon any further extensions of that part of the building. Electric lights in the roof would, I think, provide for the lighting of this reading-hall at night, with the least possible danger from fire; in which event, I hope to see the hall open in the evening. With processes of instruction which make success more and more dependent upon the free use of the Library by students, it seems to me a misfortune that the Library hours are limited to daylight during the short winter days, when most of the work is done. I can conceive that moral as well as intellectual good should come from the more liberal plan. I was much interested last year at Oxford to see the good use to which the old Radcliffe building had been put, by making it an evening annex to the Bodleian.

With this arrangement of the hall, I had reserved in my mind the series of lower alcoves— removing the present central cases and substituting tables—to contain a succession of collections of the most useful books in all departments of knowledge, each alcove being given to a particular branch, of which the students could have unfettered enjoyment. I think there can be no difficulty about sufficient oversight; and I have confidence that it will stimulate inquiry, and give new resources to the instructors. I would not have these collections permanent, but shifting from year to year. Ten and even twenty thousand volumes can thus, I judge, be most profitably disposed.

In the adjacent room,—formerly the entrance-hall of the original building,—the space has already been divided into three ample stalls, with conveniences of shelves and table, for the use of scholars who may come to the Library for protracted investigations, or of the professors seeking more quiet than can be found in the public hall.

The new shelf-lists of the Library, perpared as rapidly as the new classification goes on, will be a most useful topical key to its resources. Indeed, the careful reassortment of the books now going on will in more ways than one be of assistance to all concerned with the Library, whether as officers or users.

I should be glad to see more constant use made of the Library by the whole body of instructors. The services of the staff are freely rendered to them. The printed bulletins are promptly despatched to them; and, in cases where closer watch of additions is of advantage, they can have the galley-strips also. I have taken pleasure in sending them immediate notice of the arrival of new invoices, that they may be the first to inspect the books. I shall be glad, as far as possible, to provide facilities for demonstrating methods of research for the higher classes.

On a suggestion received from Mr. William Cook, Instructor in German, I introduced during the winter a slight device, which has since been adopted in other libraries. Slips of paper, headed *Notes and Queries*, followed by a few words of direction, were prepared, and a row of hooks was arranged in a conspicuous place to hold them. A slip having been filled out with a question, and hung up, anybody who possesses the information wanted answers the question on the same slip, or refers the inquirer to the sources of information. The device has answered a good purpose, and I am glad to see that no unworthy advantage has been taken of it to ask silly or trivial questions.

Beyond the regular attendants upon the advanced instruction of the University, there is a considerable body of literary and scientific workers in Cambridge or its neighborhood, and, with the increase in the advantages of such a residence, the number is likely to increase. I have welcomed such to the Library, with pleasure; and, in cases where it seemed apparent that the cause of true learning would be advanced, their applications for the privilege of borrowing books have been forwarded to the Corporation, and upon approval granted. I know no cause to regret the courtesy which that board has shown in such cases.

It has occurred to me that each graduating class could very gracefully leave some memorial of their college years in Cambridge, by becoming, as a body, the patron of some department, or of a subject in some department, of the Library. The literature of the currency question as a topic rife in men's minds to-day, the history and antiquities of Cyprus, the electric light, are subjects which a class, leaving this year, for instance, might well make permanent provision for in the Library, as interesting topics in their year of graduation. A class would thus link its name permanently with the history of the Library in some special branch of knowledge.

The figures of the accessions of late years (given below), which I have derived since 1870 from Mr. Sibley's careful reports, represent the additions, with the duplicates thrown out; but a system of crediting accessions when received to the general account, and debiting them when disposed of, is better for our purpose, and in this way the figures for the present year are made out. Practically, however, Mr. Sibley's figures may stand, since the array of duplicates which he had thrown out were all disposed of in the autumn of 1876, and the proceeds have been bestowed upon new books. The accumulation of duplicates since that date is small, and it has been kept down by exchanges with other libraries, with which running accounts have been opened. The three principal libraries of this vicinity can well reciprocate in this matter, and thus obtain a considerable relief from the burden that useless duplicates entail. I hope, in the future, to send to the several libraries of the departments whatever of our duplicates would there be useful.

The accumulation of pamphlets in the Library is now large and valuable. I doubt if it is surpassed in value by any other in the country. My predecessor entertained a fit sense of the undeniable importance of them; and, as he worked for many years with insignificant means for the purchase of books, labor bestowed upon this department gave the only appreciable evidence of increase. With his proclivities for the study of American history, he selected the most valuable pamphlets upon that subject, and put them in sufficient binding for the shelves. They served to fill out the proportions of that department with a completeness no other section of the Library can boast; and they also for several years, very properly, swelled the count of volumes in his reports.

The constant use which is made of the pamphlet files, and the significance of their titles in the catalogue, as inducing such use, calls for a distribution of them as books, suitably bound and placed in their classifications; and I hope gradually to accomplish this for such as may seem by their importance to demand it. Meanwhile, pamphlets containing discussions of current topics are now made promptly available as books, by being placed between covers, which are kept in stock for the purpose.

The large mass of important pamphlets now tied in bundles, the long list of serials now received in paper, and the evidences of need of rebinding which are observable everywhere along the shelves, indicate the desirability of a University bindery; and I render the establishment of one feasible. The actual expenses for binding in some other of the departments,—the Law Library, for instance,—and the urgency for incurring such in others,—like the Museum and Observatory,— indicate that all departments of the University would profit by it. Perhaps, with the completion of Sever Hall, rooms fitted for bindery work will become available in some of the older buildings. Having seen the bindery of the Boston Public Library grow from small beginnings to an establishment employing fifteen hands, and turning out fifteen thousand volumes a year, I speak from experience when I say that the advantages of a University bindery over the employment of outside binderies would be three: *first*, less cost per volume; *second*, much better work and material than it is possible to secure by the most particular specifications; *third*, convenience of access, and greater security for rarities. I have procured accurate estimates of the first outlay necessary.

The following figures represent the amount of binding done for the College Library during late years:—

1869-70	441 volumes.		1874-75	1,647 volumes.
1870-71	2,125 "		1875-76	1,504 "
1871-72	2,944 "		1876-77	1,277 "
1872-73	324 "		1877-78	1,627 "
1873-74	2,537 "			

These figures do not include the binding done abroad of books purchased here; but they do include the binding of pamphlets, selected for their importance. Of the 1,627 volumes reported this year, 1,181 were bound outside the premises, and are exclusive of this preparation of pamphlets.

The last absolute count of the College Library was made in August, 1873, when the footings showed 134,275 volumes. Last year, Mr. Sibley estimated the Library at 164,000 volumes, and as many pamphlets. I judge that this enumeration of volumes fell considerably short of the actual number, as no account was made of the large number of serial volumes and periodicals, counted upon receipt as pamphlets, and subsequently bound and placed upon the shelves, without a change of count, as books. When the reclassification of the Library is completed, we shall be able from the shelf-lists to make a trustworthy count, and to report it with accuracy year by year.

The accessions of the past year foot up 8,362,—a number largely in excess of any growth of late years. It is but just to say that this includes duplicates and bound serials,— not exceeding together 500 volumes, however,—which are not embraced in the following figures of reported past accessions:—

1870	1,520 volumes.		1874	4,754 volumes.
1871	3,091 "		1875	5,828 "
1872	4,462 "		1876	3,752 "
1873	3,604 "		1877	3,741 "

Add to this total of 8,362, the accessions through the year to the various departmental libraries:—

Law School	557
Scientific School	97
Divinity School	114
Medical School	7
Museum of Zoölogy	373
Observatory	320
Bussey Institution	79
Peabody Museum	24
	1,571

And we have a grand total of 9,933 volumes, by which the Library of the University, as a unit, has been increased. This progress may be considered as quite equal to the normal increase of any other library in the country, not duplicating under the copyright law, and not catering by duplication to the popular wants of large communities. Of this number a considerable portion came from benefactions. Our records show that during the year nearly five hundred different bodies or persons, representing nearly every section of the globe, contributed to our growth. It should be borne in mind, however, that the entire accessions are in reality gifts, since there are no means of adding to the Library, except from funds of individual benefactors. About one-third of the year's accessions of the College Library are direct gifts of books, a proportion sometimes exceeded in the past, as will be seen by the following comparisons:—

	Volumes bought.	Given.
1869-70	197	1,323
1870-71	1,575	1,516
1871-72	3,303	1,159
1872-73	2,578	1,026
1873-74	3,601	1,153
1874-75	2,699	3,129
1875-76	1,992	1,760
1876-77	2,984	847
1877-78	5,566	2,796

Of pamphlets, the accessions of late years stand as follows, for the College Library:—

1869-70	3,700	1874-75	4,665
1870-71	4,974	1875-76	2,954
1871-72	5,020	1876-77	2,270
1872-73	4,615	1877-78	4,750
1873-74	4,000		

These additions give the Library of the University, at the close of the past academic year, the following extent,—estimating rather under than above the probability, where positive data fail:—

	Volumes.	Pamphlets.
College Library	175,000	170,000
Law School	16,907	
Scientific School	2,083	146
Divinity School	17,000	
Medical School	2,000	
Museum of Zoölogy	11,970	5,000
Observatory	6,662	
Botanic Garden	2,921	1,193
Bussey Institution	2,077	681
Peabody Museum	270	305
Total	236,890	177,325

This puts the Library of this University far ahead of any other collection of books, in connection with other institutions of learning in this country. Two other general libraries exceed it. The Boston Public Library, on the 30th of April last, had 345,734 volumes, of which 220,000 or 225,000 volumes may be considered in relative character the equivalent of this collection, the rest being duplications, mostly of popular books. The Library of Congress is a trifle less in extent, and stands second; but its duplications under the copyright act are very large.

There are two special departments of the College Library needing more attention than, in the present transition state of the book collection, the staff can bestow upon them. As soon as practicable, they must be put in better condition. They are those of maps and coins. The catalogue, printed under the direction of one of my predecessors, Mr. Benjamin Peirce, in 1831, of the rare collection of "ten thousand maps, charts, and views," collected by Professor Ebeling, of Hamburg, and constituting part of the gift of the late Israel Thorndike, is still a sufficient finding-list to that collection; and the section *Maps* of the card catalogue opens the resources of the Warden collection, a part of the gift of the late Samuel A. Eliot, and of others added since. The whole collection needs, however, to be rearranged, and to be supplemented by later issues. The collection of coins is partly arranged, in a case made for the purpose, and of these a MS. catalogue was made in 1859, by Mr. William Eliot Lamb. The later accumulations are considerable, and need to be as well cared for. During the year they have been increased by a collection of Roman coins, the gift of Mr. Robert N. Toppan.

Upon various collections of manuscripts, broadsides, scraps, engravings (apart from the Gray collection), there is much labor yet to be bestowed. One insecurely preserved collection seemed to imperatively demand immediate attention. I refer to the very large collection of printed accounts, reports, programmes, broadsides, and notices, illustrating the history of the College and University; and I have taken steps for the better ordering of them at once. It seems fitting that the Library should be in some sense a memorial of the graduates; and the good work for the preservation of all the publications of the graduates, begun and so enthusiastically carried forward by my immediate predecessor, I hope to sustain.

The work of the College Library staff, both in the catalogue rooms and in the delivery room, has gone on during the year with unavoidable obstructions, owing to the confusion incident to the rearranging of the books. The present catalogue was begun in 1861, and there still remain over twenty thousand volumes of the more difficult of the older books, whose titles are yet to be incorporated in the new catalogue, under author and subjects. A marked copy of the old printed catalogue of 1830-34 is at present the only clue to them; and for using that the author entry needs to be known. For the present, this "old work" is substantially at a stand; but I have arranged that it shall go on hereafter parallel with the reclassifying of the books, so that each department, as perfected in the new arrangement, shall stand completely embodied in the catalogue.

Mr. Fiske has furnished the following synoptical work of this department, since he joined the staff:—

CATALOGUE WORK, 1872-78.

YEARS.	Old Volumes.	Current Accessions.	Old Pamphlets.	Current Pamphlets.	Total.	Cards Written.	Old Cards Corrected.	Total.	Cards Distributed in Case.
1872-73	576	3,230	333	1,992	6,131	19,001	. .	. .	. .
1873-74	597	4,078	211	1,824	6,710	24,566	. .	. .	. .
1874-75	1,175	7,812	704	2,660	12,351	36,993	. .	. .	55,223
1875-76	5,458	5,199	1,014	1,850	13,521	40,429	19,148	59,577	46,023
1876-77	10,003	4,083	1,631	1,785	17,502	38,171	18,925	57,096	44,220
1877-78	6,379	5,382	485	1,120	13,366	44,914	18,142	63,056	57,115

The work of cataloguing pamphlets (except so far as the more important ones of the current accessions, and occasionally some from the back files, are put in covers to be classed as books) is now discontinued, till some systematic grouping of them as prospective books can be devised. There are no considerations except economy for treating pamphlets other than as books; and the users of a library are never thoroughly equipped for investigation as long as any distinction is made between them. A librarian's principle is to keep the pamphlet collection as small as possible, not by discarding any, but by amalgamating them with the books, as far as it can be done.

The figures representing the writing and distribution of cards are portentous. In the new catalogue cases, an increased capacity of about fifty per cent was provided for; but with additions to the cards, averaging 50,000 a year, and with the increase of the space they occupy, resulting from the introduction of guideboards, the present cases will not suffice for many years, and there is no convenient space for their enlargement in the delivery hall, as at present constructed. An extension of it, northerly, along the wall of the original structure, with a glass roof, will have to be seriously contemplated, when the time comes for remodelling that part of the building.

I did not begin until February last to provide for a regular registration of the use of the Library, so that the figures given below do not represent a whole year. The record covers only such books as are delivered over the counter to the readers, either for taking from the building, or for use at the tables; and they do not include the large hall use of books of reference and new books, nor of the books temporarily shelved apart as collateral reading for the elective courses, nor of the currently received periodicals. I give them by months, as indicative of the relative value of the different months as reading periods, premising that the eight months probably do not yield results more than equal to those of the four earlier months of the academic year, not embraced in the record:—

	Loaned.	Hall Use.	Total.
February	3,073	1,303	4,376
March	3,959	1,585	5,544
April	3,362	1,191	4,553
May	2,833	1,299	4,132
June	2,133	675	2,808
July	1,018	167	1,185
August	934	269	1,203
September 1-25	874	235	1,109
Totals	18,186	6,724	24,910

In December, 1877, we began a separate record of the loaning of reference books overnight, and the slips show about 3,000 such deliveries for the rest of the year. They are not included in the above figures. This is an extension of use in addition to that of previous years, as is believed, and one which, I think, is destined to increase largely.

JUSTIN WINSOR, *Librarian.*

GORE HALL, Sept. 28, 1878.

14. COLLEGE AND THE OTHER HIGHER LIBRARIES

I am to speak to you as a librarian—possibly as an over-confident one—upon the relations of the College library to the university and of the higher libraries to their constituents. This means the relations which active repositories of books bear to those, who as a rule are the skilled intellecutal laborers of our communities, either in their formative or riper conditions. They may be workers in the professions usually so called, or they may be pursuing those callings, where intelligence works under the help of acquirements in a way to place many another vocation upon the same old-time vantage ground. It was long ago apparent that the original professions no longer hold their triple supremacy. As long as the literature of Law, Medicine and Theology were the only literatures appertaining to what men think and do for a living, libraries were necessarily the monopoly, outside of literature itself as a study, of the Lawyer, the Physician and the Theologian.

The vast domain of pure and applied science, covering almost every aspiration and material want of humanity, and the fields of philosophy in all its aspects, never before so connected with daily living, have in these latter days brought into the closest relations with life, a vast number of books essential to the new conditions of human existence. And they have also brought into prominence a new phase of literature, the professedly evanescent part of the library, necessary to-day, but so far as ministering to the progressive wants of life, forgotten in a decade. As some merchandise is made to sell, so some books are written to be superseded.

When literature, as such, had a habit more marked than to-day of constantly returning upon itself; when the lore of theology buried the Bible in its drifts; when the precepts of medicine filled folio upon folio; when law was pre-eminently the record of precedent,—Libraries were their nurseries, and they were the nurseries of little else. Succeeding generations went to the same store-house. To-day a great library retains its hold upon a community only so far as it keeps abreast of that community's progress. An important American library stopped its purchases for fifteen years and everybody forgot it. What was Science fifteen years old! What was History without Sedan and Gettysburg! What was Literature without the last sensation! So have libraries come to be a part of one's living. And how changed, consequently, the functions of a librarian. Once the warder of a castle, who parleyed distantly with those that knocked; now, the expounder, the prophet, the missionary—or he should be—whose gates cannot be too widely opened, whose sympathy cannot be too broad. It has changed his life from that of a self-absorbed recluse to one of active exuberance, and if to make himself felt in the organization of life is a triumph, to one of a certain supremacy.

New conditions always bring new dangers, as new transformations bring new pests. These dangers may be the eddies, which, whirling him about, make him unmindful of the sources of the stream that is bearing him on.

I have had a celebrated specialist say to me, "I wish all there is in your library over ten years old was burned up. It is all useless." That was because he holds different theories now from what he did then; because he thinks he has grown, when, perhaps, he has merely warped the other way. He may cry, as Rob Roy did, in the verse of Wordsworth,

> "What need of books?
> Burn all the statutes and their shelves;
> They stir us up against our kind,
> And worse against ourselves!"

So sure is it that Science, sooner or later, repeats its old homilies; and the librarian knows what the record of the past is worth. If he has that conserving catholicity of judgment,

Source: *Library Journal* 4 (1879): 399-402 [A paper read before the American Social Science Association, at Saratoga, Sept. 10, 1879].

which teaches him as well to look back as to look forward, his wide experience, contermi-
nous with all learning, ought to preserve him from such error.

Ask, if you will, any keeper of a large collection of books, open to much general
use, what experience in it strikes him most, and he will tell you it is the immensely wide
range of human interests, so far as the reading of books shows it. The bulk of the percentage of use can be, of course, assigned pretty accurately in fixed proportions; but the
remaining portion covers assimilations of mind, by no means of least importance, and which
will be a constant revelation to you.

Every experienced librarian has established two canons, both of doctrine and of
discipline.

First. Nothing that is printed, no matter how trivial at the time, but may be some
day in demand, and, viewed in some relations, helpful to significant results. Therefore, if
his store-house and treasury admit of the keeping and caring for, the librarian feels the
necessity of preserving all he can.

Second. Let him amass all he will, he knows some investigator will find gaps that he
has not filled. There is no library in the world so well able, as a rule, to satisfy all the
demands of scholarship and diversity of inquiry as that of the British Museum; and yet
the head of that library, my good friend, Mr. Bullen, testified not long since before the
Society of Arts that never an inquirer came to that library, determined to exhaust his
subject, but he found there were phases of it he could not sketch; there were thoughts
he could not illustrate; there were apposite books not yet discovered, and even not yet
written.

The present has been aptly described as the conflux of two eternities, and we may
say the sparkles of life are the abraded fragments. And so the modern library is the meeting of what has been and is to be–the accomplishment and the potentiality,–and the
scintillations scattered over the cope of our intellectual existence, come from the friction
of the two.

The librarian lives in an atmosphere of possibilities; but there is also about him an
ether, charged with his own electricity, that makes in every alcove, the dead alive! In the
wisdom born of his surroundings, he well knows that libraries, while taking on an activity
begotten of the closer connection which they are acquiring with experience and daily
thought, cannot, if they would, slough off the associations of the past. It is given to him
to defend the one and to deny the other. If science belittles the history of its own beginnings, he knows it to be wrong-headed, and can recall where it has gone back on its own
track.

The librarian has from this experience no sympathy with that unbalanced condition,
which prompts solely the aspiration that men may

> "Rise on stepping-stones
> Of their dead selves to higher things."

While he gives that a due place in his cult, he has the talent of looking back. Therefore
it is that while the librarian in his present emergent condition is proclaiming a mission of
progress in the world, he has another equally imperative duty in attending to the neglected
and in remembering the forgotten!

And as the librarian, so in some sense the library; for as a convocation of books
takes on the machinery of administration, the hand that is on the throttle valve directs
what its power shall be. And this is the instrumentality that is now beginning to exercise
its legitimate functions in our educational systems. Time was when the student in college
came up to the library once or twice a week on sufferance, under the impression that it
would never do to have too much of a good thing. "Boys!" cried the warder of one of
the first of our college libraries, within the memory of the present generation, "Boys!
what are you doing here–this is no place for you?" The poor craving creatures slunk away
to Euclid and Horace in the seclusion of their bedrooms.

I have no disposition to disparage the results of collegiate education in such days
and under such dispensation. It is an old story, as well as true, that innovation is not
always improvement; but that does not prevent innovation becoming necessary, because

readaptation must follow upon changed conditions. The same impulse, which is converting the fixed curriculum into the variable system of elective studies, while it tends to banish text books, throws open the alcoves of the library, as never before.

I look upon this new departure as likely to be permanent, or at least not to change but with the ways of our intellectual life. I see it in a habit consonant with our legitimate expectations, because it agrees with the independent spirit of modern thought; and because it gives a glow in the pursuit, flushing the follower in an unwonted way.

It has yet to be more generally recognized that the hunting down of a subject through the resources of a great library, has an exhilaration that spurs on, because of the condition always attending a combination of skill and chance. This was not possible, when books were less diversified and when libraries had not rendered themselves accessible, not through main avenues only but by a great variety of by-paths—for such is the result of the subject catalogue, an idea in its development almost exclusively American.

Not one of the great European libraries is thus equipped as we judge it to be necessary; but the best of them are looking forward to it. The Bodleian has already begun the work. The British Museum hopes to make available in this way its reserve of manifold-written titles, which now represents its shelf-lists. As my friend, Mr. Garnett, the Superintendent of its great Reading Room, said recently, "An immense lee-way remains to be made up in the great European libraries." This gentleman has well reasoned out the question—so long a vexed one—of the printing of the Museum catalogue. It is really going to be resolved into one of purely mechanical construction. Print is to take the place of manuscript, not because the public demand it, but because the Museum building will hold the one, and will not expand to the dimensions of the other; and this expansion is to be something appalling if subject-clues are to be added to their present Authors' Catalogue. Even in print the destined size is portentous. As it stands their simple authors-entry catalogue may be simmered down through the process of type from two or three hundred volumes, still large folios. Considering that anywhere from ten to thirty years may be required for this transformation, the accessions of that interval would add nearly as many more. The undertaking, moreover, would involve the expenditure of about half a million of dollars. It would be very easy to calculate the bulk both of titles and expense, if this authors-entry catalogue should be supplemented by a subject index, which to be thorough should at least equal it. Therefore it will be seen that the equipment of a large library for a thoroughly satisfactory use of it raises at once practical questions of no mean magnitude.

Of late years, literature, science and art have, almost without precedent, been brought into review by synoptical, critical and cyclopedic survey. Every topic has had its bibliographical measure. While Europe has been content with this, America has been showing the way to make direct application of it in its individual libraries, In order to vitalize dormant energies, that need contagion to quicken them; in order to economize labor, and to apply principles of coöperation, American librarians, instead of standing aloof from one another and rounding their little lives to the dimension of but a single experience, have drawn themselves together, to teach and to be taught, by a process of reciprocal imbuing. No librarian grows to the full measure of the spirit that animates him; but the community he serves derives its advantage.

Until subject catalogues became what they are—and they are by no means yet what they should be,—and until librarians became helpers as well as keepers, it was not possible for libraries to be turned into these intellectual hunting-grounds. I often think as I see a young man casting about at the catalogue case for the best way to grapple with his elusive theme; as he comes to me with a question that shows he is off soundings and is guiding himself by applying his wits to the phenomena about him,—that there may be better discipline to teach him intellectual self-reliance, and better experience to sharpen his intuitive powers,—but I hardly know where. You remember that someone advised—Scott, I think—that there was no better mental experience for a young man of a bookish tendency with a purpose in it, than to be turned adrift in a good collection of books, and to be left to find his way with a new sensation at every turn; to pursue, as it were, in Thoreau's phrase, a meandering brook rather than a straight-cut ditch, which is too often what education becomes. I know nothing better, unless it be that the young man has a kindly mentor at hand,—some sympathetic professor, say, who goes beside rather than ahead, sharing the excitement. I have seen such professors and they are the life of the college. There is no task-work in such company.

If this philosophy be true, it needs only to be shown, as I trust time will show, that the results are praiseworthy beyond compare, and the method becomes fixed in our college systems. The library will become the important factor in our higher education that it should be. Laboratory work will not be confined to the natural sciences; workshops will not belong solely to technological schools. The library will become, not only the store-house of the humanities, but the arena of all intellectual exercise.

15. THE COLLEGE LIBRARY AND THE CLASSES

I fancy that among institutions there is scarce a stolider than the average college library, and I know no reason to account for it but the old one of the laughing shoes of the cobbler's children. A collection of good books, with a soul to it in the shape of a good librarian, becomes a vitalized power among the impulses by which the world goes on to improvement. A stagnant library, musty and dank, open at hours which suit the convenience of an overworked professor rather than inviting everybody at all hours, is an anomaly. The object of books is to be read—read much and read often. There is enough of folly in books no doubt; much of impertinence; much of vacuity, since some evil is always inseparable from every good; but its proportion is far less than in oral instruction, as the latter goes, whether in the desk or around the social circle. With all the crude writing in the world, it is in far smaller proportion to good writing than poor talk to good talk. What is concrete of knowledge, or better, of experience, is crammed into books, and what else there is in them can be avoided, if we choose,—but in talk not easily. And yet this library instruction in colleges is not made to tell as it should.

The main thing to know is, what book can accomplish what work, and how it can be brought to bear. Who teach this? Who knows it to fit them to teach it? Who is bold enough to throw text-books to the dogs, and lead his class through the recesses of a library?

Professor Henry Adams opened a new mine at Harvard when he led his students among the sources of history, and directed them to do their own culling, and to make their own text-books. He implanted a new interest in the work, and showed what a library is for. At the average college it is thought that if anybody gets any good from the library, perhaps it is a few professors; and if anybody gets any amusement, perhaps it is a few students, from the smooth worn volumes of Sterne and Fielding. What it is to investigate, a student rarely knows; what are the allurements of research, a student is rarely taught. What would have been thought five-and-twenty years ago of some such proposition as this:

PROFESSOR (loquitur). "Gentlemen, we will take up in March the period of the Norman Conquest of England. Mr. Bright, you must be prepared on Bulwer's "Harold" to analyze the events and compare them with what you deem the best contemporary authorities. Mr. Somers, you take Kingsley's "Hereward," and criticise his estimates of the Saxons, and point out his divergencies from historic truth. Mr. Hammond, I leave for you Napier's novel of "William the Conqueror;" you may treat the book in any way you please as illustrative of the time. Mr. Shortman, I want you to compare Tennyson's "Harold" and Leighton's "Sons of Godwin" as plots, where the movement is more or less regulated by historical records, and give us a picture of Saxon England at that time, as you read it in these respective dramas. The rest of you, gentlemen, I refer for study to the authorities. A to H will work up the contemporary ones, which you will find referred to in the notes of Turner and Palgrave. Mr. Allen, we shall expect from you a list of notable *desiderata* in these early sources where you may find the college library to fail. We shall want to know all about Wace's "Roman de Rou" from you, Mr. Fellows. From you, Mr. Davis, we shall expect a presentation of the social institutions of the Anglo Saxons, and Sharon Turner will start you in the investigations. I to Z will master the modern authorities. Mr. Loring will take Palgrave, and we shall then know how the political institutions of the time were developed. Messrs. Stone and Strong, you are to pit yourselves, one against the other, in your judgments of the Conquerors. You will find Freeman sufficiently anti-Norman, and Thierry will show you the general opinion of them held on the Continent. Of course, there are Hume and Lingard, and Knight and the Pictorial History—all of you must familiarize yourselves with these writers; and we shall expect criticism and discussion; and the results, if you do your work well, ought to engage us for several weeks. I shall be happy to assist any one. You must live as much as you

Source: *Library Journal* 3 (1878): 5-6.

can in the college library. Read general books, cyclopaedias, consult historical atlases, and get the period first mapped out clearly in your own minds; then fill in the details. Make all the use you can of the college librarian. It is his business to advise you. The class is dismissed."

Is there any doubt now in these latter days what a college library is for? Can any corporation do better with their money than to buy the books to supply these deficiencies? Thus can the library fill up subject after subject; and fortune will go hard with these young men in the future if the department they worked to found or develop is left without patrons among the graduates, who will look after its condition as a memorial of the class.

16. THE CHARGING SYSTEM AT HARVARD

In an article in the August number on "Principles Underlying Charging Systems," the writer states very fairly the respective advantages of the two ways of charging books—in account with the borrower and with the book. In a small library, where the librarian's impressions and memory will serve him in regard to the kind of information derived systematically by the book-account, it may do to take advantage preferably of the borrower-account system; but the moment the business increases beyond such mnemonic recognition a fixed system to record such facts becomes necessary to him if he would administer his library in a businesslike way. Then the advantages of the borrower-account system must go by the board, except so far as the librarian can mentally preserve them through his own observation. Under some circumstances, however, the two can be united with great advantages; but it is essentially impracticable in a large library of much business, where the borrowers are so numerous that it cannot be assumed that any one of them is known to the attendants, and credentials (cards) are required in all cases. We are experiencing the advantages of the two in combination very decidedly here at Harvard. The old method in use was a ledger-account with borrower, requiring their signatures against every title charged. It was slow and annoying, and did not furnish the needful data on which to base action for improving the circulation and defining the administration. I had myself naturally a predilection for the book-account slip system, such as was developed upon the foundation laid by Prof. Jewett at the Public Library in Boston. But it was at once forced upon me that new conditions must suggest the system to be adopted. There was no gain sufficient to offset the annoyance to borrower to be derived by issuing borrowers' cards, for the constituency was not large enough to preclude the recognition by the desk attendant of every user of the library; and without such a card the slip-system account with books could not be carried out successfully; and even with it, in the case of the professors, whose use of books is practically unlimited, the card could hardly suffice for the record. It was clear, then, that the old system should not be wholly given up, but that certain elements of the Boston system should be engrafted upon it.

Our present plan is this: Call-slips are used, but they are not printed ones; nevertheless I believe that with a mixed, and in part illiterate clientage, like that of a large popular city library, the printing is a needful help to keep the routine in good shape. The moment the book is delivered the borrower departs; there is no longer delay in signing and waiting the turn to sign.

Here I think there is a failure in the above named paper to recognize the great point for the slip-system as opposed to the ledger. The slip-record has all the disadvantages named, and the ledger certainly can be consulted more rapidly, but not so much quicker with an expert as might be supposed. In cancelling loans the ledger has the advantage; but this is not an advantage that interests the borrower, for that labor can be done from the book he returns after he has departed. With the charging, however, it is quite different. With the ledger the page must be found or the entry made while the borrower stands by. With the slip, its retention suffices, and the patron is free. The writer is correct in asserting that any thing will be pardoned by the borrower sooner than slowness; and the advantage in this respect is wholly with the slip-system. I found at Boston that detention was reduced to the minimum, so far as cancelling and charging went. The delay incident to finding and fetching books is common to the two systems. From the slips, at the attendant's leisure, the individual's account is posted in a ledger. The slips are then assorted by their book-numbers.

Thus I gain all the points of the two systems, and at no more cost than a library like this can afford. From the ledger I learn each borrower's reading, can tell him what books he has out, can check him in getting a larger number than he ought to have. From the slips I can tell where any book is, can notify borrowers of the expiration of their time, can learn the circulation of particular books and the comparative issues of all classes, and I can examine the library and account for the books without calling them in—a proceeding never attempted in a large library till I set the fashion at Boston in 1869. This point is omitted by Mr. Dewey among the advantages of the book-account system, but it is perhaps *the most important of all*. Stock-taking in a

Source: *Library Journal* 3 (1878): 338-39.

large library with a borrower-account record is practically impossible without a cessation of the circulation. Think of looking over more than 100,000 individual accounts to find a title, as would be required now at the Boston Public Library!

From the ineffectual slips—those not securing a book—I can discover where duplicating is desirable. It is of course a more perfect system than the Boston system, because it answers more questions without taking any more of the borrower's time, and he is not bothered with a library-card to look after. I much question, however, if in a library like that of Boston it would not cost far more than it comes to, and the added facility of answering some of the questions is certainly more likely to be of use with us than at Boston.

17. SHELF-LISTS vs. ACCESSION CATALOGUES

I take issue with the Supply Department in the desirability of distinct accession catalogues. I had experience with one for ten years at Boston, and was often troubled with the amount of labor required to keep it up—it took one attendant's whole time latterly. It was a device bequeathed to me by my predecessor, and I was reluctant to displace it; but in all that period I never knew it resorted to for information that could not just as well have been put on the shelf-lists. Indeed the shelf-list, or the book in question, or the card catalogue—usually the first—must always primarily be consulted as an index to the accession catalogue when any question as to the history of a particular book comes up. Of course, by giving this catalogue up—as I had begun to do before I left Boston, and I believe since then it has been further disused—I lost the ability to know just the order in which all books came into the library, a piece of knowledge, however, that I never once required to know. I also lost the record in one place of the titles of any single gift of books, when they were of a miscellaneous character, but I do not remember of being at a loss for such record. On the contrary, if A. B. was a numismatician, and was in the habit of giving books in his department to the library at intervals, the accession catalogue would not, unless it was indexed, afford a list of their titles, while the shelf-list would, or approximately so, the library being classified. Almost all the questions arising about a particular book can be more readily answered by inscribing the required information on the shelf-list, with not more than one half the labor, since about one half the writing is duplicated in the two. The same form of combined shelf-list and accession catalogue, which I devised for the Jamaica Plain and South End branches—the last departments started during my superintendency at Boston—I have adopted at Harvard, giving up here the Record-book (accession catalogue) which had been in use previously. The headings of this new shelf-list are for the left-hand page: *Book-number* (*i.e.*, order on shelf); *no. of vols.; title; place;* and *date.* And for the right-hand page: *Sign; date of accession; source* (*i.e.*, whence received); *fund or gift; remarks.* There are thirty-two lines on the page. A title, not volume, is given to a line.

It will be observed that where both records are kept, the writing on the left-hand page, as indicated above, is common to both, and has to be duplicated.

The shelf-number of course answers all the purpose of the accession number as a link of reference, and the latter is not used—another item of labor saved.

Of course a class-list, where relative location is used, is equally effective as a shelf-list for the combination, so far as the regular purchases of the library go; the file of bills or invoices shows the growth of the library in its chronological aspect; and a separate record of gifts—if one is kept—completes the record.

My opinion, then, derived from ten years' experience in the library of the widest range of perplexities of any in the country, is that the pure accession catalogue demands an amount of labor which produces no corresponding advantages, and that the items of value on it can be far more conveniently preserved on the shelf-list or class-list.

Source: *Library Journal* 3 (1878): 247-48.

18. THE COLLEGE LIBRARY

President Eliot, in writing of the Harvard Library in a recent report, spoke of its "having a profound effect upon the instruction given at the university, as regards both substance and method: it teaches the teachers." And yet, I fear, we have not discovered what the full functions of a college library should be; we have not reached its ripest effects; we have not organized that instruction which teaches how to work its collections as a placer of treasures. To fulfil its rightful destiny, the library should become the central agency of our college methods, and not remain a subordinate one, which it too often is. It is too often thought of last in developing efficiency and awarding appropriations; committed very likely to the charge of an overworked professor, who values it as a help to his income rather than an instrumentality for genuine college work; equipped with few, or even without any, proper appliances for bibliographical scrutiny; and wanting in all those administrative provisions that make it serviceable to-day and keep it so to-morrow.

There is often a feeling that books are, or ought to be, sensible enough to maintain their own ranks, without the need of a drill sergeant. A good deal of the librarian's work is doubtless that of the drill sergeant; but the genuine custodian of a library knows that his best work is a general's, who has campaigns to plan and territory to overrun; in other words, he has got to force his ranks into action, and make each book do the work for which it was made. Books skulk. Few are aggressive and compel attention, unless the librarian puts each on its own vantage ground.

In all this the librarian becomes a teacher, not that mock substitute who is recited to; a teacher, not with a text book, but with a world of books. The man is but half grown who thinks a book is of no use unless it is read through and would confine his acquaintance to the few score or hundreds of volumes that he can conscientiously read from beginning to end in a lifetime. One may indeed have a few books that remain a constant wellspring to him; but these should be very few, unless he wishes to have his conceptions dangerously narrowed. There is nothing so broadening as an acquaintance with many books, and nothing so improving as acquiring the art of tasting a book, as the geologist takes in the condition of a landscape at a glance. Let your few bosom books qualify your intellectual nature; and then give yourself the food you will grow upon by the widest discursiveness. The way to avoid being apalled at the world of books is what the library of the college is commissioned to point out. Nothing is more certain than that the socalled text book is really more the author's predilections of a subject than a true exposition of it. I would not certainly underrate the advantage often to come from any subject being passed into the alembic of an author's individuality; but it is not all: the subject as a virgin creation still attracts us. We must often get it from many angles, and it is the many books that give us this.

I will now now stop to discuss the thraldom or, if you choose, the practical necessity of the class system. It is quite true, however, that the arguments for it have resulted in the text book— something that hits an average, with a void on either side of it.

I will not say that the library is the antagonist of the text book; but it is, I claim, its generous rival and abettor, helping where it fails and leading where it falters. If this is so, it follows that we must build our libraries with class rooms annexed, and we must learn our ways through the wilderness of books until we have the instinct that serves the red man when he knows the north by the thickness of the moss on the tree-boles.

I do not write this as a piece of idealism. I know it to be practical. It needs indeed time, money, industry, skill, patience, but it can be done. You may count the time and doubt the expediency; you may reckon the money and ask where it is to come from; you can promise industry; you hope for skill; you may question if your patience will hold out; but, with all these saved or acquired, it can be done.

The proposition then is to make the library the grand rendezvous of the college for teacher and pupil alike, and to do in it as much of the teaching as is convenient and practicable. This

Source: *College Libraries as Aids to Instruction*. Circulars of Information of the Bureau of Education, No. 1-1880. Washington: Gov. Print. Off., 1880. pp. 7-14.

cannot be done with a meagre collection of books indiscriminately selected, with an untidy, ill lighted, uncomfortable apartment. The library should be to the college much what the dining room is to the house—the place to invigorate the system under cheerful conditions with a generous fare and a good digestion. It may require some sacrifices in other directions to secure this, but even under unfavorable conditions the librarian can do much to make his domain attractive. As he needs the coöperation of his colleagues of the faculty, his first aim is to make everything agreeable to them, and himself indispensable, if possible. College faculties are made up much as other bodies are—the responsive and sympathetic with those that repel and are self-contained. A librarian shows his tact in adapting himself to each; he fosters their tastes; encourages their predilections; offers help directly where it is safe, accomplishes it by flank movements when necessary; does a thousand little kindnesses in notifying the professors of books arrived and treasures unearthed. In this way suavity and sacrifice will compel the condition of brotherhood which is necessary and is worth the effort.

With the student also the librarian cannot be too close a friend. He should be his counsellor in research, supplementing but not gainsaying the professor's advice. It would be a good plan to take the students by sections, and make them acquainted with the bibliographical apparatus, those books that the librarian finds his necessary companions, telling the peculiar value of each, how this assists in such cases, that in others; how this may lead to that, until with practice the student finds that for his work he has almost a new sense.

I am afraid few librarians not brought up amid an affluence of such reference books understand all that they can accomplish. It is too much to expect more than a very few college libraries to be equipped with such books by the thousands—twenty-thousand would not be too many for perfection—but there is much that is bought for libraries that would be best postponed until the librarian can offer such instruction to the students with a well balanced if not large bibliographical and reference collection at his hand.

Let me enumerate a few of the books that every librarian will cite among those of chiefest importance to him, and such as it is a pity every student has not a working knowledge of.

When we consider the broad field of all languages and all subjects, we must probably give the first place to Brunet's *Manuel du Libraire*, the last edition of which (Paris, 1860-1865) is now being completed with some supplemental volumes. A book must have a certain prominence before Brunet chronicles it. This work is in its main body alphabetical by authors, but there is a classified topical key in the last volume. In some respects there is a more ample record in *Grasse's Trésor de livres rares et précieux*, but it is without subject clews.

If we deal with foreign languages and literatures, we must know also how to use Quérard's various bibliographies—his *La France littéraire* and *La littérature francaise contemporaine*, which with Lorenz's *Catalogue général*, 1840-1865, make a record covering 1700-1865. In German the chief help is Heinsius's *Allgemeines Bücher-Lexikon*, beginning 1750, has the preference for those who wish to use a subject index. Notice of other languages is hardly called for with the present purpose.

On the English helps I must be fuller. Watt's *Bibliotheca Britannica* is arranged by authors and by subjects, but contains nothing later than 1820. Its topical arrangement gives it often advantages over Lowndes, who cannot in all ways be said to supersede it. Bohn's edition of Lowndes's *Bibliographer's Manual* is the best to have, with all its faults; but it is an arrangement by authors only. Its eleven parts as issued are sometimes bound in six volumes. Lowndes published the work originally in 1834, and Bohn began the new edition intending simply to revise and add to Lowndes's entries; but as the work went on, Bohn extended his scheme, and the later volumes are much fuller than the first, and they contain the record of various writers whom Lowndes had ignored. In this way it is a pretty good register of authors who appeared before 1834, chronicling for about thirty years later their newer publications and editions of older works. The article on Shakespeare, for instance, is much elaborated, and is one of the best of the Shakespearian bibliographies, and it extends into other languages. The eleventh part of Bohn, in his sixth volume, is the only convenient record we have of the publications of societies and printing clubs, of private presses, and of similar exceptional issues.

Allibone's *Critical Dictionary of English Literature* is indispensable. It is useful biographically as well as bibliographically, but as there was an interruption in the printing the user must bear in mind that up to the letter O the record is not later than 1858, while after that it is in some parts as late as 1870. The author frequently gives under another writer, whom he may be treating of, sometimes with appositeness and sometimes with hardly any, addenda to articles which had already passed in the printing. Though a large part of the third volume is made up of indexes, which nobody uses, no index is given to these contributions, and they are lost unless the user makes his own index to them. They are of this kind: Under Syntax, the pseudonym of Combe, the record of his publications is continued, and as John Camden Hotten chanced to edit an edition of Dr. Syntax's *Tour* occasion is taken to introduce a long list of Hotten's editions, to supply a deficiency under H.

These two books, Allibone and Bohn, are those chiefly to be commended; but for the publications of the day they need to be supplemented with Whitaker's *Reference Catalogue of Current Literature* for English books and with Leypoldt's *Uniform Trade List Annual* for American ones.

For books distinctively American in text or print, and which were still in the market in 1876, the *American Catalogue* is as nearly a complete guide as it is practicable to make. This catalogue will have, when completed, a topical index. Such a subject aid is at present found to a much less extent, but for small libraries quite sufficient, in F. B. Perkins's *Best Reading*. For older English books, particularly for those of too transitory an interest to find place in the bibliographies, there may be occasion to consult the various publications known as the *London, English,* and *British Catalogues*; also, such similar publications as Low's *Index* and the *Bibliotheca Londinensis*; and even the lists of current books printed from month to month in the *Gentleman's* and the *London Magazines* in the last century. So, for the older American books, one has to consult the list giving those back of 1776, appended to the last edition of Thomas's *History of Printing*, Trübner's *Bibliographical Guide*, and Roorback's *Bibliotheca Americana*, 1820-1860, continued by Kelly in his *American Catalogue.*

The skilled librarian sees that I have given but the rudimental sources for research, and that the foreign languages admit in some cases of even finer details than the English. I have mentioned such, however, as it were well everybody having to do with books should know something of.

It is further true that there is generally a great lack of knowledge of the most common books of reference, with little understanding of the help they can be in literary research for the sources of knowledge. I always know a man who has learned to work in a great library by the aptness of his choice of books of reference in any emergency. All things considered, the most useful of these books, and the surest to respond to one's wants, is Larousse's *Grand dictionnaire universel du XIXe siècle.* It is an immense conglomeration of matter, and its fine but legible printing occupies sixteen large quarto volumes. Its cost may shut it out from the smaller libraries, but it is worth some sacrifice to get. The *Encyclopaedia Britannica* can be much more easily dispensed with, and, notwithstanding the authoritative character and fulness of its articles, it will not compare with Larousse for genuine encyclopaedic value.

I can hardly conceive a college library in fit trim that has not one or more of the principal encyclopaedias now current, like Appleton's *New American Cyclopaedia*, Chambers's *Encyclopaedia*, and Johnson's *New Universal Cyclopaedia*—each good in its way. Appleton is naturally preferable for many American topics and is better supplied with illustrations. Chambers is better on British subjects. Johnson, however, gives you more for your money than either of the others, and is an excellent working reference book. Of those in foreign languages, after Larousse, the great German *Conversations-Lexikon* of Brockhaus, which is in some sense the parent of the modern cyclopaedia, is the first choice. There are various other cyclopaedias which are desirable companions, and some of them have a distinctive value. It is perhaps not of so much consequence which one we use as it is to use some one constantly. They often help one by their references to the best literature on a subject. For instance, in all matters appertaining thereto we shall find very full and well assorted references in McClintock and Strong's *Cyclopaedia of Biblical, Theological, and Ecclesiastical Literature*; a chief use of Allibone's *Dictionary of Authors* is for its references. For a compact general dictionary of biography and mythology, Thomas's *Biographical Dictionary* has no superior, and he guides you to the sources of his information. Hoefer's *Nouvelle biographie générale* has ample notes for further inquiry.

The indexes of the important periodicals should always be kept in mind. There are two convenient lists of such indexes, one in the initial publication of the new Index Society. Wheatley's *What is an Index?* and the other in the little *Handbook for Readers*, issued by the Boston Public Library. Poole's *Index to Periodical Literature*, though nearly thirty years old, is a necessary adjunct to the reference shelves, and the new edition, now in progress under the joint action of American and British librarians, will add a new resource for the inquirer.

Of the great mass of library catalogues, a few principal ones stand out as distinctively and characteristically useful, and experience soon discloses them. As a general rule the subject catalogue of a large collection is a peculiarly American product; though some of the principal European libraries are giving signs of efforts in a like direction. Meanwhile in Britain, the Advocates' Library at Edinburgh, the Bodleian at Oxford, and several sectional publications of the British Museum are of constant use in a well equipped catalogue room. The publications of the latter institution include their catalogue for the letter A, which Panizzi put a stop to forty years ago; the catalogues of the King's and of the Grenville collections; and the very useful list of twenty thousand volumes which form the handy reference collection of their great reading room.

Of the continental libraries it is enough for our present purpose to name the chronological and classified catalogue of French history and biography, prepared at the great library in Paris.

Of the American library catalogues I can be more particular. Those of the *Public Library of Boston* are probably best known, beginning with the Bates Hall Indexes, two volumes, and including those of the *Ticknor* and *Prince Collections* and of the *Barton Collection*, still unfinished. This library has also issued for more general use annotated *Class Lists of History, Biography and Travel, and Fiction*, making, with their critical, descriptive, and advisory notes, the earliest examples of what has since been called the Educational Catalogue.

For assistance to scholars, however, we can hardly boast anything better than the great *Catalogue of the Boston Athenaeum*, of which three volumes, bringing it to the letter M, are now published, and into which Mr. Cutter, an exemplar in such work, is putting his careful and discriminating scholarship.

The *Subject Catalogue of the Library of Congress*, 2 volumes, 1869, and later authors' lists with subject indexes disclose the assiduous care which Mr. Spofford is bestowing upon the national collection.

The student, however, will rarely find for his ordinary work any catalogue to stand him in better stead than Mr. Noyes's classified *Catalogue of the Brooklyn Library*, and he will regret its present incompleteness, which, it is to be hoped, will not long continue. The Brooklyn Library will not rank with our larger libraries, but it is a good one, and this catalogue forms a better key to it than belongs, in print, to any other of our collections. It follows the Boston catalogues in giving annotations, though not to the same extent; but its references to periodical articles are more systematic, and in this respect it constitutes much the best single continuation of Poole's Index. It can be supplemented in some ways by the *Catalogue of the Public Library of Quincy, Mass.*, which has other features to warrant its taking a place on our nearest reference shelf. I should not pass from this topic without mentioning the *Catalogue of the Astor Library*, 4 vols., 1857-1861, with a supplement in 1866, an authors' list, with a condensed index of subjects; the *Catalogue of the Philadelphia Library*, 3 vols., 1856, which is well indexed.

There is no occasion now for my mapping out the limits of the science of bibliography, but I simply give a reference to the article upon it in the *Encyclopaedia Britannica*, 9th ed., vol. iii. It is the key to all knowledge and the sparer of unfruitful pains. Can there be any instruction fitter for our colleges? There is nothing to indicate its scope later than Dr. Petzholdt's *Bibliotheca Bibliographica*, 1866, and an examination of this thoroughly German specimen of erudition will teach one what it is to be a bibliographer. Dr. Petzholdt divides his subject into eight heads, covering all languages:

1. General literature.
2. Anonymous and pseudonymous works.
3. Incunabula.
4. Works prohibited by censors.
5. Works on or by particular persons.
6. Engraved portraits.
7. National literature.
8. Classed literature.

There are two minor lists of classed bibliographies, sufficient for most purposes, in Nichol's *Handbook for Readers at the British Museum* and in the *Boston Public Library Handbook* already referred to. Supplementing these, the librarian will do well to watch the *Bulletins* and other *Bibliographical Contributions* of Harvard College Library, the Boston Public Library, the Boston Athenaeum, and the Lenox Library. Nor can the librarian fully keep abreast of the literary progress without a file of the *Publishers' Weekly* of New York, the *London Bookseller*, the *Bibliographie de la France*, and similar publications of the other modern languages.

I have dwelt upon these extraneous helps because they are something that care and money can procure at the outset. The librarian's great labor, however, the ever accumulating evidence of his devotedness, is something that money will not buy off-hand, but comes, after much pains and never ending assiduity, in the catalogue of his own library. I can hardly here fully indicate the variations of the vexed question of the catalogue, which librarians will always discuss and rarely come to conclusions upon. It may be desirable that some determinations should be reached, but it is by no means necessary to the end in view. All catalogues, if there is a reasonable application of common sense in their construction, are fitted to do good work, and there is no doubt one whose principles have not been mastered. That comprehensive Report on American Libraries, issued by the Bureau of Education at Washington in 1876, contains a paper on catalogues by Mr. Cutter, and a code of rules for cataloguing, admirably exemplified by the same authority. This code, which is so thoroughly fashioned that it has become an authority everywhere, will disclose to any one who examines it a new field of intricate knowledge, and it will broaden the conceptions of any one who is destined to a life of mental action.

If the librarian and his coadjutors, the instructors of the college, are to work for a common end effectually, the collection gathered about them must be catalogued. This means no rough work of the auctioneer's kind, but scholarly and faithful inquiry embodied in a fixed and comprehensive method. Every book must be questioned persistently as to its author, its kind, its scope, its relations to all knowledge. Answers to all these questions must be made record of, once for all. Let not the cost frighten; a library without such an index is no library, but a mob of books.

My own preference is to have the authors and subjects catalogued in one alphabetical arrangement, on what is called the dictionary system, of which the best examples are found in the printed catalogues of the Boston Athenaeum and of the Boston Public Library. The plan doubtless has disadvantages; but for the general user it presents clews that are most easily followed, and carries in large part its own key. For the skilled and habitual user, classed catalogues, especially those in which related subjects stand in close propinquity, may be more satisfactory; but such users are always rare. Both kinds, in fact, need a complemental index to restore the balance lost in the light of the other. In this way the two are put on planes of substantial equality, and the matter of choice between them becomes largely a question of predisposition. For the dictionary catalogue the key should be a tabular classification, showing the relations of allied topics, with an index of synonymous terms. For the classed catalogue the key should be an alphabetical list of topics, entered under every conceivable synonym.

There is a kind of indexing too seldom done in libraries, and yet it represents a present need, constantly emphasized. Live questions of the day, and literary questions brought into prominence by passing events, are matters that recur to students in their outside reading, and they constitute some of the more profitable subjects for themes and forensics. Articles and chapters bearing on such questions are usually buried in periodicals or books of miscellanea, sufficiently gone by to be not easily recalled. The librarian who has pursued a habit of indexing such articles as the numbers pass by, is always much better prepared for all such questions than he who lets the memoranda pass into dim corners of his unassisted memory.

I here leave the question of the relations which the college library should bear to the general conduct of the academic instruction, commending it to the serious attention of all whose lot has brought them to undergo the yoked labors of our colleges. The new interest that has of late been awakened in libraries as educational agencies does not, I feel sure, leave out of consideration that kind of library which seems so peculiarly fitted for sharing largely in the general appreciation. The college library, I trust, is starting on a new career.

19. THE DEVELOPMENT OF THE LIBRARY

It is nearly two centuries and a quarter since a tiny college of the wilderness floated along your water-front. It carried two teachers. One, a black-robed priest, had passed a novitiate in Latin and Greek, and had drunk inspiration from the fountain of the Fathers. His maturer life had been passed in the woods, a student of its wild denizens. He had sought the mysteries of their varied tongues till he could embalm in native cadences the great truths of his religion. His faith was symbolized in the crucifix dangling from his neck. Within the folds of his cassock rested the well-thumbed manual of his hourly devotion,—the be-all and end-all of his saintly life, the little library of this pristine university.

His companion was a vigorous spirit, equally adept in driving a bargain for peltry with the savage, and in discerning the points of the compass in a lichened tree-bole. He could tell what to expect in the up-country by scanning the river which came from it. His perceptions could place the great divides which turned the river channels to one ocean or the other. The outward aspects of nature were to him, what supreme truths and human aspirations were to the priest.

Thus this little primitive college, borne on the littoral current which sweeps to the great southern bend of your life-giving lake, fitly prefigures the counter resources in mind and matter, which form the bewildering diversity of our modern, encompassing education. In the folds of our devotion to all that is helpful in the emanations of man's intellect, and beneath the symbol of our faith, we lay nearest our hearts the wealth of our libraries, just as the devoted Marquette enfolded the spiritual manual upon his palpitating breast. In the lessons of our laboratories we find the prescriptions of natural law, just as Joliet found them in the air, the water, and the sky.

Two centuries and a quarter of struggling and vitalizing growth has done this for us, as it did to those pioneers, a preparation to subdue the earth, and to drink the libations poured by the bountiful past. From the breviary of the missionary to the possibilities of our modern libraries, is a reach only equalled by the passage from the simple instruction of those lowly teachers to the complex variety of the new learning.

There are few more interesting problems to the student of the new learning than the part which libraries are playing in its development. There are two necessary concomitants of a large collection of books. These are a bibliographical apparatus and the growth of special departments. Without the aid of bibliographical studies, no large library can be well formed and no such collection can be properly handled. No library but those whose distinction is their size, can attract much attention, unless it becomes exceptional in some directions. Bibliography and specialism are also the two readiest props of scholarship, and nowhere more than with us; and this is particularly true of bibliography. The learned of the old world look with some surprise on the recent advances in this respect which have been made in this country. We have seen and are seeing our account in it. Such studies have enabled us to outgrow the reproach which, fifty years ago and more, was a common one, that nowhere in this country could we verify the first-class investigations carried on by European scholars. The late George Livermore, in 1850, emphasized the stigma by saying—and he spoke the truth—that so cardinal a little book in the creation of the Yankee character as the "New England primer" could, nowhere in this country, be historically considered, because of the lack of books necessary to elucidate the allusions in it. Mr. Justice Story, speaking under the shadow of the Harvard library, said the same thing of Gibbon's great history.

If this was more a reproach then than now, it should be remembered that the first duty of a new country is to establish a good *average* of education, and that the creation of signal instances of the ripest scholarship comes later. A country like ours, receiving a constant influx of ill-educated aliens, has a more conspicuous duty to the state in making good citizens of them than in creating pure scholarship. Wealth creating a leisured class, the patrons and purveyors of learning, has only

Source: *Library Journal* 19 (1894): 370-75.

come to us in a conspicuous way since our civil war, and it has brought with it the need of scholarship.

It by no means follows that the creation of a large body of educated people is the sole source of remarkable scholarship. The scholar may easily appear of his own option; but he is buttressed in a community that respects him. I met, a few years ago, one of the best students of our constitutional history, writing his book in a society that offered him no encouragement and was destitute of libraries. There was something pathetic in his joy for an hour's intercourse with one who could give him a sympathetic response. Such a student, buying his own books and hampered in the selection of them, contrasted with one familiar with the resources of a well-equipped public library, may mean two things. It may signify a debasement of the intellectual vantage-ground, so as to affect scholarship; or, what is occasionally the case, it may put the scholarly mind on its mettle, and nourish its best endeavors. But such isolation from books is never a safe experiment, and never a successful test of mental endeavor in more than a few introspective studies.

The amassment of large private libraries is no longer a necessity of scholarship. The student is more and more learning to depend on large collections of books which the public fosters. There has been in the older communities a decided check of late years to the formation of private collections. I am told by law publishers at the east, that it is the western lawyer who buys books, while the eastern advocate depends on the social law libraries. It is my observation that with classes four or five times as large as they were in my day at Harvard, the number of young men among the students laying the foundation of their own collection of books is fewer now than then. It is notorious that today in England the collecting of books by the educated and leisured classes has gone by. If a man is found forming a library, he is a banker or a brewer come to the financial front, who thinks it a passport to social distinction. Earl Spencer told me a few years ago that he never added a book to the famous library then at Althorpe, and as I looked it through I could well believe there had not a book been put in it for half a century. I have looked at some of the best libraries in English country houses, and I have found but one or two, notably that of the Duke of Westminster, which indicated that the best current literature, as distinct from bibliographical fads, were contributing to their growth. The average English gentleman, with the training of Oxford and Cambridge, is content to depend on a weekly box from Mudie. Twenty years ago the London publisher, Pickering, said that he could not count on selling more than 250 copies of a good new book, and Quaritch to-day says he could not live except for his American orders.

Meanwhile the British Museum is printing 60,000 titles a year of its current accessions. Leaving out of account the mass of books in foreign tongues, it was recently held by a competent judge that the British Museum did not have more than half (or at least three-fifths) of the books in English which have been printed. It is not too much to say that the best library of English-speaking peoples is more or less of a makeshift. Mr. Bullen, the late keeper of the printed books in that library, recognized this when he testified before the Society of Arts, that on few or no subjects to be investigated could the British Museum afford the scholar *half* the necessary books. The late Winter Jones, for many years its principal librarian, told me once that not one thorough student in ten could find there all he wanted; and yet the British Museum is said to contain not much short of 2,000,000 volumes, and is possibly exceeded only by the Bibliothèque Nationale in Paris. I have learned to distrust comparative library statistics; but we cannot certainly on American soil point to any collection one-third as large.

The growth of American libraries, however, has been rapid, and far beyond expectation. Five and 30 years ago, when the Boston Public Library was finally organized, it was calculated that a building capable of holding 200,000 volumes would suffice for a century. In less than 20 years it fell to my lot (being then in charge of that institution, to double its capacity, and now in less than 40 years, or much less than half the allotted time, it has been found necessary to erect a building of eight or 10 times the capacity of the old one. Less than a score of years ago the library of Harvard College was given an addition to its building to double its shelf-room. To-day it has to store away in boxes its superfluous books. Not long ago I was directed by the president of the university to plan a new building with everything commensurate for a college of 5000 students; and the result was a scale of structure which would give acceptable room to 600 readers at the same moment, and would hold a million and a half of volumes with a prospective capacity of three millions—a great hive, the queen bee of which is a single folio come down to us through more than two centuries and a half, the sole relic of the library of John Harvard.

Twenty years ago Mr. Spofford reckoned that the library of Congress would reach half a million of volumes at the present time. It more than reached it in eight years. It was but the other day that the final stone was laid on the great building at Washington destined to hold the principal American library. The structure is claimed to have a capacity of at least five or six million of volumes; but I suspect that with modern devices for compact stowage, its capability as a store-house may be carried much beyond these figures. Perhaps it can be made to reach an extent something like five times the size of any existing collection of books, or just about equal to what a library must be, if it is to contain every book that has been printed.

If no great library has to-day more than a quarter or a fifth of the vast product of the press during these four and a half centuries since Gutenberg, is there a chance that in this new world we can hope to bring from their obscurity all that is not irrecoverably lost of those other three or four millions of volumes? The abyss of ages has doubtless swallowed some part of this literature, never to give it up, but it is probable that the greater part of it is scattered in many libraries or in obscure household repositories, and only needs to be brought together.

American competition in the European bookmarts, which has done so much in 50 years, not only to enhance prices, but to bring books from their hiding-places, may do something to recover for us this vast reserve of literature. The great area of our national library building, how-ever, is doubtless to be filled chiefly by the teeming products of the press in the future. Some-thing like 40,000 or 50,000 volumes of all kinds a year pass into the library of Congress, under the American copyright law alone.

These vast figures make the library problems, which the coming librarians are to confront, greatly interesting. There was a time when Englishmen thought the Bodleian contained every book worth having. Fifty years ago Panizzi came to the British Museum, fresh from an acquaintance with what the great continental collections preserved. He drew up a list of that library's deficien-cies, and British insularity stood aghast at the revelation. The assiduity of Jones, Bond, Thompson, Bullen, and Garnett, have ever since been doing much to remedy the defect.

These future problems, if great and in some ways difficult, are far from being appalling. Great occasions produce great resources, and historical crises raise up adequate men. I see no reason to believe that learning and education will not be in the future more deftly as well as more exhaustively served in an administrative sense, with these enormous segregations of books, than they are to-day with out far smaller collections. I see no reason to believe that libraries can outgrow our ability to handle them.

We have not yet reached the capabilities of cataloging and indexing, and have got to use more frequently the printed title, not altogether for its legibility, but for its compactness. When the British Museum authorities saw that their prospective 9000 huge volumes of its manuscript catalog was going to take for its convenient display a space three times the size of its own reading-rooms, they were forced into print. It was cheaper than building a new structure. We may be sure, also, that we have not begun in mechanical devices to take advantage of all that the Edisons have yet done, or may do, to find appliances to diminish labor and expedite service. Twenty years ago I outlined an automatic device for the delivery of books; and its principles have been re-adapted in a moving, endless chain, which is to render rapid the distribution of books in the new library at Washington.

I look to development in such directions that will make the library of the twentieth cen-tury, with a capacity and demand quadrupled over those of to-day, more easily administered in the serving of books, and more thoroughly subordinated to intellectual requirements in their catalogs, than any small library is to-day. Such developments will come in time. To Franklin the world owed 160 years ago a step in university extension, when he founded the Philadelphia library, more imposing than any that is making to-day. When he tamed the lightning, we may yet see what he rendered possible through electricity for library administration.

Nearly a score years ago I was present among a small circle of friends, when Graham Bell made a rude instrument in the rooms of the American Academy in Boston give out "Home, sweet home," as played on a distant piano. A year or two later, after I was one of the first to put the telephone to practical use in the Boston Public Library, I recounted its possible future to a dinner party, at Althorpe. The incredulous English thought my presumptuous fancies but the foolish rampage of an irrepressible Yankee. We know what has come of it.

We don't know what will yet come of the phonograph. Edison's first instrument was sent to Boston, to be shown to some gentlemen, before its character had been made known. I never expect again to see quite such awe on human gaces as when Gray's "Elegy" was repeated by an insensate box to a company of unsuspecting listeners. I look to see its marvellous capacities get utilized in the service of the librarian.

The scientists tell us, that palpitations once out upon the air never die; and that, had we instruments delicate enough to register them, we might yet hear the footfalls of Plato walking in the Academe; the denunciations of Brutus on the rostrum; the prayer of Columbus at San Salvador; the periods of Garrick at Drury Lane; the calm judgments of Washington in the Federal Convention. Perhaps we might listen more attentively yet to the splash of the paddle of Marquette and Joliet in that infant college, wandering along these neighboring shores. We must wait many developments of the way in which science is to walk, lock-stepped with the ardent librarian.

This library of the future is doubtless to be very costly, and we have got to compare the flame and the candle. The British Museum is to spend half a million dollars in printing its 3,000,000 titles. A recently erected library is to be lighted at an annual expense of $15,000— whether the necessity of such expense is wise may be a question. Nevertheless, a great librarian is an expensive necessity, and it is far from easy for the man of affairs to comprehend it. The processes of bulking, which reduce averages of expense in commercial measures, work quite otherwise in making money, foolish in making libraries. A certain rich man founded a college, and selected a librarian. This officer proposed to buy a bibliographical apparatus to aid him in selecting a library. "No," said Croesus. "I don't know anything about bibliography. Buy books as you happen to want them!"

A man of wide experience in affairs consulted me about a trust for a library in a metropolitan city. He had no doubt that the money would enable him to lead the world in libraries, and that the start of the great Paris library, with its two millions and more of books, was no discouragement. He would not only equal the old libraries in books, but he would have their manuscripts copied, and would even print such as no publisher would touch. When I examined the balance-sheet of the trust, I found that, after he had built his building, he could not compete for income with a third-class institution, as libraries do.

A distinguished advocate of the chief bar of the United States, in attacking the same trust on behalf of the heirs-at-law, is said to have claimed that such an endowment as the trustees held was out of all proportion to the needs of a library, and it would soon find that there were no books left to buy. Learned as this counsel was, he never suspected that there were still five or six millions of books which the biggest libraries had never yet succeeded in buying.

A distinguished Anglo-American, who spread his benefactions on two continents, once employed an agent to gather a library for his native town. He restricted him to an average cost per volume of one dollar, and no more. I remember the distress of this agent, when he told me of the bushels of cheap books he had to buy in order to give him the chance of buying a few more costly and indispensable books of reference, and still keep his average at a dollar. It is certainly one thing to bank for governments wisely, and quite another to cater with sagacity to the intellectual wants of your native village.

But the millionaire has his mission, if he is not always wise in it, for he must be depended upon to do what learning will not do. From a million to two millions, and more, have been privately bestowed on American communities in the endowing of libraries, in six or eight different instances, within a score of years. We can have nothing in this country like the sequestrations which have so conspicuously augmented some of the chief libraries of Europe, but of late we have begun to experience the gravitation of private collections of special interest toward our public libraries. It was a saying of Thomas Watt, the bibliographer, that the excuse for the existence of private collections is, that they may eventually be engulfed in public ones.

We have seen scholarship better equipped among us for what Mr. Lenox studiously preserved for us; for what the Barton collection has done for Shakespearean studies, in Boston; for what the White collection has done for students of the French Revolution and the Revolution, at Cornell; for the Dante collections at Cambridge and at Ithaca; the garnering of Von Mohe and Bluntschli at Yale and at Johns Hopkins; the geological and geographical library of Professor Whitney at Harvard; and the Spanish collection of George Ticknor, at the Public Library of Boston— not to name others. It is in Americana, however, that our libraries can naturally best compare with those of the Old World. The Ebeling, Worden, Bancroft, and Force collections have put all students of American history under obligations. They have seen with regret the Prescott, Brinley,

Barlan, Field, and Murphy collections scattered under the hammer, and cherish the hope that the Carter-Brown and Charles Deane collections may yet be possessed by the public.

The world has fewer more precious possessions than the books of a scholar, tinged with his mental contact. I remember seeing once in the London library in St. James' Square, a closet full of books, which had been lent to Carlyle, and carefully preserved, because when he read them he had entered his pungent exclamations and pithy comments on their margins. In recognition of this audacious habit, it had been the policy of the librarian to send to Carlyle every new book which he thought would interest him, because he was sure to scatter his disdain on the blank spaces. What these marginalia were we can imagine if we glance at the books streaked with his belligerent spirit, and shown in the collection used in writing his Cromwell and Frederick, which he bequeathed to the Harvard library.

The most significant development of the college library during the last score years is that which has worked parallel with seminary methods, and which has made laboratories out of collections of books. The elective system and the dispelling of vote-learning has reacted in the library, and the library has influenced them.

I may be in error, but I venture to say that this close mating of library uses with college work first took shape in Harvard college library, not 20 years ago. When the process of closely applying particular books to help instruction was then proposed, it was not received with much favor, and most of the teachers discredited the innovation. The plan was a simple one. The teacher was to name to the librarian the books to which in his lectures he was to refer, and these, taken from their places in the general library, were to be made accessible to the students in a given alcove. My recollection is that not more than a score or two of books were thus designated in the beginning, by two or three instructors. It took a year or two to make a real start; but to-day not a teacher of the two or three hundred at work in the college but is eager for this chance to promote his pupils' study. So, instead of a dozen or two books, we count now in the shelves 7000 or 8000 volumes particularly applicable to the instruction. With allied reference books there are 25,000 to 30,000 volumes open to the immediate contact of the interested student. The system has gone a step further in the creation of class-room libraries, close at hand in the hour of instruction, and ten or a dozen of these supplemental collections show from a few score to a few thousand volumes each. All this has conduced to an enormous increase in the use of books, and our statistics reveal that a very small proportion of the students are not frequenters of the library.

Nor is this all, which is, in these latter days, done to facilitate the use of the books. Systematic instruction in bibliographical research keeps in the van of every subject a cloud of skirmishers, who bring in title after title for the consideration of the library authorities. Thus, the whole system becomes a practical endowment of research, and the library becomes a central agency in college work. It "teaches the teachers," as President Eliot has said of it.

There is at this point one particular question—With this importance in the broad system of instruction, does the library always get its due share of the money resources of the college? Are not too often the advantages of its improvement weighed against those of a new chair? If another institution creates a professorship of Tamil, cannot the library wait till we create *our* chair of Tamil? Do the authorities always consider that every diminution of the library's essential allowance is simply a check upon the proficiency of *existing* chairs?

Is it too much to say that the library is the very core of the university? I once said, "The library should be to the college much what the dining-room is to the house—the place to inaugurage the system under cheerful conditions with a generous fare and good digestion." There cannot be too much care bestowed in making this place of intellectual sustenance attractive. Grateful appearances beget grateful humors.

The fact is, a librarian needs every advantage he can possibly command, if he is going to make his library of the utmost profit. He must be himself a standing invitation to the library's hospitality. I remember one day, shortly after I took charge of the library at Cambridge, seeing an old man bearing a head that no one could forget, with its black cavernous eyes and white shaggy locks—the most picturesque character that we have ever had in our Harvard faculty; I remember seeing this old man climbing clumsily up a steep stair to a cock-loft. I asked where he was going, and was told that in the crowded state of the library the collection of books in modern Greek, being used by no one else, had been placed in this upper loft, and that it was the old man's habit to go there and seek quiet among the books. Shortly after, I inspected the collection and found it a motley assemblage of volumes in bad bindings or in none. I ordered them to be tidily bound, and placed in a fitting room. Thereafter Professor Sophocles was my friend. "I want to tell you a story," said he to me one day, in that deep sonorous tone which gave his talk so much Rembrandtish character. "My father," he went on, "asked to be chosen the chief man of the village where he lived in Greece. There was another man who had the same wish. One night there came to my father's home two men, scowling and saying nothing. They had knives in their girdles. 'How much did my rival promise to pay you if you killed me?' asked my father. They told him. 'Humph!' he replied, 'I will pay you twice as much to kill him!' They left on a new errand."

This was the way my venerable friend had of making a ghoulish tale serve for a bit of advice. If an inquirer comes to the librarian to lay him bare to his knife, send him away with twice the reward. Compound, if you can, the interest on the visitor's investment.

A librarian often wonders that a student can go through a four years' course without really becoming proficient in the use of books; without learning that it is not always the reading of books that most enriches, but the skillful glancing at them. We do not want to go a journey with a stallion to find if he can throw his feet in a two-twenty gait. We must jockey in books— make them show their paces over a half-hour course—and leave the plodding reader to be lost in the bewilderment of sentences.

It is a librarian's luxury when a man comes to him who knows how to master a book and to dominate a library. If our colleges would pay more attention to the methods by which a subject is deftly attacked, and would teach the true use of encyclopedic and bibliographical helps, they would do much to make the library more serviceable.

The time lost in *floundering* among books would fringe the dreariest existence with many graceful amplitudes of learning, if men were taught to investigate as they are taught to swim. Floundering is not study. Then there is the waste of time and energy in rediscovering what is already known. The wise student looks for the blazed pathways of those who have gone before him.

A university scope in instruction, selection in studies and the pursuit of special aims, are certainly doing much to make us produce celebrated scholars and enlarge the bounds of knowledge; but I trust that we may never cease to value the generous and all-round training of the small college. It is of inestimable value to us Americans that we have these small colleges, and I always feel a pang when one of them puts on university airs. It is the function of such colleges and their libraries to make educated gentlemen, to whom no knowledge is superflous, who respond to every intellecutal sympathy, and who make of social intercourse a well-spring of learned delights. It is the function of the university to enlarge the bounds of knowledge, to make one acquirement the stepping-stone to another, to lay tribute upon nature and probe the obscurities of learning. Heaven defend that they should not make gentlemen *and* scholars; but the amenities of our social existence are much more dependent on cultured gentlemen whose education does not aspire to the deeper scholarship.

I know of a university town where the atmosphere is saturated with the damps of specialisms; one wonders if Sanskrit or hypnotism, or electrodynamics exist for the world's sake or the world exists for them. It is the fashion of this community to maintain dinner clubs among its professors, and once a fortnight these clubs listen to an essay on the peculiar specialty of its host. He gives in the latest intelligence in his little world. Somebody has discovered an abnormal vein in a butterfly's wing. Another puts his lens on a literary critic and makes him hateful. A third tells how a Roman folded his napkin. It is a rule of these clubs that there should be no two members devoted to like studies, and when the essay is read each of these specialists trains his own little gatling-gun upon the poor essayist. The show is sometimes brilliant; sometimes it wearies a trifle. The scintillations sometimes light up unwonted depths, and I go home in a state of amazement at the mutiplicity of the mind's angles. Intellectual life certainly gets new significance as one vantage-ground after another is brought into use in the contemplation of a topic.

I go again to a table full of gentlemen, who make no profession of advanced learning. I have on my right a banker who has just read a novel in which he finds a misconception of a curbstone operator. Someone across speaks of an horticultural exhibition, and my friend tells the story of the introduction of the chrysanthemum from Japan, and is led to speak of Parkman's success in the hybridizing of lilies. My left hand neighbor says he has been at Belle Mead and ridden behind Iroquois. My Wall street friend knows the pedigree of Iroquois, and tells me who his grandsire was.

Our host is reminded of a celebrated horse of Colonial days who carried Gen. John Winslow on some famous ride. My moneyed neighbor immediately fills out the story of the Acadians, and traces back the tale of the Cajeuns in Louisiana.

"My friend," said I, turning to him, "what don't you know about?" "Oh, I graduated at a little college in the New England hills, where we turn out educated gentlemen, who know a little of everything and not a great deal of anything; who can talk with a Pundit or a Sioux and make him believe he is talking with a brother."

Thus both dinner-table experiences illustrate what is the difference between the educated gentleman and the special scholar. Is not one as necessary to our civilization as the other?

I have said nothing of the relations of the college and books to the most momentous problem of our day.

Squirarchy and birth, which ruled our nation once, have given place to a new order. Political economy in its sociological aspects has become a study of contemporary manifestations. It is no longer the geologist alone who takes his pupils afield. The professor of social economics finds his "strata" in graded benefactions, and his "faults" in broken lives. We cry much about education as the safety-valve of this mighty change, and say that university extension is a saving grace. Along with it all has come the wonderful growth of our free-library system. In Massachusetts the state stands ready to help any town to have its library, and few there are without them. All this cannot mean, I think, that books and education are losing their hold on the people. We are sometimes alarmed at the coming among us of vast hordes of aliens. We should not forget that we have in this country passed through just such disturbing conditions before, when our life was not equally well prepared to deal with the phenomena. Study the history of that huge wave of Americanization which, in the last century and in the early part of this, broke like a sea against the Appalachians, swept through their gaps and moved athwart the great valley of the Mississippi, broke again upon the Rockies and toppled down the Pacific slope. How much of this surging wave was of alien blood? Look at the names on the street-signs of every considerable town, which that wave has left stranded in its passage. I doubt if, as our frontier moved west, there were fewer aliens in proportion than we find among us to-day.

I happen myself to come of the ancientest of our New England stock. I can hold my grandchild on my knee and tell it of its great-grandfather, and of *his* father and grandfather—six generations whom I have known, as much as would carry some old persons still living back to Plymouth Rock, and yet may I not well afford to welcome the alien who landed yesterday at Castle Garden? Of a family nurtured on the sea, I have come to nourish my existence on books. Is it strange that I believe the laborer of to-day will be the progenitor of future bookmen?

The students of Harvard College are seen nowadays in the manual training school. The president of a southern university, when he took me into the workshop of his institution, said to me: "We found out in the civil war what an advantage to you of the north was the spread of industrial practices among your people, and we don't propose to forget it." If it was an advantage in helping save the Union, can it be otherwise in helping to carry our life to higher results?

20. ADDRESS AT THE UNIVERSITY OF MICHIGAN, 1883

I have no mission with you this evening, but to bear the congratulations of the oldest of our Universities to the most vigorous of the younger, on this auspicious occasion. I would like to have brought with me a fitting credential in the shape of a certain huge folio, but the burden of it was too great. Some of you may have seen it, for it is a precious heirloom with us, of Harvard—a copy of Downame's *Christian Warfare Against the Devil*. To look upon its title page brings back to us something of that theological atmosphere, which surrounded those who founded a college in the New England wilderness nearly two hundred and fifty years ago. In the bold and vigorous copperplate engraving of the time we see on that title the plumed knight of the cross, clad in panoply from a worldly forge, holding at bay the imps of the evil one, brandishing their barbed tongues and bracing themselves on cloven hoofs. There is enough of the good orthodoxy of our puritan fathers, compacted within the covers of that ponderous tome to turn a deluge of modern agnosticism. Why could this weighty volume be a good credential to bring to this festival of your library?

When John Harvard, in 1638, hardly a year in the country, and but a few years after he had left those signatures at taking his bachelor's and master's degrees on the records of the University of the English Cambridge—the sole records of his existence, which the most filial curiosity has been able to find in the mother country,—and while feeling the insidious advance of that New England scourge, pulmonary consumption, made his will in the Massachusetts Charlestown, and left the half of an estate (to be classed among the largest possessed by his fellow colonists) to endow the college, then gathering on the banks of the Charles, he added to his benefaction his entire library of two hundred and sixty works; and so the college grew upon a foundation of books! When in 1764, while the provincial assembly of Massachusetts was occupying Harvard Hall, to escape a pestilential disease, which was raging in Boston, a neglected fire upon the hearth, more untameable than the sulphurous blazes of the theology about it, laid the building low and destroyed the entire library, which was housed in the building, except about a hundred volumes, which chanced to be in the hands of borrowers, and among them was this massive volume, of which I have spoken, the sole survivor now of John Harvard's two hundred and sixty books.

When in 1638, the books of the "godly Harvard," as the records call him, were borne across Charlestown neck to the infant seminary at Cambridge, the problem was not yet solved, if an adventurous woodsman by going westward, and passing perhaps the very spot, where we are now assembled, might not reach, footsore with continuous land-travel the Cathay of Marco Polo. Some imaginative geographers, had indeed for a long time severed the Continents of Asia and America by the Straits of Anian, but there was a long lifetime yet to pass, before Behring, without knowing it, sailed from the Pacific to the Arctic seas. Poor was the comprehension then of your Michigan peninsula to the young eyes, which saw a wealth of learning in the heap of books, stacked so portentously in the rude study of Nathaniel Eaton, the master of the incipient college. As we read the list of those two hundred and sixty books, we may well ask ourselves, what would Aquinas, and Beza, Chrysostom and Calvin and Duns Scotus, Luther and Pelagius, have told them of the country of the Ottawas and Miamies? Would Minsheu's *Guide to the Tongues*, to quote another of the titles, have recognized the linguistics of Aboriginal America? Would Bacon's *Advancement of Learning* (for that too was there), have solved the problem of the Mound-builders? Would Homer have told the battles of the Iroquois and the Eries? Would the gallery of Plutarch have shown to them the heroism of Nicolet and Champlain, tracking your neighboring waters? Would Horace have voiced the chants of the Hurons?

There was but one book among them which might be expected to tell them anything of this region, and that was an early edition of Peter Heylyn's *Cosmographia*, but to Heylyn the basin of the great lakes was an area, which he might have well filled on his maps with elephants and parrots, to say nothing of a throne for the great Cham of Tartary. The colonists of New England in 1638 knew absolutely nothing of this valley of the lakes and the adjacent water-shed of the gulf of Mexico. Even the French of Canada, with their better knowledge, could

Source: *Public Exercises on the Completion of the Library Building* . . . Dec. 12, 1883. Ann Arbor, 1884, pp. 26-39.

only surmise that your territory was on the line of that passage to India, of which Lachine, or the New China, was but the first stage of the westward progress. And so, ignorance of some things and pretence of others found its place in the books of the new college. Ignorance and pretence often lurk very near to our strongholds of knowledge, to-day. There is a good story told of one of Harvard's most distinguished presidents. Edward Everett was expected to respond to a toast in praise of classical learning at a dinner of the Φ B K society. As he was going to the dinner, he turned to his shelves to select a small edition of Homer to put in his pocket. There chanced by some strange juxtaposition to stand side by side, a convenient Homer and another book of equal size. By mistake he took the other. He approached the climax in his speech. He pictured the all pervading intuition of Homer. He told the old stories of valor and tenderness. He drew from his pocket the captive missionary, and holding it aloft with that tremor of the hand, which we all remember, he said, "Within the covers of this book," and then went on to epitomize the experience and wisdom of Homer. As he laid his text beside his plate, while the table rang with the applause at the completed apostrophe, an inquisitive neighbor took it up, and found it to be *Hoyle's Games*. So pretence in some form or other, wittingly or unwittingly enters the citadels of the humanities.

And what are these citadels, the best of them, compared with what they might be? Rather than answer my question by the palpabilities which you anticipate, let me, by a few venturesome statistics reply to a question which is often put to me, as I have no doubt it is put to your librarian: What is the use of so many books? Who reads them? Why not sift them and burn the trash? If there was wisdom in this inquiry, neither you nor we would have to build new libraries.

With very rare exceptions not a book has been published since the invention of printing without its use in some way. The next best thing to finding a book helpful is to satisfy yourself it is not helpful; but that may not by any means imply that it is of no value to another. Inanities indeed are a constituent part of psychological study. We have the inanities of our own day about us in walking figures; but the inanities of the days of Elizabeth are only preserved for our social studies in books, as those of Victoria and Arthur will be preserved to future times. When the Roman said: *Homo sum, humani nihil a me alienum puto*, he did not mean that his study was of his *wise* brothers only. Folly and inanity are not without their lessons. To us who are on a height, the groping progress, the slippery climbing, that generations before us have gone through, are not to be discarded in the study of humanity, or of the humanities. Such is my plea for what some are fain to call worthless books. No one so well as a librarian, who is alive in every direction to the wants of everybody, knows the importance of most, which is covered by a term, so flippantly used by a narrow experience—*trash*.

Nothing is more true than that comparatively few books add much to our store of knowledge. Most books are indeed a digest, made with more or less skill of other books or of parts of many books; but they go to make up the class of useful as distinct from original books, and they have a certain adaptability in one direction or another, which is the excuse for their being. Furthermore a book may have a curious psychological interest, independent of any addition to knowledge, which it may convey, as representing a type of mind, local peculiarities, or race-structure, which as one of a mass becomes of some importance in the study of mind. It is always dangerous to say a book is of no value. There is no truism—as I think—which a librarian is oftener called upon to assert and to illustrate, than that it is impossible to say what current ephemeral publication may not become of cardinal interest. I can well understand how a specialist looks with something of disgust upon that labor of the librarian, which tickets away the ephemera of a study foreign to his own. He is, however, quick to see the possible value of the dingy chap-books of his own study.

I am sometimes, from my observations, forced to a conviction of the narrowing influence of special studies in that they are apt to use the wrong end of the telescope in viewing other attainments. It is no small part of a librarian's duty to make a counter force in such cases and to defend on general principles all sorts of studies. Is it not too often the fault of restricted studies which makes us a cyclops with one eye, until we lose the relief of a background? It is two eyes which give sphericity to the disk. It is foil and counter-foil in study which makes the object of it seem palpable and graspable. Coleridge once said that the principle of Gothic architecture is infinity made imaginable. In the same way we may say that a widened sympathy in intellectual studies makes the vastness of knowledge comprehensible.

The most costly nuggets of English libraries to-day are the little six-penny play-books of Elizabeth's time whose countless thousands perished with the reading and whose survivors are the chance waifs, which have run the gauntlet of all sorts of vicissitudes. The purifiers and collators of our English texts have taught us their value. Perhaps no one more than Macaulay has made manifest the wealth of historic illustrations existing in the ephemera of all ages. Mr. Edward Edwards, the chief English authority on library history and economy, has said that the trash of one generation becomes the highly prized treasure of another. It is to-day the rule of the Bodleian, the British Museum, and the other great libraries of Europe to reject nothing, having long ago learned the folly of discrimination, and I am glad to say that our chief American libraries follow the same rule.

Counting by volumes, not by works, it may be safe to assume that in the last four hundred and fifty years, there have been put upon the world an aggregate of not far from 10,000,000 books—trash included; and of these scarcely more than a fifth part can be found in any one library; and probably very much less than all can be found combined in the great libraries of the world to which scholars resort. Nor can we reasonably suppose that the world was ever better able to compass all knowledge, through books, than now. We read of the enormous extent of a few ancient libraries; but careful computation does not put the amount of matter in the largest of them above the equivalent of a modern library of 100,000 volumes, and of this size there are at present not far from a hundred in the civilized world; and the great collections of London, Paris, and St. Petersburg would each swallow up near a score of these ancient collections. When the Harvard library was burned a hundred and twenty years ago, it was the largest by far in America and it contained scarcely more than 5,000 volumes; and not a library in Europe possessed over 200,000. Nothing perhaps presents our relative growth as an intellectual factor in civilization better than the fact that our chief American library of a century ago contained about a fortieth of the resources belonging to the largest of the European libraries, while we have two or three to-day which are from a fifth to a quarter as large as the greatest of those in Europe. Even within this century the Vatican, Bodleian and British Museum have been loosely held to contain every printed book. It is doubtful if the Vatican has to-day more printed books than, for instance, the Boston Athenaeum, a library of the second class with us; and the Bodleian more than the Library of Congress. We have several larger libraries in the United States than exist in Italy to-day.

The 10,000,000 volumes constituting first and last the world's stock of books since the invention of printing with an average edition of 300—which I think is low—will give an aggregate of 3,000 millions of volumes, which the press has produced during four and a half centuries, and of these 3,000 millions, I doubt if there are in the United States in public or semi-public libraries, where scholars might supplement their own private collections, fifteen millions of volumes, or say, one-half of one per cent of the grand total,—a striking estimate of the inadequacy of public collections of all sorts, to preserve a world's literature, for I take it, we account ourselves much better, as a nation, than a half of one per cent. in relation to the mass of the world's communities.

In the fifty or sixty years which followed the first work of the press, and within the fifteenth century it is usually reckoned there were at least 16,000 volumes printed at all of the presses of the forty-two cities which are known to have had printing offices. It is not an unfair estimate to place the average edition of those days at 500 copies, and this would give a round eight million of incunabula—cradle books,—of which the number which have come down to us is comparatively small. Of this 8,000,000 I doubt if there are more than a very few thousand on this continent. I do not regard the possible excess in some of the libraries of Spanish America, when I say that the largest number which I know in this part of the world, is the four or five hundred which belong to the Union Theological Seminary, of New York.

Now what are the relations of a single American scholar to this vast aggregate of ten million of books, who in pursuing any subject to its final conclusion, would not, if he has the scholar's longing instincts, let any book go unquestioned which might give him knowledge or prove the absence of knowledge.

It was DeQuincy's computation, that a man the most favorably situated, and reaching old age, could hardly hope to *master* more than from five to eight thousand books. A person having to do with many books rarely masters them, if by that term it is meant, he reads them. Such a person by practice acquires great foraging skill. He reads first, perhaps, the most neglected part of the book, its preface. From that and the table of contents he has more than half won the battle in getting the author's purpose and divisionary methods. He skims the pages, reads at length such passages as appear salient, scans the foot-notes to discover his use of authorities; runs over his appendixes to see what he leaves over. I have known such a professional reader to run over two or three thick octavos of an evening; and to assimilate enough to serve him and those who made inquiries of him, from 1,500 volumes in a year, besides giving hasty inspection of thousands more. The literary luxury of such a man was the slow devourment, once a year, word for word, of a famed novel.

Of course few books survive in interest from century to century; but the scholar's range is beyond the perennial books. Three-quarters of the books published may be forgotten in the year, and not one in a hundred survive twenty years. It has been estimated that of the 50,000 books published in the 17th century not one in a thousand is worth reprinting—which is not by any means an equivalent term to re-reading—and of the 80,000 produced in the last century, scarce 500 are known to the general run of educated people.

It is a significant fact that not a single library in the world is perfect enough to satisfy any considerable number of different specialists. I have had to do with some of the best general libraries in this country, and yet I never attempted an exhaustive investigation of a single subject, that I did not find myself at a loss both for the books which have been, and for the books which have not been written. This is the fact to be thrust in the face of those who are always demanding the thinning out of our libraries. We generally agree that a man cannot better broaden himself than by seeking contact with his fellows, and he would be far from wise, who did not sometimes seek his inferiors as well as his betters. Yet books are but people, *usually at their best*, people of many ages and from various parts. The good folk who sneer at the profusion of books, seldom sneer at the still greater profusion of men!

I once asked the late Winter Jones, when he was the principal librarian of the best working library in the world, that of the British Museum, "How often does it happen that a special student, seeking the utmost recesses of his subject, can find all he desires in your vast collection?" His answer was, "Not one such investigator in ten is satisfied." "Because you haven't the books he needs?" I asked. "Yes, partly for that reason," he replied, "but still, in good part, because the books he wishes do not exist. When you have been a librarian as long as I have," he added, "you will be convinced of the exceedingly small margin of the bounds of knowledge as yet covered by printed books."

We may well be startled at such a confession from a librarian, whose life had brought him in contact with three generations of scholars of the old world, of all nationalities, coming to explore the great national library of England.

One-fifth part of the books that have been published will not satisfy one scholar in ten, and that dissatisfaction is equally great on account of the books which have not been published! Do you wonder that the City of Boston is talking of a library building that will hold prospectively ten millions of volumes? If our material longings are not to be satisfied till we annihilate space and abolish night, is the scholarly longing to be ignored, and are we to be long content with a scant twenty per cent. of possibilities? Let us leave the problem to our successors and from the empyrean a century hence, let us wonder at *our* days of small things!

With libraries, in most ways too narrow and confined for exhaustive research, we in America are forced in every direction to take matters as second hand, not to speak of much that we miss altogether. Scholarship, so far as it recondite and based on verification, is still, I fear, in most cases beyond our reach. The most important books we doubtless have, not in every library, though in the combination of our principal ones; but the test of thorough scholarship, is the proof that the minutest details have not escaped notice; and to this, can we only in a few subjects lay claim.

Our advances in the equipment of our libraries have been great within the last thirty years, but no one who undertakes to verify the references in any great book of European scholarship, but becomes aware of the vastly better advantages, especially in other languages than English, which he has in some of the great bibliographical centres of Europe. John Quincy Adams thought fifty years ago, that it was not to our credit that nowhere in the United States, could Gibbon be tracked through his course by the verification of his foot-notes. I doubt if it can be done to-day.

While this condition may be a cause of regret, it is no cause for reproach. Libraries like those of London, Paris and St. Petersburg, are not the creation of a lifetime, and it is hardly more than that since we in this country set seriously to work to amass large collections of books. Thomas Watt said twenty years ago, that it was only a question of time when a scholar would have to visit the great libraries of America as well as of Europe to be sure of completely hunting down the authorities. Within a year I have known a Spanish scholar, who is exhausting all resources for a history of Columbus, to find it important, after Madrid and Genoa, Paris and London had been explored, to cross the ocean to see what our libraries and eager collectors had carried off as prizes from the dealers of Europe.

It is nearly thirty years since in a Paris auction room I looked on one of the bouts, which Dibdin likes to describe, when the coveted object was the oldest cartographical monument of American history, and the combatants were well-known representatives of the crown of Spain, the Bibliothèque Imperiale of Paris and a private American collector. The prize hung before the assembly. It was an oxhide on which was depicted the known world, showing at one extremity, all that had been discovered of the new found islands, as they were supposed to be, lying about Japan. The chart bore the name of its maker, one of the pilots of Columbus, and the date of 1500. The bidding was spirited, and a certain young American, who was in the room, recognized the coming glory of American libraries, when his country's champion pressed hard upon his rivals, even though his courage failed him, when the agent of Queen Isabella swept the field at four thousand, two hundred francs.

That America has struggled well to equip her scholars is only too apparent in the enhancement of the commercial value of old books, which has gone on under American competition in the book-marts of London, Paris and Leipzig. It is not unfair to say that our own eagerness has at least doubled the antiquarian prices, in most cases, and much more in some. European libraries and collectors recognize this and regard it jealously. In one department, that of early Americana, the increase in prices has been enormous, and is still going on extravagantly under the false competition, introduced in the methods, which have been employed to the general detriment of letters, in the selling of the Brinley and Cooke collections.

When the American, Obadiah Rich, set up in London as a bookseller fifty or sixty years ago, he printed catalogues which showed prices a fifth or a sixth part of the sum necessary now to secure the same books. And this scale of increase rules in every department of learning, and if not always to the same degree, certainly to a considerable degree. It has thus become a serious financial problem for American libraries to make themselves great. Fortunately, money comes easier now to them, than it did fifty years ago.

Bibliography is growing, and it is essential that it should be so, a far less special attainment than it used to be. It is in fact a study fast becoming necessary to every scholar, who without it may be lost in a wilderness of books. It may be an instance of the subduing of my nature to what it works in, like the dyer's hand, but I never read the touching recital in Evangeline of the rushing by, unobserved, of Gabriel's boat, while the maiden lay screened by the palmettos, without likening the trapper of the Atchafalaya to the uncircumspect student, who never knows how near he is passing to the object of his study. It is the aim of bibliography, as it is now understood among us, to prevent just these misfortunes, and the great agency in this revolution is the subject-catalogue. It is a matter of congratulation to us as Americans, that the potentiality of the subject-catalogue is a power of our own creation; and we have developed it, despite the disregard, not to say disapproval of the older world, which is now, however, beginning to show unmistakeable signs of their error.

There are potent reasons for the lead in this direction taken by American librarians. Our libraries are comparatively young and small. We are not hampered with traditions, come down from a period when monks were the only scholars, and monasteries the only libraries. We did not so much *possess* as we were trying to *make* a race of scholars. We were making them of everybody. We paid little regard to prescriptive rights of everybody. We could not tell where our encouragement would bear fruit, and so we worked as if everybody needed help and would take it.

There is no factor in the efficiency of a library equal to the Catalogue. It used to be the librarian. Van den Weyer in 1849, in his remarks before the Royal Commission at the British Museum, when some librarians were raising all sorts of excuses against the preparation of even Authors' Catalogues, met them very squarely when he told them, that the librarians who undervalued catalogues were aiming to make themselves personally indispensable. It was a telling blow at the traditional librarian and it was the truth. The race is not yet dead; and I could name one or two in this country.

With much that is discouraging progress is making, and librarians have no need to be disappointed in the growing sympathy with their requirements, which the last few years have shown.

The work of the librarian is only now sharing the perplexities, which all sciences experience in that transition stage when they are passing from the purlieus of pretence to the recognized status of a department of knowledge. Botany was once but the province of "all simples that have virtue under the moon." Genesis was once the text-book of Geology. A similar crassness of ignorance has surrounded and still in some degree surrounds the science of *bibliothetics*, if I may be allowed the word. Dr. Johnson found lexicography in much the same disrepute, when common notion placed it, as he says, like "a task, that requires neither the light of learning, nor the activity of genius; but may be successfully performed without any higher quality than that of bearing burdens with dull patience, and beating the track of the alphabet with sluggish resolution."

The modern library movement, which is beginning to disabuse the common mind of similar estimates, owes probably more than to any one else, the first development, which took it from its plane of empiricism up to the level of science, to the indomitable will, the clear perceptions and the great learning of an Italian outcast, who by his sheer competency, reached the chief position in the best working library in the world. The names of Antonio Panizzi and the British Museum are inseparably linked. He had not only a hostile public to confront; but he had to overcome his own official superiors, the trustees of the Museum, and he did it. Parliamentary commissions and Royal commissions started up, urged by petitions of men, who looked to the library to supply some deficiency in their own mental organism; but Panizzi's manly and honest fight evinced a potency that in the end not only forced all opposition to succumb; but also all that was generous in it to acknowledge him a victor.

It will be dry reading doubtless to most, despite the piquancy of some of the cross-examinations; but the Blue Books which contain the reports of those Royal commissions of 1835 and 1848 on the British Museum must always be resorted to in the study of library economy. I read them when I was in college, and they did much to prepare me for the life of librarian, when fortuitous circumstances placed me, without any gradation of ascent, at the head of a large library. I have read every word of those ponderous folios more than once since,—always with an increasing admiration of the courageous mental power lodged in the rugged physical form of that Italian refugee. There is no name of so potent a spell on an occasion like this, or one I would so like to leave last in your ears, as that of ANTONIO PANIZZI.

21. THE PERILS OF HISTORICAL NARRATIVE

I hope to show how the elements and concomitants of historical narrative are imperiled by perversion and accident; how their accuracy is often little more than a question of belief; how they are emasculated by what is called the dignity of history; how they are debilitated by the so-called philosophy of history; how they are modified by unavoidable change in men and manners, and subject to revision through the development and readjustment of material in the hands of succeeding writers.

There is no quality of the historian upon which so great stress is laid, nor one so little understood, as what is called his accuracy; and it seems difficult for the layman to consider it other than a positive thing. Historical accuracy is, in fact, the most fleeting of vanities. Hard, dry, distinguishable facts there doubtless are. An annalist may deal with them and seldom err. But the difference between an annalist and a historian is, that the mere facts of the first as used by the latter become correlated events, which illumine each other, and get their angles of reflection from many causes external to the naked facts. These causes are the conditions of the time, which gave rise to the facts; the views of the period in which they are studied; and the idiosyncrasies of the person studying them. Hence no historical statement can be final. Views change, and leave credulity and perversion always to be eradicated from the historian's page. Individuals are cast in varying moulds. Until Nature has reached the limit of her ethnical and personal diversities, there can be no stay to the rewriting of history upon the basis of the same data; and the problem is kept otherwise alive by the constant discovery of new material. So we may well ask if an annalist is accurate; but to put the same question respecting a historian means a great deal more; and, beyond a certain range, it is never easily answered, and rarely with satisfaction. It is this uncertainty that keeps historical study perennial. It is very easy to say that history is false. Napoleon called history nothing but established fiction. Frederick the Great spoke of it as "lies mixed with some truths." The well-known story of Raleigh in the Tower is rehearsed to point the denunciatory moral, and then we are told that this story itself has no authority, and is another of the lies. The novelist and playwright claim, or the claim is made for them, that their plots and characters are more historic than the historian's. Fielding said that only his names and dates were false, while in the histories these alone were true. Such are the commonplaces which lead many people to talk much of the superiority of Shakespeare's English history to that of the chroniclers and historians. It is superior in its way; and, with this acknowledgment, there is no proposition to discuss. We want Shakespeare, and Bacon, and Hume, and Hallam, and Macaulay, and Green, and Lecky, and we want them all. It is of no more account that their recitals do not agree in details than it is that the horses of a sweepstakes are of different colors.

We are often deceived by the disguises of truth. It is a legal fiction that the king, or the state, is always present in court. Truth stands at the bar of history in much the same way. She is hidden from us in the raiments of the historian. A famous lawyer once said that there is an idiom in truth beyond the imitation of falsehood. Therefore, whatever its obscurities, whatever the special pleas of a partisan, whatever the blur of the personal equation, truth may still be there, to be seen at times by sharp eyes in a learned head. Accuracy in a historian is a question of comparison, largely. It depends greatly upon the reader's views. Accuracy in the sense that a problem in mathematics is accurate is, in much that a historian is bound to write, wholly out of the question. You cannot deal with appearances and motives, as a historian must, and demonstrate a truth beyond dispute.

A distinguished author, who sometimes writes history, once said to me, respecting a proposition which he had made, that, if it were not true, it ought to be. It was better than truth to him, and no doubt was to his readers. What is a fact in the face of the higher law of truth? Bulwer puts it thus: "Facts, if too nakedly told, may be very different from truths in the impression they convey." A writer of history, who was trying to tell a story of the making of a new social system in a philosophical spirit, by interlarding his narrative with bits of generalizations, asked me how he could improve his books. I told him by so arranging his narrative that its philosophy would go without saying, or would, in other words, be carried by his narrative. He went for comfort to a brother philosopher, who told him to stick to his philosophy and leave

Source: *Atlantic Monthly* 66 (1890): 289-97.

out his facts. There are men who hate facts. When a novelist submitted to me a piece of history which he had been writing, and I pointed out its errors of statement, he scorned what he called "the stern brutality of facts." No one who has dealt largely with historical research but quite understands this disparagement of much that passes for judicial and learned statements; for no one knows so well as such a student that to make a statement of the circumstances of an event involves estimates of probabilities, of character, and of purpose that are not wholly to be clinched by unimpeachable evidence.

I fear that the unquestioned accuracy of history is like the vital principle of life: we seek for it, but never find it. In history, as in all else, we agree to disagree, and accuracy has more faces than Janus. It is in the nature of things that it should be so. Freeman tells us that "absolute certainty is unattainable by the very best historical evidence"; and he adds, as respects two witnesses, that exact agreement in every minute detail is held to be a little surprising. So it is that accuracy in any correlated historical statement is often nothing more than probability as it lies in one mind.

The successful historian employs the same faculties which make for the merchant his fortune. It is penetration of character, discernment of qualities, judicial sifting of evidence, judgment of probabilities, that enable the historian to give the seeming of fact; and, after all, it is but a seeming. The late Dr. Deane succeeded in making uncertain the Pocahontas story of the rescue of John Smith; but there is still left a chance of its accuracy, so that the romance will never die, and each generation will renew the discussion. It is pretty much this condition that governs all historical research, where the character of the actor or of the narrator has any play. We see it in what Niebuhr has done for Rome and Grote for Greece. Thus the historian may follow the annalist in his dates and other certainties, and at the same time be conscious that omniscience, infallibility, and the infinite are quite beyond his ken. He knows how scant his divination is as to the probable truths. He knows the difficulty of giving a just value to circumstances. He cannot tell how far, purposely or accidentally, the statements of his witnesses are misleading. Who, for instance, can be quite sure of the maps of the age of American discovery, when we know Spain always concealed her knowledge, and would sometimes resort to falsification in her hydrographical offices, in order to deceive her rivals? Nor was Portugal free from similar practices. Indeed, there is nothing more harrowing to the historical investigator than deceits of record. What was intended to befog us; and all the more readily if it has been transmitted amid the confusion of prejudice and principle in the mind of the person transmitting it. The wiles of diplomacy are proverbial. One would never suspect, from the letters of Melbourne to Lord Ashburton, that the British government held the evidence to sustain the American side in the northeastern boundary controversy. A general writes a letter on purpose to have it intercepted, and it falls into the hands of an unsuspecting historian.

The historian must encounter among his authorities the alarmist, the faintheart, and the braggart. We must not wholly believe the fugitives from Braddock's field nor the miserable wanderers from a rapine, like those who escaped from the slaughter of the Wyoming Valley. The particulars of the Norse sagas become to errant minds mere milk for babes. The mendacities of Thevat and Hennepin confound the early geography of a continent. The spurious prophecies of Montcalm, the Philadelphia speech of Sam Adams, the letters that the enemies of Washington tried to make live with the authority of his misused name, are but instances of the political chicanery that would misguide public opinion. But how much that is false is still accepted! How much history must be rewritten upon the demonstration of such falsity! Stubbs tells us that the proved discovery of the forgery of Ingulf's History of Croyland Abbey was a fact that necessitated the revision of every standard book on early English history. Our most distinguished historian was obliged to rewrite his La Salle when Margry divulged documents which he had kept out of sight.

The record may be falsified by national or local pride. Time was when the Scots claimed the blood of the Pharoahs, when the Britons made themselves the heirs of Aeneas, when the genealogy of the Spanish kings was carried back to Noah. Every hero of the Middle Ages traced up to Hector. In our day, a weak mind has discerned the blood of Odin meandering through the veins of Washington. We have within a score of years seen state pride seek to make history anew by aggrandizing the transient sojourn of Popham's followers on the Maine coast into the parent effort of New England settlement.

It is the romance of history which attracts the half educated and secures the publisher. An active man of affairs and vigorous writer, who has made some successful ventures in the fields of history, believes that we should elaborate the episodes of progress, and let the gaps and level spaces alone. Another writer, more eminent in fiction than in history, holds that no book has a reason for being which is not popularly readable. Such as these establish canons of history more for the present than for all time. It is the converse of Voltaire's proposition that history is playing tricks with the dead, and is rather beguiling the living. The fact is, however we play tricks with the dead or beguile the living, the historical narrative can have no finality. It appeals anew, in each generation, to fresh individuals, or must be told under changed conditions of society. This is a reason for its perennial character quite apart from any necessity of retracting, arising from new discoveries of material. "Truth indeed is single," says Prescott, "but opinions are infinitely various." We must not forget how important a share of any historical narrative is the opinion of the narrator; and, moreover, according to Freeman, we should not forget that "the history of opinion about facts is really no small part of the history of those facts." Farther is it true that though the historian has to do with facts, or what he supposes to be facts, he has quite as much to do with what his actors supposed were facts, but were not. Columbus, on the coast of Cuba, making his crew swear they were on the coast of Asia, and Balboa discovering what he called the South Sea, dominated the historical geography of their time.

History, so far as it embodies the study of the characters of men, deals necessarily with their motives, which are the foundations of character. How uncertain the scrutiny of personal motives is needs hardly to be said. The historian's divining-rod to find the well-spring of motive is his own predisposition, which is the unfailing cause of a diversity of views. John Adams saw a hater of New England in the royal governor of the Stamp Act times. To-day we discover in the diary of Thomas Hutchinson the most filial of natives. The speech which Webster puts into the mouth of John Adams, another imagined by Botta, and an actual record, if we had one, would be far from alike. Mitford sees aristocracy in Greece, and Thirlwall democracy; and one wonders what the fact was. Was it qualities which they had inherited from a line of ancestry that made these respective writers so at variances? There is nothing more perplexing than the delicate relations in history of cause and effect, whether in the events or in the recorders of them. There seems sometimes to be nothing to check dependent progress, if we travel back over the annals of the world. Shall we say the American Revolution traces back to the Writs of Assistance, as most begin it; to the changes of European policy which followed the Treaty of Aix-la-Chapelle, as Bancroft divines; to the revulsion of the Andros revolution; or even to that taking of the emblems of a national life in their hands, when Winthrop and his fellows brought hither the charter of the Massachusetts Company? So mysteriously generation is linked with generation, and century grows out of century. Who would have thought that when the Plantagenet, Henry VII of England, gave a patent to the Venetian, John Cabot, and his three sons, to discover western lands, he would have determined the fact of the fee in the roadway of the New York Bowery, in a suit of abutters against an elevated street railway, as really happened the other day? Or when Champlain, a Frenchman, wintered on an island in the American wilds, in 1604, he would have determined by the traces of his occupancy a question of bounds between Great Britain and the revolted colonies, two centuries later? Bosworth field and the Bowery, Catholic France and rebellious Protestants, thus contrast and connect, and their concomitant results are good instances of the mutability and dependence of history. Events in the age of their happening are one thing; events placed in the world's memory, affecting the world's opinions and experiences, are quite another thing. This interlacing of the ages makes the new telling of old stories a part of the intellectual development of the race, and this retelling is necessarily subject to the writer's personality, and to the influence upon him of his day and generation. So the Tytlers and the Rollinses pass with damson plums and syllabubs into the limbo of forgotten things.

Distance in leagues, as well as in years, makes similar distinctions. This is shown territorially and chronologically in the rules of evidence. We do not find the flavor of the common law in the historians of France. Two centuries change the rules of the witness-stand in our own communities. We cannot forget this when we deal with witnesses of a former age. A sense of right may have been different then from what it is now. The pine-tree shilling of Massachusetts Bay and the iron coin of Lycurgus convey morals as different as can well be imagined. Webster delivering his eulogy on Adams and Jefferson in Faneuil Hall, in an academic gown, and an Irish Catholic descanting at Plymouth on the message of the Mayflower to civilization, have fallen within the survey of a long life. We might believe that when Voltaire said that what is not natural is not true, he could have known of just such paradoxes; but let us think a moment, and we shall decide that what is natural is really based on the artificial notions at the time prevailing. We find it sometimes difficult to believe this. It materially makes the past to us a thing of which the past had no conception. It needs a little effort to take in the fact, says Freeman, that we ought not to forget that Thucydides himself was not to his contemporaries all that he is to us.

The child takes his first history lesson from a fable of Aesop, or he is told how the naughty cat killed the canary. He is shown a moral in the fable, and made to see total depravity in the feline act. As we grow older, the story-telling of the histories is smothered with generalities and garnished with psychology, till we are in doubt whether we are hearing a story or reading the secrets of nature as some one else understands them. We emancipate ourselves at last, and find the freshness of life in the story that travels steadily to the end, in which its philosophy goes without saying, and the narrative needs no condiment to improve its flavor. Such are the stages in the development of the historical instinct. It needs training and large familiarity to convert a maundering method into directness, force, and significance. The colt paces, the finished roadster has learned to trot. To tell the story with Herodotus is what we have come to, after all experimenting.

It is often claimed, on the contrary, that it is the power of generalization and classification which makes a great historian; but this power alone is apt to come dangerously near to cant and platitude. To dole out homilies is not spaciousness of mind. General propositions are by no means circumspection of thought. Macaulay, in his description of a perfect law-giver, strikes close to the perfect historian: "a just temper between the mere man of theory, who can see nothing but general principles, and the mere man of business, who can see nothing but particular circumstances." It is such a one who makes a story, in the telling, carry the meaning which belongs to it, in all its breadth, equipoise, and significance. Gibbon did not spend much time in accounting for the influence of events. His recital showed the connection; an epithet gave the keynote. This, too, is not the least of Macaulay's charms. Neander, on the other hand, stands opaque before his story; and it is this dominating tendency of the Germans which makes a well-composed history so rare a thing in their literature.

I remember a trick of boyhood. A certain fish, when his abdomen is rubbed, swells with the confined air, so that when he is thrown back into his element he flounders desperately in efforts to dive. When I think of the philosophical historian gamboling in constraint upon the surface of his narrative, and never lost to sight, I bring to mind this sportive freak of the boy. It is in both cases a wronging of nature. Lingard says that few writers have done more to pervert the truth of history than philosophical historians. It is not that causes and effects do not exist; but the elements of the problem do not remain constant. The times are different, the conditions of life are altered, the peoples are not the same. We are apt to say that human nature is much the same everywhere; but we are little prone to recognize how great an influence on human nature the surroundings of it exercise. We have only to look at the customs, laws, and superstitions of peoples of different regions and different ages to mark this diversity. It is enough to allow that the study of history has ripening effects upon the mind. We may get habits of practical wisdom, but Burke says that we fail to get political precepts to apply to practical issues with the immutability of law. To reach what may perhaps be called comparative history, which Disraeli traces back to Machiavel, is as far as we can go in the construction of a philosophical scheme. Robertson, who had brought his history of America down to the outbreak of the American Revolution, and had forecast the drift of his narrative beyond, was rudely balked by the events which followed. "It is lucky," he acknowledged, "that my American history was not finished before the event. How many plausible theories that I should have been entitled to form are contradicted by what has happened!" One remembers how Freeman, twenty-five years ago, talked of the disruption of the United States as an accomplished fact. The logic of events is a dangerous formula. That there is an agency, or principle, or method in historical progress that justifies historical forecast, as in the laws of storms, can, in the nature of things, be true in no broad sense. Our problems deal with the ductility quite as much as with the docility of the human mind, singly or collectively. There is a flexibility in the relations of cause and effect that is quite beyond gauging. The political prophecies that come true we remember; more that fail we forget.

The historian may be sagaciously profound without being what is called a philosopher. There is all the difference between the two that exists between a field of grain which undulates with the breeze and the same field beaten down by a storm. I do not want, says Milton, speaking of a historian, frequent interspersions of sentiment or a prolix dissertation on transactions which interrupt the series of events.

It is always easy to find instances of what is called, in the lives of men and of nations, the compelling force of natural law, the divine guidance or the devil's machinations. God in history, for instance, appears to be a noble phrase, but the ways of Providence are no less inscrutable to the historian than laws of the natural world that are not understood. What seems providential in history is but the reflex of the mind that contemplates it, and depends upon the training and sympathies of that mind; and as the training is diverse, the view is also diverse. It may have seemed providential to the American Congress that an incompetent like Howe went to Philadelphia instead of going up the Hudson to join Burgoyne, but it could not have looked very providential to his Majesty George III. The old chroniclers of the Spanish Indies saw God's work in the atrocities put upon the natives of tropical American at which the Christian shudders to-day. The untold miseries consequent upon what the world has miscalled religion, in wars, inquisitions, oppressions, inhumanities, appall us; and we are almost forced to ask ourselves at times if the benefits of religion in private life can compensate for its public practice through the ages. It need hardly be said that religion is something quite apart from men's definition of it; but it must also be said that when one age see God in history, the insight is based upon the opinions of a fleeting and changeful period, while the inconstancy of motive, purpose, will, and circumstances is the only thing that is changeless. The theories of Comte, Buckle, and Spencer are interesting; but the life of the world goes on willfully, nevertheless. The South should create lassitude, but the sluggard is in the North. The North should have the warrior; but he appears in the South. Sluggard and warrior, misplaced according to theory, appear in the nick of time for some effect, and the current of history runs up hill, when it should run down. We may strike an average from the wildest helter-skelterism, and this average may be reasonably steady if long enough followed; but an average is not a law,—it is the proof of the absence of law. Moral philosophy may draw its examples from history; but history is no scheme of moral philosophy. Events are provokingly willful. "It is better as I have told it," said Voltaire, when his facts were disproved. The inevitable does not happen. Take a battle. Its course ought to be thus and so. The position of the troops, the superiority of arms, the talents of the commanders, the rights of the cause, all indicate the inevitable; but the other thing happens. The fate of political parties turns on a slander or a rainy election day. Rome ought to fall, and the geese save her. Columbus stretches his course to the Florida coast, and a flight of birds turns him to the West Indies, and saves the Atlantic seaboard for another race. But for a hazy day Champlain might have gone into Boston harbor, and the Jesuits instead of the apostle Eliot might have struggled with the Massachusetts Indians. But for the breakers off Nauset the Mayflower might have landed the Plymouth Pilgrims to grow peaches on the Jersey coast.

There is no question likely to present itself to the mind of the young student of history more officiously than this. Is there a science of history?—and no question which one who has long worked as a historical student would so willingly shuffle out of sight. There are, to be sure, in historical studies some of the semblances of the frailties of science. We have occasionally to take a working hypothesis and hold it as long as we can, and historical opinions are often as unstable as the experimental sciences. Thirty years ago, Buckle endeavored to convince the world that history had mainly to deal with man's subjection to natural laws. Ritter had already recognized a certain potency in man's surroundings, but he acknowledged, nevertheless, that a man's will is a certain and often a compelling factor in his destiny. The laws which govern the progress of mankind, if we must believe Buckle, are as constant as those which send the satellites about the planet; but the potency of human volition is not so easily set aside.

Daniel Webster, in an address before the New York Historical Society in 1852, endeavored to make clear the steadfastness of historical experience as springing from the essential characteristics of human nature everywhere and in all ages; but he proceeded to qualify the statement, until it lost most of its force so far as it exemplified historical teaching. "It may teach us," he said, "general principles of human nature; but it does not instruct us greatly in the various possible developments"; and inasmuch as possible developments are the salient points of historical progress, the exceptions confront us more vividly than the law. Buckle holds that national movements are determined solely by their antecedents; but if antecedents have such an accumulating force that they become potent by overpowering masses of men, we should have none of those revolutions like that of the English colonies in America, where a vigilant and determined minority threw a continent into a civil war. Even Buckle, as has frequently been pointed out, after he had amassed his data and formulated his theory, discarded them, when he came to show that individuals really controlled in large part the history of Spain and Scotland.

The treatment of the historical narrative by a mere *littérateur* is almost as bad as that by a mere philosopher. He makes perspectives which do not exist. He forgets things which he cannot readily and gracefully weave into his web. He writes politely oftentimes when he should write judicially. He hesitates to unhorse the traditional hero. Irving held it unwise to destroy the world's exemplars, however the truth might demand it, and he exemplified his practice in his life of Columbus. Such a writer holds candor to be obtrusive, and sees no difference between a host's drawing-room and the court of history. Gervinus has said that the historian must have the courage of the moth, and burn his wings to approach the light.

Writers of a timid sort hold that to be a detective is to lower the dignity of history. Their art eschews what the camera sees, and trusts to the polite eye. Nature hides her ungainliness to the slow eye. It is the business of an artist to second Nature; it is the work of the historian to expose Nature. The ivy beautifies the tower, but we have to strip the vine to repair the edifice.

Scientific research is developing, in these latter days, a body of correlated material in which the historical student finds much to study. It is doing far more. It is raising a body of intermediary elucidators, who prepare it for the popular sense. The fact that the historian's search is symbolized by the camera disposes of that old-time notion of the dignity of history. The camera catches everything, however trivial, and shows its relation to the picture. Robertson was perhaps the last of the great English historians to discard the help of the antiquary and of personal memoirs. Voltaire set the fashion of emphasizing the life of the people. In him the court and the army first lost their prominence. He at last viewed the course of history from the plane of his own century. Carlyle fell into line, and the Germans, in their *Cultur-Geschichte*, have carried the same process to the fullest development. Macaulay, having ridiculed the exclusiveness of the oldest school in an essay on Sir William Temple, exemplified other views in his own history. Buckle is as timorous here as he is bold in his main drift. He would reject personal anecdotes as belonging to biography, and not to history. The faithful student, however, knows what history suffers by any such deprivation. It rests on a personal anecdote that Columbus, to prosecute his voyage, deceived his own crew; but it is nevertheless as essential to the historical narrative as the assistance which he forced from the monarchs of Spain. It may rest on personal anecdote that Columbus deceived himself when he forced his followers to subscribe to a belief in their being on the coast or Asia; but we need such anecdotes to show that the effrontery of his character was quite another thing from the courage and trustfulness of being in the right.

Nothing is more certain in the world's history than that the far-reaching cause may not rest in a great undertaking, but is found in the trivial happenings of humble people. It is of the rivalry of two small Greek tribes that we read in Thucydides. Anglo-American historical literature begins, for New England, in the best sense, with the history of Plymouth Plantation by William Bradford,—a record of the trials and discomforts and faith of a very small body of unknown, expatriated English yeomen; but generations of a great people have given that record largeness; and we shall search far to find a similarly noble account of the beginnings of any other people.

In conclusion, I may confess that I have made of history a thing of shreds and patches. I have only to say that the life of the world is a thing of shreds and patches, and it is only when we consider the well-rounded life of an individual that we find permeating the record a reasonable constancy of purpose. This is the province of biography, and we must not confound biography with history. Their conduct and their lessons are different and independent. The man is a part of his age, but he requires a different gauge. The age is influenced by the man, but it is fickle where he is constant, halting where he is marching, and active where he is contemplative. Neither the man nor the age can fall behind the years, but, like cannon-balls linked by a rod, the onward course of the twain is marked by different revolutions, and no one can tell which will strike the target first.

PART III
BIBLIOGRAPHY

WINSOR'S MANUSCRIPTS

Justin Winsor was involved in a massive amount of correspondence during the course of his life, and much of it has been preserved. Three major repositories now hold most of this material. In the Boston Public Library are found the records of Winsor's superintendency of that library, 1868 to 1877, and some miscellaneous material. At Harvard, one will find the papers relating to his management of the Harvard University Library, 1877 to 1897, plus a substantial amount of material related to his professional activities, both as a historian and as a librarian. Finally, in the Massachusetts Historical Society Library, one will find a substantial collection of material related primarily to his historical research and editorial work.

Two other collections deserve brief mention. They are the American Library Association Archives, which are now preserved at the University of Illinois Library and which contain some scattered but important Winsor papers; and the Melvil Dewey Papers housed in the Columbia University Library, which contain important letters to and from Winsor. Readers wanting a detailed list of the many manuscript collections that touch, even if only slightly, on Winsor's life should see Joseph Boromé, "The Life and Letters of Justin Winsor," Ph.D. dissertation, Columbia University, 1950, pp. 595-98.

Justin Winsor's annual reports at the Boston Public Library and the Harvard University Library were, during the last third of the nineteenth century, considered invaluable guides to the operation of libraries. Winsor was constantly dealing with problems that were not only important to the Boston Public Library and to the Harvard University Library, but that were also of considerable consequence to librarians everywhere. As a result, a few specific notes must be devoted to the reports. Winsor's reports at the Boston Public Library are contained in the Sixteenth to the Twenty-fifth Annual Reports of the Trustees of the Boston Public Library, and were issued by the Library between 1868 and 1877. In addition, Winsor chaired the Examining Committee for 1867, which prepared the highly significant *Report* of that year (reprinted in this volume). This was part of the *Fifteenth Annual Report of the Trustees of the Public Library for the Year 1867* (Boston, 1867, pp. 11-64). Winsor's reports at the Harvard University Library cover the period 1878-1897. They were originally published as part of the *Annual Report of the President of Harvard University*, and then were reprinted separately as the *Report of Justin Winsor, Librarian of Harvard University*. Each of these, numbered one through twenty, was widely read by academic librarians in the United States and abroad. The *Twentieth Annual Report* was outlined by Winsor shortly before he died, and was finished and published by his assistant, William H. Tillinghast.

Justin Winsor was a prolific and dedicated author, and the complete corpus of his published works would consume a very large space in this book. However, since a full and annotated list of all of Winsor's works is to be found in W. F. Yust's *A Bibliography of Justin Winsor* (Cambridge, MA: Library of Harvard University, 1902), we have listed only those items authored by Winsor that dealt with librarianship and that constitute significant contributions to the literature of the day. Those wishing a complete list should see Yust's bibliography.

* * *

Abbreviations Used

LJ — *Library Journal*
LW — *Literary World*

* * *

1871

"The Boston Public Library." *Scribner's Monthly* 3 (1871): 150-56.

1876

"Free Libraries and Readers." *LJ* 1 (1876): 63-67.

"Library Buildings." In *Public Libraries in the United States of America: Their History, Condition and Management: Special Report, Part 1*. pp. 465-75. Washington: Gov. Print. Off., 1876.

"Library Memoranda." In *Public Libraries in the United States of America: Their History, Condition and Management: Special Report, Part 1*. pp. 431-33. Washington: Gov. Print. Off., 1876.

"A Word to Starters of Libraries." *LJ* 1 (1876): 1-3.

1877

"Fiction as a Starting Point in Reading." *Boston Daily Advertiser*, 9 June 1877.

"Libraries, American versus European [on library catalogs]." *Boston Daily Advertiser*, 21 March 1877.

"Libraries and Catalogues." *LJ* 1 (1877): 247-49.

1878

"The British Museum and its Catalogues." *LW* 9 (1878): 66-67.

"The Charging System at Harvard." *LJ* 3 (1878): 338-39.

"The College Library and the Classes." *LJ* 3 (1878): 5-6.

"A Librarian's Catholicity." *LW* 9 (1878): 93-94.

"Library Lectures and Other Helps." *LJ* 3 (1878): 120-21.

"Library Questions and Answers." *LJ* 3 (1878): 159.

"A Plan of the new 'Pooles Index.'" *LJ* 3 (1878): 143.

"Shakespearian Catalogues, 1801-1814." *LW* 9 (1878): 77-78.

"On Women as librarians in America." In *Transactions and Proceedings of the Conference of Librarians Held in London, October, 1877*, p. 177. London, 1878.

1879

"The Beginnings of Our Public Library System." *LW* 10 (1879): 121-22.

"College and Other Higher Libraries [read before the American Social Science Association, Saratoga, 10 September 1879]." *LJ* 4 (1879): 399-402.

"The Library Movement Thirty Years Ago." *LW* 10 (1879): 330-31.

"M. Vattemare and the Public Library System." *LW* 10 (1879): 185-86.

"The President's Address [to ALA meeting in Boston, 1879]." *LJ* 4 (1879): 223-25.

1880

"Bookbuying Thirty Years Ago." *LW* 11 (1880): 25-26.

"Boston Libraries Thirty Years Ago." *LW* 11 (1880): 109-110.

"The College Library." In *College Libraries as Aids to Instruction*. U. S. Bureau of Education, Circular of Information, no. 1, pp. 7-14. Washington, 1880.

"The Harvard University Library." *Harvard Register* 1 (1880): 3-4.

"Libraries in Boston." In *Memorial History of Boston . . .* , vol. 4, pp. 279-94. Boston: James Osgood and Co., 1880.

1881

"President's Address [to the ALA meeting, Washington, February 1881]." *LJ* 6
(1881): 63-64.

1882

"Annotated catalogues," *LJ* 7 (1882): 4-5.

"Annual Address [to the ALA meeting, Cincinnati, May 1882]." *LJ* 7 (1882): 123-24.

1883

"Address of the President [to ALA meeting, Buffalo, August, 1883]." *LJ* 8 (1883):
163-65.

"The Functions of a Library in a Community of Scholars [address at the Harvard
Divinity School]." [Abstracted in] *LJ* 8 (1883): 33.

1884

"Address [upon the opening of the new library building at the University of Michi-
gan]." In *Public Exercises on the Completion of the Library Building* ...
Dec. 12, 1883, pp. 26-39. Ann Arbor, 1884.

1890

"Cathedral and Other English Libraries." *Nation* 51 (1890): 284 [Reprinted, *LJ*
15 (1890): 302-65].

1891

"America in Italian Libraries." *Nation* 53 (1891): 9-10.

"The Condition of Italian Libraries." *Nation* 53 (1891): 26-27.

1893

"The Future of Local Libraries." *Atlantic Monthly* 71 (1893): 815-18.

1894

"The Development of the Library [address upon the opening of the Lunt Library,
Northwestern University, 26 September 1894]." *LJ* 19 (1894): 370-75.

WINSOR'S PUBLISHED WORKS ON AMERICAN HISTORY

For two decades, Winsor held in his possession the keys to one of the nation's finest collections of historical manuscripts, maps, and rare books. His was an opportunity of which he took full advantage; indeed, without such rich historical sources, he might never have undertaken his monumental editorial and research projects. The following list of historical works omits Winsor's numerous critiques and occasional writings. For a complete accounting of his scholarly labors, see Yust's bibliography.

1849

A History of the Town of Duxbury, Massachusetts, With Genealogical Registers. Boston: Crosby & Nicholls, 1849.

1852

Journal of an Expedition against Quebec in 1775, under Colonel Arnold by Joseph Ware, of Needham, Mass., to Which Is Appended Notes (by Justin Winsor) and a Genealogy of the Ware Family. Prepared for the New England Historical and Genealogical Register. Boston: 1852.

1879

Historical Sketch of the Colony and County of Plymouth. Boston: George H. Walker, 1879.

1880-1881

The Memorial History of Boston, Including Suffolk County, Massachusetts. 1630-1880. Edited by Justin Winsor, Librarian of Harvard University. Issued under the Business Superintendence of the Projector, Clarence F. Jewett. 4 vols. Boston: James R. Osgood & Co., 1880-81.

1884

A Bibliography of Ptolemy's Geography. Cambridge, MA: University Press and John Wilson and Son, 1884. [Library of Harvard University. *Bibliographical Contributions*, No. 18.]

1885

Report to the Legislature of Massachusetts Made by the Commissioners upon the Condition of the Records, Files, Papers, and Documents in the Secretary's Department. Boston: Wright & Potter Printing Co., 1885.

1886-1889

Narrative and Critical History of America. 8 vols. Boston and New York: Houghton, Mifflin and Co./The Riverside Press, Cambridge, 1886-1889.

I.   *Aboriginal America.* 1889.

II.   *Spanish Explorations and Settlement.* 1886.

III.   *English Explorations and Settlements in North America, 1497-1689.* Copyright, 1884.

IV.   *French Explorations and Settlements in North America and Those of the Portuguese, Dutch, and Swedes, 1500-1700.* Copyright, 1884.

V.   *The English and French in North America, 1689-1763.* 1887.

VI.   *The United States of North America, Part I* [Revolutionary War]. 1888.

VII. *The United States of North America, Part II* [Confederation and Constitution to 1850]. 1888.

VIII. *The Later History of British, Spanish, and Portuguese America.* 1889.

1886

The Kohl Collection of Maps Relating to America. Issued by the Library of Harvard University. Cambridge, MA: 1886 [Library of Harvard University, *Bibliographical Contributions,* No. 19].

1887

The Manuscript Sources of American History. An Address before the American Historical Association, May 21, 1887, by the President, Justin Winsor, with the Action of the Association Thereon. New York: 1887 [also printed in the *Papers of the American Historical Association,* III, p. 9-27. Washington: 1889].

1889

Calendar of the Sparks Manuscripts in Harvard College Library, with an Appendix Showing Other Manuscripts. Cambridge: Library of Harvard University, 1889 [Library of Harvard University, *Bibliographical Contributions,* No. 22].

1890

"The Perils of Historical Narrative." *Atlantic Monthly* 66 (1890): 289-302.

1891

Christopher Columbus and How He Received and Imparted the Spirit of Discovery. Boston and New York; Houghton, Mifflin and Co./The Riverside Press, Cambridge, 1891.

1892

The Pageant of Saint Lusson, Sault Ste. Marie, 1671. An Address Delivered at the Annual Commencement of the University of Michigan, June 30, 1892. Ann Arbor: The Board of Regents, 1892.

1894

Cartier to Frontenac. Geographical Discovery in the Interior of North America in Its Historical Relations, 1534-1700. With Full Cartographical Illustrations from Contemporary Sources. Boston and New York: Houghton, Mifflin and Company/The Riverside Press, Cambridge, 1894.

1895

The Mississippi Basin. The Struggle in America between England and France, 1697-1763. With Full Cartographical Illustrations from Contemporary Sources. Boston and New York: Houghton, Mifflin and Company/The Riverside Press, Cambridge, 1895.

1897

The Westward Movement. The Colonies and the Republic West of the Alleghanies, 1763-1798. With Full Cartographical Illustrations from Contemporary Sources. Boston and New York: Houghton, Mifflin and Company/The Riverside Press, Cambridge, 1897.

GENERAL BIOGRAPHICAL ACCOUNTS

Adams, James T. "Justin Winsor." *Dictionary of American Biography* 10: 403-404.

Axon, W. E. A. "Justin Winsor: In Memoriam." *Library* 10 (1898): 1-6.

Biagi, Guido. "In Memoriam: Justin Winsor." *Revista della Biblioteche* 9 (1898): 11-12.

Bolton, Charles K. ["Justin Winsor."] *New England Historical and Genealogical Register* 52 (1898): 403-404.

Boromé, Joseph A. "The Life and Letters of Justin Winsor." Ph. D. dissertation, Columbia University, 1950.

Channing, Edward. "Justin Winsor." *American Historical Review* 3 (1898): 197-202.

Cutler, Wayne, and Michael H. Harris. "Justin Winsor." In *Dictionary of American Library Biography.* Littleton, CO: Libraries Unlimited, 1978. pp. 570-72.

Cutter, Charles A. "Justin Winsor." *Nation* 65 (1897): 335.

Fay, L. E. "Librarian as Scholar." *School and Social Science* 37 (1933): 511-16.

Foster, William E. "Five Men of '76." *ALA Bulletin* 20 (1926): 312-323.

Foster, William E. "Justin Winsor," [*Providence Public Library*] *Monthly Bulletin* 3 (1897): 295-296.

Foster, William E. "Justin Winsor, 1831-1897." *Bulletin of Bibliography* 8 (1914): 2-3.

Kilgour, Frederick G. "Justin Winsor." *College and Research Libraries* 3 (1941): 64-66.

Lane, William C., and William H. Tillinghast. "Justin Winsor: Librarian and Historian, 1831-1897." *Library Journal* 23 (1898): 7-13.

Lowell, A. Lawrence. "Justin Winsor." American Academy of Arts and Sciences, *Proceedings* 34 (1899): 641-45.

Metcalf, Keyes D. "Six Influential Academic and Research Librarians." In *Libraries for Teaching; Libraries for Research: Essays for a Century.* Chicago: American Library Association, 1977. pp. 127-40.

Peabody, Francis G. "Justin Winsor." *Harvard Monthly* 25 (1898): 128-130.

Peabody, Francis G. *Justin Winsor, Memorial Address in Appleton Chapel, 26 October 1897.* n.p.; n.d.

Potter, Alfred C. "Justin Winsor." *Centralblatt fur Bibliothekswesen* 15 (1898): 60-62.

Rathbone, Josephine A. "Pioneers of the Library Profession." *Wilson Library Bulletin* 23 (1949): 775-79.

Scudder, Horace E. "Memoir of Justin Winsor." Massachusetts Historical Society, *Proceedings*, 2nd ser. 12 (1899): 457-82.

Sharma, R. N. "Winsor: The Quintessential Librarian." *Wilson Library Bulletin* 51 (1976): 48-52.

Tillinghast, William H. "A Sketch of Mr. Winsor's Life," *Harvard Graduates' Magazine* 6 (1897): 188-91.

"Tributes to Justin Winsor by Samuel A. Green, Charles W. Eliot, Mellen Chamberlain, Charles L. Smith, Albert Bushnell Hart, and William W. Goodwin." Massachusetts Historical Society, *Proceedings*, 2nd ser. 12 (1899): 30-44.

Whitney, James L. "Justin Winsor." American Antiquarian Society, *Proceedings*, n.s. 12 (1898): 229-34.

Winship, George P. "Justin Winsor." *Cyclopedic Review of Current History* 7 (1897): 1029-34.

Yust, W. F. *A Bibliography of Justin Winsor.* Cambridge, MA: Library of Harvard University, 1902.

Collier, Francis G. "A History of the American Public Library Movement Through 1880." Ph. D. dissertation, Harvard University, 1953.

Ditzion, Sidney. *Arsenals of a Democratic Culture: A Social History of the American Public Library Movement in New England and the Middle Atlantic States from 1850 to 1900.* Chicago: American Library Association, 1947.

Garrison, Dee. "Cultural Missionaries: A Study of the American Public Library Leaders, 1876-1910." Ph. D. dissertation, University of California at Irvine, 1973.

Harris, Michael H. *The Role of the Public Library in American Life: A Speculative Essay.* Urbana: University of Illinois, Graduate School of Library Science, Occasional Paper No. 117, 1975.

Harris, Michael H., and Gerrard Spiegler. "Everett, Ticknor, and the Common Man: The Fear of Societal Instability as the Motivation for the Founding of the Boston Public Library." *Libri* 24 (1974): 249-75.

Waldlin, Horace G. *The Public Library of the City of Boston: A History.* Boston: Printed by the Trustees, 1911.

Whitehill, Walter Muir. *The Boston Public Library: A Centennial History.* Cambridge, MA: Harvard University Press, 1956.

AMERICAN LIBRARY ASSOCIATION PRESIDENT

Bishop, William W. "The American Library Association: Fragments of Autobiography." *Library Quarterly* 19 (1949): 36-45.

Bowker, Richard R. "Seed Time and Harvest: The Story of the A.L.A.." *ALA Bulletin* 20 (1926): 303-309.

Gambee, Budd L. "The Great Junket: American Participation in the Conference of Librarians, London, 1877." *Journal of Library History* 22 (1967): 9-44.

Holley, Edward G., ed. *Raking the Historic Coals: The ALA Scrapbook of 1876*, Beta Phi Mu Chapbook No. 8. Chicago: Lakeside Press, 1967.

Maddox, Lucy J. "Trends and Issues in American Librarianship as Reflected in the Papers and Proceedings of the American Library Association, 1876-1885." Ph. D. dissertation, University of Michigan, 1958.

Miksa, Francis. "The Making of the 1876 Special Report on Public Libraries." *Journal of Library History* 8 (1973): 30-40.

Thomison, Dennis. *A History of the American Library Association, 1876-1972.* Chicago: American Library Association, 1978.

Bolton, Charles K. "The Harvard University Library." *New England Magazine*, n.s. 9 (1893): 433-99.

Brundin, R. E. "Justin Winsor of Harvard and the Liberalizing of the College Library." *Journal of Library History* 10 (1975): 57-70.

Carney, Frank. "The Harvard Library under Justin Winsor." *Harvard Library Notes* 3 (1939): 245-52.

Currier, Margaret. "Cataloguing at Harvard in the Sixties." *Harvard University Library Notes* 4 (1942): 67-73.

Currier, Thomas F. "Cataloguing and Classification at Harvard, 1876-1938." *Harvard Library Notes* 3 (1939): 232-42.

Cutter, Charles A. "Dr. Hagen's Letter on Cataloguing." *Library Journal* 1 (1877): 216-20.

Cutter, Charles A. "The New Catalogue of Harvard College." *North American Review* 108 (1869): 96-129.

Elkins, K. C. "President Eliot and the Storage of 'Dead' Books." *Harvard Library Bulletin* 8 (1954): 299-312.

Lane, William C. "The Harvard College Library, 1877-1929." In *The Development of Harvard University Since the Inauguration of President Eliot, 1869-1929*, edited by S. E. Morrison. Cambridge, MA: Harvard University Press, 1930. pp. 608-31.

Lane, William C., and William H. Tillinghast. "Justin Winsor's Administration of the Harvard Library, 1877-1897." *Harvard Graduates' Magazine* 6 (1897): 182-88.

Lovett, Robert W. "The Undergraduate and the Harvard Library, 1877-1937." *Harvard Library Bulletin* 1 (1947): 221-37.

Metcalf, Keyes D. "Spatial Growth in the Harvard Library, 1638-1947." *Harvard Library Bulletin* 2 (1948): 98-115.

Potter, Alfred C. *The Library of Harvard University: Descriptive and Historical Notes*, 3rd ed. Cambridge, MA: 1915.

The authors, books, and subject headings appearing on pages 78, 79, 80, 81, and 102 have not been indexed here, nor have the annotations or the bibliographic references in Winsor's essays on college libraries and historical narrative (pages 146-47, 151-55, and 169-74).